Up Came a
SQUATTER

MAGGIE BLACK is a writer whose work up to now has been mainly about development among poor and disadvantaged peoples in Africa, Asia and Latin America. Her most recent book – *International Development: Illusions and Realities* (New Internationalist 2015) – explores the contradictions whereby a process intended to improve economic well-being inflicts destruction on powerless minorities. This has proved a surprisingly useful apprenticeship for a study of her great-grandfather's pioneering life in Victoria, with its themes of Aboriginal exclusion, 'improvement' of the land, and the emergence of a new colonial society. Among her other works are *A Cause for our Times: Oxfam's first 50 years* and *Children First: The story of UNICEF* (OUP, 1992 and 1996); and several books on water and sanitation, including *The State of the World's Water* (UCP, 2016).

D1609949

Up Came a
SQUATTER

NIEL BLACK
of Glenormiston, 1839–1880

Maggie Black

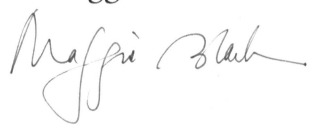

NEWSOUTH

STATE LIBRARY
VICTORIA

A NewSouth book

Published by
NewSouth Publishing
University of New South Wales Press Ltd
University of New South Wales
Sydney NSW 2052
AUSTRALIA
newsouthpublishing.com

Published in association with
State Library Victoria
328 Swanston Street
Melbourne Victoria 3000
Australia
slv.vic.gov.au

© Maggie Black 2016
First published 2016

10 9 8 7 6 5 4 3 2 1

National Library of Australia
Cataloguing-in-Publication entry
Creator: Black, Maggie, 1945– author.
Title: Up came a squatter : Niel Black of Glenormiston, 1839–1880 / Maggie Black.
ISBN: 9781742235066 (paperback)
       9781742247946 (ePDF)
       9781742242521 (ebook)
Notes: Includes bibliographical references and index.
Subjects: Black, Niel.
  Scots—Victoria—Biography.
  Squatters—Victoria—Biography.
  Squatter settlements—Victoria.
  Frontier and pioneer life—Victoria.
  Sheep farming—Victoria—History.
Dewey Number: 994.5092

Cover design Susanne Geppert
Internal design Avril Makula
Cover image (FRONT) Cooper, Duncan. 1850, Panorama of Challicum, Victoria, ca. 1850, 5, watercolour painting. National Library of Australia, PIC Volume 176 #R.312.
(BACK) The residence of Niel Black Esq, wood engraving by Frederick Grosse, based on drawings by Nicholas Chevalier, undertaken during the visit of Prince Alfred the Duke of Edinburgh in 1867. *Illustrated Australian News*, 4 February 1868; IAN04/02/68/SUPP/5, State Library of Victoria.
Printer Griffin Press

UNSW
AUSTRALIA

CONTENTS

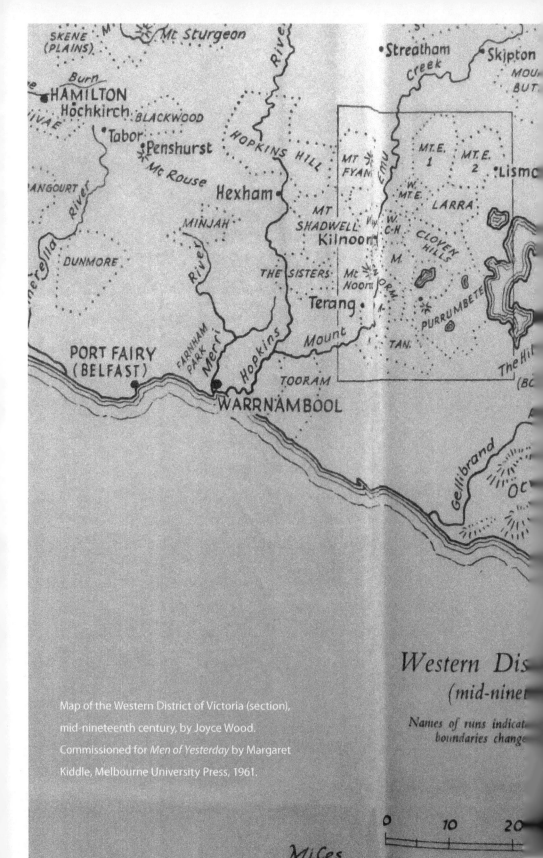

Map of the Western District of Victoria (section), mid-nineteenth century, by Joyce Wood. Commissioned for *Men of Yesterday* by Margaret Kiddle, Melbourne University Press, 1961.

Buninyong

Mt Buninyong

Moorabool River

MELBOURNE

River Yarra

WYNDHAM Werribee Plains

Werribee

WERRIBEE PARK

Williamstown

GOLF HILL DARRIWIL

Darriwil R.

Batesford

BARWON PARK

GEELONG

AVALON

Pt. Henry

Port Phillip

ke

ngamite

Birregurra

Lake Colac

OLAC
(YTE ROOK)

River

Barwon

INGLEBY

Barrabool Hills Germantown

Waurn Ponds

L. Modewarre

Cape Schanck

ges

ape Otway

MOUNT FYANS

Emu Creek

MT ELEPHANT NO.1

MT ELEPHANT No.2
(TITANGA, GALA)

Lismore

W. MT. E

LARRA

of Victoria

entury)

rather than extent;
ut the period.

WOORI-WYRITE

W. CLOVEN HILLS

CLOVEN HILLS

GLEN ORMISTON

MENIN-GOORT

Mt Noorat

Terang

MARIDA YALLOCK

Ewan's Hill

Camperdown

Mt Leura
(Timboon Hill)

PURRUMBETE

Lake Corangamite

MOUNT

KEAYANG

TANDAROO

40   50

FOREWORD

NIEL BLACK arrived in Melbourne in 1839, a Scottish farmer eager to acquire a large expanse of pastures. He owned no sheep or cattle. Not really wealthy but backed by partners at home, he had just enough money to buy livestock and enough experience to succeed. In retrospect it was one of the most fortunate times in the history of the western world to commence such a quest.

The Aborigines who had occupied the district for ages were too divided by their own enmities to resist effectively. Many were killed by the white invaders, and many succumbed to fatal diseases and alcoholism. Their land, with the consent of the government in Sydney, could be occupied or 'squatted on' at token cost, and the necessary shepherds and shearers were not costly to hire: many were former British convicts who accepted the loneliness of bush life. Into this district of raggedly dressed settlers rode Black, a 35-year-old bachelor, a tall man made even taller on horseback by his top hat and black tail coat. For years he lived in a simple hut shielded from the weather by a plastering of mud and clay. In this vivid, fast-moving book Niel Black comes to life.

A skilled squatter, so long as he coped with droughts and diseases, could make a small fortune. Black made a large fortune. We forget that first-class wool held an importance it has largely lost. Synthetic fibres had not been invented. In the long European winters, the woollen blankets, rugs, caps, dresses, sweaters, waistcoats, jackets, suits, flannel underwear, stockings and trousers were substitutes for central heating. The tens of millions of Europeans who worked in the open air favoured wool, if they could afford it. As a commodity it was expensive enough to afford the high cartage costs. Thus Niel Black's consignments of wool went by dray to port and so by sailing ship past Cape Horn to the mechanised woollen and worsted mills of England. By 1848 Australia had far supplanted Spain and Germany as the great wool exporter, and Port Phillip Bay sheltered a small fleet of wool ships.

Here for the first time is his personal story, told by Maggie Black, one of his descendants. It is unusual because of the successes and tragedies it describes and the moral dilemmas embedded in Black's Australian career. Moreover this book rests on an astoundingly large collection of letters written or received by him. He must have penned – I guess – a few million words and they cover hundreds of topics extending from the daily life of Aborigines and shepherds to the astonishing bushfire of Black Thursday in 1851 and his visits to Scotland in a search – at last successful – for a wife. Perhaps no other flourishing entrepreneur in this land can ever have found the time to write so much.

A long-serving politician, he feared 'naked democracy' and the political 'scoundrels' he saw emerging during the gold rushes. As Maggie Black reveals in her fluent prose, he made enemies and told them so to their faces. He was a serpent in the eyes of one, a vexatious man in the eyes of others. Also very generous at times, he lent money to enable humble employees to buy their own sheep. One gratefully approached him in 1846 with the news that 'he has this year shorn 5200 sheep of his own'. In a typical Scottish district, such a proprietor would have ranked with the gentry.

Niel Black had loyal friends and many well-wishers. His funeral in 1880 must have impressed those who watched it pass through the countryside. It left his mansion at noon – the wealthier mourners travelling in horse-drawn carriages and the poorer on foot – and reached the cemetery in Terang nearly two hours later. I assume that much of the country it passed through was his own.

Geoffrey Blainey

Chapter One

'A RUN UNEQUALLED IN THE COLONY'

ON 3 DECEMBER 1839, Niel Black – a determined, confident, God-fearing Scot – set out on horseback westwards from Melbourne. He had sailed from the Clyde in April, arriving at Port Phillip as his final destination in October. By December he was impatient to be off on his first expedition to the bush. Another day was lost to a summons to appear in court for failing to register two dogs he had brought with him thousands of miles across the sea. Raised in Argyll, the 35-year-old tenant farmer had been a breeder of stock and a holder of scattered grazing lands throughout his adult life, so a long, solitary horseback journey in wild country was something he regarded as routine. Rather than await companions, he preferred to face the hazards of the interior alone. He travelled light – a compass, a tether for his horse, a pair of pistols, matches, a spare shirt and a pair of stockings.[1]

For weeks he had been raring to go out and see the nature of the land that would make or break his fortune. But there was much to detain him: his people and freight from Scotland to land, lodgings to find, introductions to proffer, hands to shake at Government House, bills of exchange to sell, equipment to buy, and bounty to claim on his indentured servants – he was entitled to a grant for bringing out emigrants, and he made certain of claiming it from the authorities. He had also had to help with the premature lying-in, in a stable, of Jane McNicol, wife of Duncan, one of the shepherds he had brought with him. Fortunately, both mother and baby girl – named Christina – came through their ordeal unscathed. Then he had been obliged to hire a lawyer to get his stockman released: Peter McIntyre had been arrested on a trumped-up charge of stealing a horse. And critically, it had taken time to find a suitable mount. As all horse-flesh seemed ludicrously expensive, he had difficulty finding one at a price he was prepared to pay. A tall man and well built, he needed a strong horse and wanted a game one. For Niel Black of Niel Black & Company, no ordinary hack would do.

As he and his horse struck out into the immensity of the bush, the many anxieties he had felt in the weeks since he first stood on Australian soil fell away. His spirits were elated by the sense of space and freedom. 'I traversed plains thousands of acres in extent, and as level as a billiard table without almost a tree … If "distance lends enchantment to view" I had it in perfection, and I must confess, the extent of country and the distant hills richly covered in wood rendered the scene very imposing, calculated to make one feel how trifling a creature man is amid the mighty works of creation.' Black recorded his impressions that evening in an inn at the crossing point on the Werribee River. If the land impressed him, man's mark upon it did not. 'The Golden Fleece', he wrote, 'is a mere hut, [and] between the split slabs which – stuck in the ground – compose the walls, a hen with a brood of chickens might find her way in and out.' The Fleece had fine furniture but as a billet was very uncomfortable. He was 'obliged to double up with an entire stranger in a shack that would be thought too bad for a pig at home'.

The next day he continued travelling to the north-west. In the afternoon he came to the Moorabool River, where, due to his own misjudgment, his splendid horse nearly drowned. It had recently rained, but Black did not think the river particularly swollen or fast-moving. 'I had rode the whole day and saw neither house nor human being till I came to this river, on the opposite bank of which stood a small hut – the sight of which cheered my spirits.' The temptation to cross was overwhelming. 'After putting my pistols, powder and Lucifer matches on the top of my shoulder underneath the coat to keep them dry, I pushed in. The first plunge brought me up to the mouth and rendered my matches useless and my weapons inoffensive.' After retreating once more to the bank, he 'cooeed, and the hutkeeper came to my assistance. He stripped naked and came out on the stream as far as he could. My tether was long, and I at last succeeded in giving him one end, and tying the other round the horse's neck.

'Out went horse, saddle and cloak, and soon reached the other side. The horse headed the stream, the man pulling the rope with might and main.' But unable to get his footing on the bank, the horse became entangled in drifting wood. 'He at last lay dead on the water and I considered him lost. In despair I

3

threw a piece of wood at him; he made a desperate spring and his spirit and mettle brought him clear over it.' Somehow the girth slipped back over the horse's haunches, the branch freed itself, and by an extraordinary effort the horse struggled up a steep bank, and stood at last unharmed on the top. Black scrambled across on some tree trunks, 'and was regaled with a quart of tea, a mutton pye and plenty of damper'. This near-disaster determined him never again to put his horse into an Australian river without knowing exactly where and how he could come out.

After eating the food and resting his horse, he gave the 'old soldier' five shillings and set off once again. In wet clothes and with no way to light a fire, he needed shelter for the night. As dark descended, he picked out some landmarks in the gloom, and thankfully made his way to a 'Highland-man's home station'. Here he put his horse to feed, after covering 53 miles at a stretch. After damper and tea, and a glass of whisky consumed before a roaring fire, Black tumbled into bed, 'ending the adventures of my second day'. These left a powerful impression: they could have marked both beginning and end of his pioneering quest.

The following day he rode along a muddy dray track and reached different territory. Here were the runs and stations he had come to see, occupied by members of the new Port Phillip species of Scottish pastoralist-entrepreneur he had come to join. 'Scenes more rich and beautiful than those I passed through today cannot be imagined. It partook more of the character of fine old English lawn and parkland than anything I can remember in Scotland ... passing in perfection, even while in a state of nature, [their] soft, rich, and pleasing beauty.' His northernmost point was Ballarat, a 10 000-acre run held by Archibald Yuille, brother-in-law of John Anderson, one of Black's mercantile mentors in Britain.[2] From here he travelled south through Buninyong along the valley of the Leigh River, an area opened up only the year before, in 1838. Although Aboriginal people still occupied many of their traditional haunts, Black did not record seeing any. Perhaps they kept their distance, and from this he concluded that they were 'a very timid race'.[3] On this and most of his other forays they are absent from his landscape descriptions.

At Yuille's station he hired a spare overseer, another Scot; at other stations he inspected sheep and noted how flocks and their diseases were managed. Everywhere he picked his fellow settlers' brains for information. He also arranged to lend his Scots shepherds and their wives to Yuille until such time as he needed them. This removed them from temptation offered by other employers in Melbourne – he noted that many people lost their servants soon after they arrived – and helped take their minds off the anxieties of the new life they had entered into. This kind of arrangement was common among early pastoralists, Scottish immigrant workers being always in demand. He found many people known to him directly or indirectly among settlers, managers and servants. Some had already won a reputation for their flocks and runs, including George Russell of the Clyde Company, stationed at Golfhill; Campbell of Otter, a laird from the same part of Argyll as Black; and Henry Gibb, a poor orphan at home, now a superintendent earning good money in the Portland Bay direction. Most had not come directly from Scotland like himself, but across the Bass Strait from Van Diemen's Land. Following Major Thomas Mitchell's 1836 discovery of the country he named 'Australia Felix' south of the Murray River, the image of a grassland El Dorado had taken hold in both Sydney and Hobart, and the trickle of 'overlanders' following Mitchell's tracks and of graziers bringing sheep across the strait had rapidly grown.

As Black travelled down towards the Barwon River, an area where Aboriginal peoples had put up fierce resistance to Europeans in 1837, he was increasingly treated to 'bouncing' – bragging – of how the squatters dealt with 'natives'. He listened and noted, but kept his counsel. Staying in 'Crayoh' (Corio, later Geelong) – a 'great city', having 'four stores, as many private houses, an Inn and a stable' – he had his first encounter with the young blades from different areas, the 'Colac mob' and the 'Buninyong mob'[4], carousing at the Woolpack Inn. At 35 he was older than most of them, and he did not appreciate their rowdy drinking sprees, especially when they spilled over into the Sabbath. He was not prudish, but earnest and committed, a typical taciturn Scot. Black had not ventured out to the Antipodes on a young man's tearaway adventure. He had come to found a proper business, and he had responsibilities of which he was keenly aware – to his partners in Liverpool and Glasgow, his family in Argyll, and to the men and women from the Highlands he had persuaded to leave hearth and home and come with him 'to hunt their Fortunes, Strangers in a foreign land'.[5]

Riding out and visiting stations, he observed how young graziers lived. Many 'have miserable huts and take a detestable pride in roughing it. They eat damper and drink tea three times a day … They have no furniture, no windows to their huts. In short, it is the greatest possible achievement to live entirely void of every comfort.' Black was not the only early settler to comment on the way these young squires of the bush, many well born and much better educated than himself, competed to be the most ill-kempt and squalid.[6] He also noted occasional 'instances of the reverse': neat cottages shingled and floored, with 'glass windows opening like doors', and well-laid-out gardens with every kind of fruit and vegetable, 'rose bushes innumerable and flowers in abundance'. What a contrast did the tables at such cottages offer: at one, dinner consisted of 'roast fowl, mutton pye, roast mutton, green peas, turnip and damper', only lacking potatoes because they were not yet full grown.[7] Black was quite clear which model of bush housekeeping he intended to follow.

On 12 December 1839, he rode back into Melbourne, and over the next few days, in snatches of time when not out at stock or land sales, he wrote up his journal. His entries are coloured with a vivid sense of surprise, enthusiasm and misgiving. Some newcomers were being led astray, making bad bargains in an atmosphere fevered by rampant speculation; one in his lodging he described as half-demented by anxiety brought on because he had been duped in the purchase of cattle. There was even a case of suicide at the Lamb Inn in Collins Street. Black was shocked by colonial amorality: 'There is but one thing on which I find persons all agree and that is that you are to believe nobody.' Newcomers were tricked into bargaining for stock or goods they found tempting, pushed up by false bids from conniving friends of the seller, and ended up parting with their cash for absurdly inflated prices. Everybody competed at cheating, and no-one seemed ashamed of it. They thought it excusable 'because they came here to make money. The desire to overreach is incredible and there is no such thing as a market price for anything. Every man takes what he gets if sell he must, and takes *in* when and whom he can.'[8]

Black found himself besieged for advice by associates from home, asked to accompany someone to buy a horse, another to view sheep or land. His knowledge of livestock and ability to bargain was sought after, as was his canniness in spotting the over-rash venture or the duplicitous dealer. Things were turning out to be a lot harder than newcomers had been led to expect.

The ideas planted by Black's advisor, Captain Duncan McKellar, who had run flocks successfully in the Sydney direction, were inapplicable to Port Phillip in its present state. To get operational 'may well be termed an arduous undertaking, tho' he makes it appear as simple as tumbling into a sofa to enjoy a siesta on a hot day'. However, up-country Black met men who were doing well, even if they were not making money on the munificent scale the gullible in Glasgow and Edinburgh – including him-self – had expected. Despite complaints about weather, hardship, ex-convict workers and the colonial government in Sydney and London, their flocks were productive, as were their returns. His calculations suggested that he could make 30 per cent on invest-ments in stock over three years.

Black's next expedition, setting off on 17 December, five days after returning from his first, was in the same direction, but deeper into the bush and further west into the Portland Bay district. This time he had a specific destination, a sheep run and flocks put on the market by George MacKillop of Hobart and his partner, James Smith. MacKillop, an ex–Indian Army officer and grazier-speculator, had hired a schooner in March 1836 and sailed from Van Diemen's Land with 500 sheep. These he had managed to land intact from the sandbank in Port Phillip Bay on which his boat foundered.[9] He later returned to Hobart, putting his sheep under a superintendent, Frederick Taylor. James Smith set up in Melbourne as an insurance broker, and though he was game for a share in MacKillop's speculation, he was not on intimate terms with sheep. In early 1839, Taylor moved the expanded flock 130 miles west of Melbourne to a new run along what eventually became known as Mount Emu Creek.[10] This area was studded with extinct volcanoes, therefore very fertile, and the local tribes strongly resisted giving it up.

Taylor was well known for adopting methods against them that Van Diemen's Land had made notorious, methods the colonial authorities had pledged themselves not to allow the Port Phillip settlers to repeat.

Neither MacKillop nor Smith ever visited the run they called Strathdownie, leaving everything in Taylor's capable hands. As with many grazier-entrepreneurs, they were absentee owners, the sheep purely a business investment. By the end of 1839, MacKillop, who had made a name for himself as an explorer in Gippsland and done well out of his years in the colonies, wished to go home and live a life of well-heeled retirement in Bath. Taylor had fled across Bass Strait to avoid the attentions of the Protector of Aborigines. The substantial run, an indeterminate acreage described as 'Taylor's country' along 'Taylor's River' (Mount Emu Creek), with 20 men in Taylor's employ,[11] was not being well managed by those left in charge, and the flock's condition was deteriorating. Rather than replace Taylor, the partners decided to sell out while prices were high. Here, in Black's view, was a good prospect – even if the 7000–8000 sheep advertised were more than he could afford.

Everything in Port Phillip was selling at inflated prices, but Black was prevented by the terms of his partnership from operating on credit – as others did according to a system he thought 'fearful and dangerous'. He did have the advantage of paying cash, of which there was a shortage, and he would use it to good effect. He wanted a good stretch of country, far into the bush where it would not be put up for sale on behalf of the Crown for many years. He had learned what he could about runs in different terrains, near and far from the only budding towns – Melbourne, Geelong and Portland. He had explored stock prices and carrying capacity, diseases and risks, and was steeling himself to take the plunge. If the run in the Portland Bay district was as promising as it sounded, he would go for it.

———————•◆•———————

Black's anxieties were heightened by the fact that he was not operating solely on his own behalf. In December 1838, a company had been formed in his name, in which shares of £1500 each from himself and three others were invested.[12] These others were not from among his own tenant-farming and small merchant relatives in his native patch of the Cowal peninsula in southern Argyll. Instead, Black had managed to enlist partners from mercantile families of the landed 'inheritor' class. Merchants in Glasgow and Liverpool were beginning to regard ventures in Australia as a possible addition to the East Indies and Calcutta trade. Prospects in Port Phillip were boosted in 1838 by the publication of Major Mitchell's *Three Expeditions into the Interior of Eastern Australia*, with its fulsome descriptions of the abundant pasturelands he had found in 'Australia Felix'. So Black's presentation of himself to would-be investors as a managing partner in a potential sheep operation fell on fertile ground. To have won such partners was a feather in his cap, despite the misgivings of Niel's oldest brother, Walter, who feared that his ambitious younger sibling had overreached himself.

One partner was Alexander Struthers Finlay, son of a hugely successful and well-known Glasgow industrialist, Kirkman Finlay. Alex Finlay lived at Castle Toward, a magnificent pile built by his father on a headland in Cowal not far from the Blacks' homestead at Ardentraive. His sister Janet was married to Walter Black's landlord, John Campbell of South Hall. The other key partner was Finlay's old schoolfriend Thomas Steuart

Gladstone, a first cousin of William Ewart Gladstone, the future prime minister, then a rising politician. TS Gladstone and his uncle William Steuart were shooting in the Highlands as guests of the Finlays when they encountered Walter Black on a boat ferrying people around the coast.[13] Gladstone fell into conversation with Walter about the agricultural depression in Scotland, and learned that his brother Niel wanted to try his luck in Australia.

Brothers Walter, Archibald and Niel Black were then jointly engaged in a grazing and livestock business, following in the footsteps of their father, who died in 1806 when Niel was only two. An old schoolfriend of Walter's, Captain McKellar, recently returned from New South Wales, had fired Niel up with the idea of going to Australia. McKellar's fireside stories of the instant fortunes to be made from wool made a deep impression on someone still young, energetic, unattached and seeking his main chance in life.[14] After Walter's encounter on the ferry-boat with Finlay's guests, Niel Black went off to see TS Gladstone at his house of business in Liverpool. Somehow he was sufficiently persuasive to convince Gladstone, with Finlay's support, to back him. In December 1838, the deed of 'co-partnery' was signed, the fourth investor being Gladstone's uncle William Steuart. Niel sold up his share of the Black family business to commit the same £1500 as the others. He was to receive a salary of £375 a year as manager.

In the bitter cold of a stormy January, he set about booking his passage, finding and engaging men to take with him, and collecting introductions, including one to Sir George Gipps, Governor of New South Wales, from Lord Normanby, the Colonial Secretary in London. He sailed from Greenock on the Clyde on 11 April 1839, aboard the *Ariadne* under Captain

George Macleod. He took with him Donald Black, an older first cousin who suffered from a congenital limp and was disregarded at home; three indentured dependants, with several more to follow a few weeks later;[15] freight worth £73, including shearing tools and ploughing equipment; a copy of Captain McKellar's *The Australian Emigrant's Guide*; and a stag hound procured at the last minute from the Earl of Breadalbane's kennels.[16]

The *Ariadne* put in at Cape Town, Adelaide, Port Phillip and Sydney. On 30 September 1839, the day after Black arrived in Sydney, he began to write a journal in a leather-bound notebook he had bought at a stationers in Glasgow. Until April the following year, he made almost daily entries in this book, until it was filled and sent off to Walter, and then in a follow-up volume. Before this date, nothing exists in his hand – a fine, flourishing hand, developed to impress. In his journal, to compensate for homesickness and a lack of intimate companions with whom to share his thoughts, he confided his impressions of this new world. He made no effort to gloss or conceal his experiences, but he did avoid stories that might alarm at home. His account was intended only for a tiny circle centred on Walter – who, he hoped, would follow him out to Port Phillip if the business turned out well. In these two notebooks, he found a new vocation: a love affair with the written word. Although he never again kept such a journal, the habit of writing was set, along with a fluency of style and wry touches of humour which later illuminated his prolific correspondence.

Black maintained this correspondence for the rest of his life, especially with his most active and sympathetic partner, TS Gladstone. From these letters emerges a detailed picture of this particular member of the upcoming squatter class, his opinions and his goings-on. Black was neither a gentrified younger son nor an ex-military officer; neither a trained professional nor an artisan; neither a young blood nor yet a middle-aged married man. A mere tenant farmer but an 'improver' to his core, he had arrived in the embryonic Port Phillip District at a time when it was as yet unbound by any definite political or social system. From the moment of his arrival he set out to transform his own situation in life and that of his loyal servants, and in so doing, he became embroiled in the young colony's struggle to prosper and take on a distinctive colonial plumage.

For his second expedition to the bush, Black had a companion: John Carre Riddell. An educated younger son of a Scottish family of standing, Riddell arrived in Sydney in August 1839 to set up as a grazier. Advised to try Port Phillip instead, he and a cousin, Thomas Hamilton, purchased horses and pistols and rode south to Melbourne.[17] Black invited Riddell to join him on his expedition as a potential co-purchaser of MacKillop and Smith's flocks. As a gentleman's son and therefore more clubbable than Black, Riddell was also a social asset along the route.

They travelled through Geelong, where they breakfasted with Captain Foster Fyans, Police Magistrate, and on to the Austin brothers' station at Winchelsea (later Barwon Park), then to Hugh Murray's at the southernmost point of Lake Colac. From there they travelled through the Stony Rises south of Lake Corangamite, passed Mount Leura, and arrived at Dr Robert Officer's head station. This was near modern-day Camperdown on the run managed by Henry Gibb. From there 'Taylor's country' began,[18] and it was a further nine miles to MacKillop and Smith's home station on Mount Emu Creek, just below Mount Noorat.

Edward Micklethwaite Curr in his *Recollections of Squatting in Victoria* provides a vivid description of the typical habits and attire of the squatter of those days. 'Blue serge suits in lieu of coats, cabbage-tree hats, belts supporting leather tobacco pouches, sometimes a pistol … breeches, hessian boots and spurs' completed the costume of the swaggering bushman.[19] But this was not a form of dress that Black adopted. He went about, unfashionably, in the time-honoured black hat and dark clothes of the old country, keen to create the impression, among both officials and the senior cadre of settlers, of a solid and sober gentleman-citizen. When he and Riddell were riding between Hugh Murray's at Colac and the Manifolds' at Lake Purrumbete, John Manifold – who was out with a party of workers – was amazed to see a man in top hat and black tail coat ride up to the banks of the flooded Pirron Yallock Creek, take off his clothes, strap them to his saddle and then swim across with his horse.[20] This, he discovered later, was Niel Black on his way to Strathdownie 20 miles further on.

At all the stations along the route, free hospitality was on offer. Later, some of those who endured heavy traffic through their country began to charge for bed, forage and board, but not at this time. A companionable mob of whoever had turned up at Golfhill or Purrumbete would consume an evening meal of mutton chops, tea and damper, and at night, beds would be brought out to cover the hut floor. Several times Black found himself sleeping alongside six or eight other travellers. Whatever he felt about rowdy socialising, he took part nonetheless: it was ill-advised to be standoffish. Most fellows were carefree and sat up drinking and smoking till all hours: 'Anxiety for a future day seems to be as little known among Bushmen as it ever was among a parcel of sailors, and they are all gentlemen. It is a rare chance to meet a person in the Bush who is not a gentleman's son, or at all events had a good education.'[21] In the morning, a basin of water would be placed on a stool outside the hut for washing, and food would be served – 'to have breakfast where one sleeps is one of the laws of the Bush'. Running sheep in Port Phillip in late 1839 was still a carefree, cavalier pursuit, although things would soon sober up when bubbles burst, prices slumped and many a dilettante squatter was ruined.

Over two further days, Black and Riddell rode through 'some of the finest country that ever the heart of man could desire to look at'. The great sweep of luxuriant grass, 'so rich and close' that it dragged back their horses' hooves like snow, fed their pastoral imaginations. Riddell was reminded of the Marquis of Hastings' 'paltry park of 500 acres'; Black compared it to the 'grounds about Inveraray Castle when under a full crop of hay, if the lime trees were removed'. Again, no mention of any Aboriginal presence in the landscape. Black also noted that, mainly due to lack of water, 'two-thirds of even the best of it is unavailable in its present state'. And the grasslands were fragile. 'The lands where sheep and cattle are depasturing lose that rich and fertile appearance they had previous to the eating of the grass.'[22] Many early graziers let their sheep eat out the pasture in one place, and moved the flocks through the landscape further west to another stretch of grassland like nomads. They were all about 'opening up' and 'pastures new', not about 'settlement' or 'improvement' – ideas that governed Black's outlook.

Having arrived at the prospective run, Black spent the next few days surveying its flocks, huts, lands and appointments, and in the evening discussing prices. Sometimes he rode out in the company of Taylor's overseer, William Blackie, sometimes with his own overseer, Robert Anderson, who arrived from Ballarat on Christmas Eve. He was shocked to find how the sheep fared. 'We were led to believe at home that stock here was nursed with the most tender care, in place of which … they are neglected and abused to an incredible extent.' This would affect the terms he offered. Henry Gisborne, Commissioner of Crown Lands, was camping in the vicinity, and Black visited him in his tent. The 'natives at Portland Bay', Gisborne told him, were 'very trouble-some'. The advantages of taking up an existing run, rather than carving out a new one as he had originally intended, increasingly impressed Black. Here, resistance by Aboriginal people had been drastically reduced. Taylor had killed off the local tribe while they were sleeping at a waterhole, assisted by squatter neighbours and their men. This slaughter had taken place about two months before,[23] and news of it had spread. The likelihood that local inhabitants in this vicinity would be 'less troublesome' than in country further west was obvious to Black, who did not want blood on his hands.

Christmas at Taylor's home station provided a solemn moment: 'We had our dinner, and wine and spirits afterwards, but we were easy served each of us quietly, and in thought only (not pronouncing the words aloud) drank the home and friends we left behind, while each absorbed in silent thought filled up his own catalogue by the light of a blazing fire. Thus was spent my first Christmas in a foreign land.' However, in the men's quarters, the Christmas liquor caused pandemonium. 'About 1 o'clock, a woman ran into our hut roaring murder and asking if there was a man among us to save it. At last the Superintendent dressed and went out. He succeeded in taking a loaded gun from one man and a loaded pistol from another. I shall not attempt to describe the scene. Drunkenness and the woman occasioned it. She was kept as a mistress by one of the servant men (a thing quite common here), and they were striving whose wife she'd be for that night.' A party of mounted police were conveniently camped nearby on their way to Portland, so they came in and put one man in irons. This incident decided Black that he wanted nothing to do with Taylor's employees – ex-convicts from Van Diemen's Land.

The following day, 26 December, he went over the rest of the run and was once again enraptured. 'It extends over 8 or 10 miles, and is one of the finest in the colony. We afterwards came to Gibb's station. It were useless to describe the lands we travelled in both places, actually finer, richer and more beautiful than the finest park land I ever saw at home, grass in many instances up to the flaps of the saddles. But let it be remembered that I have travelled hundreds of miles before I saw this, and a very great proportion of this fine land is totally useless for want of water.' Black was a good judge of country, and he had found what he was looking for.

He returned to Melbourne on the evening of 29 December and, in the absence of MacKillop, lost no time in opening negotiations with James Smith. Black was determined to gain the run, for several reasons. Not only was the land well-watered and unrivalled for grass and fertility, but it was far enough from both Melbourne and Portland not to be put up for sale by the land office any time soon.[24] Unlike many of his fellows, he expected to live on his run, managing it himself, rather than stay in town and leave such work to a superintendent. Finally, he anticipated few Aboriginal troubles, given the demise of so many at Taylor's hands. Black noted in his journal that 'The poor creatures are now terror-stricken and will be easily managed.'[25] This was the main reason he gave his partners for fighting so hard to gain this particular stretch of country.

Having seen many newcomers cheated, Black was wary. He understood the difficulties of dealing in an environment where everyone enjoyed seeing an unseasoned buyer driven high and thoroughly fleeced. 'When a customer offers, a trial takes place of how much can be made out of him, and if a very large profit can be realised, a bargain is struck.' For several extremely hot days, Black and Smith negotiated, Smith first agreeing, and then coming back with a higher price per sheep, or demanding that pregnant ewes be counted twice, and again being beaten down. Black was racked with anxiety. He had been to countless sales of stock and knew what he was doing, but at any moment some other newcomer might appear who cared nothing for viewing the run or stock and might risk a fortune on the seller's say-so. However, he was offering cash and he was used to bargaining. He even threatened to go across the strait to Hobart and treat directly with MacKillop if Smith refused to close. Finally, after six days, the weather broke, the rain poured down and terms were struck. He went to bed exhausted and slept the clock around.[26]

Coming out on the *Ariadne*, Black had been befriended by several other passengers. Many were now finding things difficult. One such shipmate was Captain John Eddington, an ex–Indian Army officer, accompanied by wife, mother-in-law and several children. Eddington was stone deaf, having lost his hearing in 1818 when a cannon exploded at the siege of Nagpur. Inhibited in dealing on his own account, he accepted Black's offer of 1000 of MacKillop and Smith's sheep, which he would purchase and Black would manage. Riddell agreed to take half the rest. The run's licence would be 'given in' and its assets – huts, buildings, equipment – were to be Black's, the price to be settled at a valuation. An important advantage to Black of these arrangements was that all the sheep would graze on his run until such time as his own flocks multiplied. Since licences to graze Crown lands required the area to be adequately stocked, he would thus be able to hold a licence for a larger extent of land than he would be entitled to for the number of sheep Niel Black & Company could afford. He intended to establish a run for Eddington on land at his boundary, with his cousin Donald Black as manager.

The final price per sheep, including unborn lambs, was 23 shillings and sixpence. Although this price was high, it was reasonable at the time. He wrote to Gladstone on the day the deal was clinched, the first extant letter in his outgoing correspondence: 'The sheep I think dear enough but it is no small advantage to get possession of one of the finest runs in the colony.'[27] Within a couple of years, values would plunge and sheep become almost worthless. But at the dawn of 1840 and at the end of shearing when the price was at its seasonal lowest, Black was content. It was not the sheep themselves but the run that neither MacKillop nor Smith had ever set eyes on that he bargained so hard to get.

Once more when he was keen to be off and take up his territory, Black was delayed in Melbourne by court proceedings – this time far more serious than non-registration of his dogs. Some weeks before, Peter McIntyre – an experienced stockman and a valued member of his small Scottish band – had got himself into serious trouble.

On landing, Black had lent McIntyre to someone to 'work' a young horse. McIntyre regularly took the horse to the bush beyond Melbourne's outskirts, along with others grazing their mounts. One day he let the horse loose to feed without tying down the tether, and the animal ran off. While chasing after it, he was inveigled into a trap. Out of breath after running for more than a mile, he came across a horse tethered to a tree, and untied it in the hope of using it to go after his own. A man nearby said it was his horse, and McIntyre asked if he would help. The man agreed as long as they first went to fetch a saddle. But it emerged that he was a member of the mounted police in mufti, who then accused McIntyre of stealing his mount and, together with a bunch of colluding associates, clapped him in jail. Since a policeman's horse was Crown property, its theft was a felony. The reward for the apprehension of such a criminal was generous, so much so that it provided a strong incentive to make false accusations – hence the set-up. If McIntyre was convicted, the punishment would be dire.

At McIntyre's first appearance in court, Black managed at the very last minute to procure a competent counsel. The bent policeman was cross-examined, and – with Black putting up a £60 bond – McIntyre's release was secured on bail until a full trial in late January. Now, as Black was preparing to take up his run, this trial was about to take place. A week before it opened, news came that the Crown Prosecutor was sending the case to Sydney. Black believed that in Melbourne, McIntyre could be acquitted, but in Sydney he would stand no chance at all. Starting at the top rank of officials, he went to see Superintendent Charles La Trobe, then worked his way down through every relevant officer in an attempt to get the case heard in Melbourne, but without success. He then rode out to Ballarat, where he had sent McIntyre to work for Archibald Yuille, and suggested that he cut and run, leaving himself to sacrifice the bail and get him a passage home. But McIntyre refused. 'If God would have it so that he is to suffer for a crime which is imputed to him without

20

cause, he would put up with the worst of it.' His defence would be his innocence.[28]

On 29 January 1840, the case came to court, and the Crown Prosecutor again insisted on its removal to Sydney. The judge deferred the case till last, and McIntyre was put in irons and sent to jail overnight. The following day, the judge listened to Black's argument that, in Sydney, the chances would be against him 'because there, they have to deal only with rogues and cannot suppose such a thing as a case appearing worse than it really was'. Wonderfully, the judge agreed that the case should be heard then and there. But when the evidence was called for, it transpired that the Crown Prosecutor had sent it to Sydney and failed to make copies. With no charge to answer, the case was dismissed. After 'two of the most anxious days I ever spent', the saga was over. Black sent McIntyre off to Ballarat on horseback within minutes of his release so as to put him safely out of the way.

That evening Black went to celebrate at the Lamb Inn, the roistering place for gentlemen-squatters. His companion was 24-year-old Claud Farie, newly arrived from Glasgow carrying an introduction from TS Gladstone, the Farie and Gladstone families being friends. While they were there, up rode James Watson, an early settler who had struck out west in 1838 and carved out the first run on the Hopkins River, 20 miles beyond Mount Emu Creek. A shepherd had just been gruesomely killed close to his station and he had decided to quit, so he put up his stock and station for sale there and then at the inn. With Black's assistance, Farie bought 1000 sheep, 800 lambs, six bullocks and a dray, and a hut and 50 hurdles for £2700. 'Thus Mr F has got himself settled and he has not done a single pound's transaction for himself.' Farie, despite their difference in background, was to become Black's valued and faithful friend.

For the previous week, preparations had been underway to start moving all Black's people, supplies and effects 130 miles to the west to take delivery of his run. One dray borrowed from Captain Eddington, full of baggage and protesting women, had already left, along with a new filly – 'very handsome and in foal' – purchased at the last moment. Black followed on to Henry Anderson's station further up the Leigh Valley with another dray to collect Farie's men and those Black had lent to Yuille. Having united the drays, Black saw them off from Ballarat in

Black recorded the purchase of 'Cleopatra' in his journal on 1 February 1840.
On 22 February, another entry notes that he and Donald Black made a stall in the woolshed 'for putting in young mare to break her in to ride'.
Niel Black papers, Box 31, MS 8996, State Library of Victoria

the charge of Robert Anderson and Donald Black. 'There are now twenty-four of them in all, travelling together like a band of Gypsies', he wrote on 6 February. Some complained bitterly about the long journey through a dangerous and unknown land. 'The symptoms of smouldering discontent were evident among some of them, but I soon got them off.'

He then invited Henry Anderson to accompany him as his valuer at the handover. On Saturday 8 February, they struck out across through the area known as Wardy Yallock to the west, and then south from Mount Emu. Having watered their horses on the eastern bank of a wide bend of Mount Emu Creek, they crossed 50 miles of bare plain before arriving at the green sward of Mount Noorat. For some days, Black took pleasure in showing his run to Anderson, Farie, Riddell and various other bush visitors. To make a break with the past, and to honour William Steuart, his senior partner, the run was renamed Glenormiston, after Steuart's estate in the Scottish Borders.

On 11 February, Black rode out to meet the 'band of Gypsies'. The five-day journey from Ballarat had been a true endurance test. Three days had been spent jolting through the plains at a snail's pace, pulled by bullocks exhausted from heat and lack of feed and water, and at night, sleeping under tarpaulins. But the caravan arrived at the Glenormiston home station without mishap. After a hearty meal, their mutinous tempers improved. 'I must say,' recorded Black, 'upon the whole, that their behaviour has been highly creditable, for they have been tried with many temptations, but yet they are all mine, and I have no doubt that they will serve me faithfully.'

The next day, the 'disposing party' arrived, and the valuation began. The sheep were counted, and the woolshed, superintendent's house and shepherds' huts valued, as well as the garden full

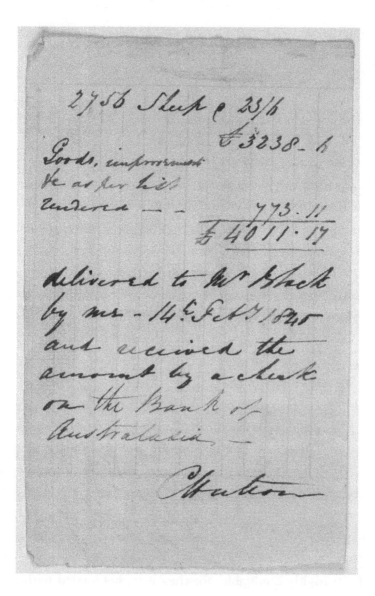

'The best run in the colony': receipt for '2756 sheep @ 23/6', 'Goods, improvements etc as per list rendered' was issued for the payment of a cheque for £4011 17s at the handover of the run on Mount Emu Creek, to be renamed Glenormiston, on 14 February 1840.

Niel Black papers, Box 31, MS 8996, State Library of Victoria

of tobacco and the cultivated crops. Around 80 people had to be sheltered and fed during this time; Taylor's men would leave after the handover. On 14 February the transactions were complete, a receipt was made out for Black's cheque – £3238 6s for sheep, £773 11s for 'Goods & Improvements', £4011 17s altogether – and at midday the selling party left.

The next day the new order at Glenormiston began. Things had been let slide, and hard work by everyone – including Black – was required. Several acres were under cultivation with wheat, oats and barley for livestock; potatoes and vegetables; and tobacco for dressing scabby sheep. The crops were overdue for harvesting and spoiling in the ground. Scaffolds were made for drying out, and the homestead was protected from fire by burning a strip of grass around it. Within two days, hot winds were blowing and the dread of fire was upon them. Black rode out eight miles to assess the danger, and sent Robert Anderson to clear bush around a spring to move a flock onto it for safety. He was used to fighting heather fires in Scotland, but these grass fires behaved differently and his people were terrified.

'About 6 o'clock wind changed and a volume of smoke surrounded us and caused a darkness and gloom through which we could not see each other at 100 yards' distance. Women all crying; some of the men proposing to try to burn a wider circle about ourselves, others praying not to attempt it. Horses tethered in the direction of the fire – sent to remove them. There was no personal danger, as by crossing a creek of water half a mile distant we were all safe, but the World around us had a most dreadful appearance, and it appeared to me that I never saw the hand of Providence so plain in anything as at this instant. A drop of rain we had not seen for weeks before, and just at the moment when certain ruin seemed impending over us and we unable to do anything for ourselves, drops of rain began to fall and in a few minutes were succeeded by a heavy shower.'[29]

Within a few days, the harvest was in. All in all, Black had made a good start in excellent country, and even the hand of the Almighty seemed to be on his side.

Chapter Two

'QUIETLY SLAUGHTERED IN UNKNOWN NUMBERS'

EARLY IN HIS SEARCH for a run, Niel Black had decided that – despite his original assumption that he would venture into the unknown and open up new territory – he did not wish to engage in the kind of action against Aboriginal people this entailed. He wrote to Gladstone: 'It is regarded as an imposs-ibility to take up a new Run without being necessitated – for the protection of life and property – to shoot many of these poor ignorant creatures. They are thus deliberately thought quietly slaughtered in unknown numbers.'[1]

During his encounter with the young squatting fraternity carousing and boasting of their exploits at the Woolpack Inn in Geelong, light had dawned on him about the murderous behaviour routinely engaged in by some of those whose ranks he was about to join. He entrusted to his journal the realisation that anyone who carved a new run out of the bush needed a conscience 'sufficiently seared to enable him without remorse to slaughter natives right and left'. He described how they often speared and stole sheep, and went on: 'the settlers agree that lead [bullets] is the only antidote that effectively cures them of this propensity'. Murders to this effect were sometimes carried out 'by whole sale'.[2]

Black thought the young squatters' stories were probably exaggerated because they were all told by 'bouncing', or boasting, obliquely 'in hints and slang phrases'. This was because it was too risky to talk openly about such exploits in case they came to the ears of the recently appointed Protectors of Aborigines. Black thought, or hoped, that the truth was less dreadful than the guarded boasts implied; but the real scale of these killings was impossible to know. That the results of their forays should be talked of like the bag at a shoot, with a total lack of conscience, was a shock to Black. 'I believe that great numbers of these poor creatures have wantonly fallen victims to settlers scarcely less savage tho' more enlightened than themselves, and that two-thirds of them do not care a single straw about taking the life of a native, provided they are not taken up by the Protectors.'[3]

Although by this time Black had been entrusting his detailed impressions of the colony to his journal for over two months, he had never previously mentioned 'natives'. Although not at the forefront of his concerns, they must have featured in his pre-departure enquiries, in shipboard conversations, and in discussions with those from whom he learned the lie of this new land after his arrival. He would have seen them camping on the outskirts of Melbourne and in the town itself. He knew that they would pose some degree of hazard to his project. But in his early priorities, they did not feature. Nor did he see himself as being at risk of attack when he set off alone into the bush. He carried a pistol, as he would have done in Scotland. But of threat from local Aboriginal people he makes no mention, nor of any glimpse of them along his way. Only after he had visited run-holders near Geelong and listened to the 'bouncers' at the Woolpack Inn did he refer to those who had been lords of their own soil for thousands of years and were now being violently expelled from their homelands and hunting grounds by intruders such as himself.

Black's observations provide a window onto how one closely involved contemporary viewed – and took part in – the clash between graziers and Aboriginal people in the early years of the Port Phillip settlement. What he described in his journal and letters, as well as what he omitted, derived from ideas and perceptions indefensible by the standards of today, reflecting a mindset very different from our own. His attitudes were not as remorseless as those of many of his peers, but nor were they as benign as those of a handful.

At the time of Black's arrival in Port Phillip, British colonial policy towards indigenous peoples everywhere was undergoing change. In Van Diemen's Land, where many of the Port Phillip graziers had cut their settler teeth, they and their ex-convict shepherds had killed off the local peoples with impunity. Their slaughter had been an accepted corollary to the acquisition of

grazing land. Such a dehumanised attitude towards the indigenous people they found in situ had, in the Americas and South
Africa, for centuries gone hand in hand with the forced acquisition of land for white settlement. 'Black' or 'native' wars had
routinely been fought by frontiersmen and gunslingers, with
the complicity of the state. But by the 1830s, extermination of
Aboriginal peoples was beginning to be greeted with abhor-
rence in Britain. The rise of evangelicalism, and its humanitarian
accompaniment – reform in prisons, factories and mines, and
an end to cruelty of all kinds – spilled over into colonisation.
Unprovoked aggression against indigenous people for the purpose of their displacement to make way for European settlement
was under attack.

The long agitation for the abolition of slavery in the British
Empire had only reached legislative fruition in 1833. Actual eman-
cipation came in 1838, and the cause of Aboriginal protection
rose in tandem. Many anti-slavery campaigners were leaders of an
Aborigines Protection Society established in London in 1837. As
a result of their pressure, a House of Commons Select Committee
was set up to make recommendations on how settlement in newly
acquired colonial territories could be pursued without inflicting
'desolation and ruin' on 'defenceless and uncivilized Tribes'. This,
the Society insisted, was possible, despite the erroneous belief per-
sisting that their extinction was 'an appointment of Heaven, and
every effort to avert their doom must be unavailing'. This sentiment, which many colonists in Australia would have echoed, was
deplored by the Society as 'impious and atrocious'.[4] The pressure
on policy was effective. Although such ideas may not have been
widely absorbed in the population, or among Scottish emigrants
to Port Phillip, they would have been familiar to the educated
and churchgoing by the time Black left home.

30

In Black's native Argyll, a process of depopulation by only slightly less brutal means had been underway since his father's childhood. The 'clearances' that began in the mid-eighteenth century removed indigenous Gaelic-speaking farmers from land they had tended for generations, to make way for 'improvers' using scientific methods of breeding and pasturing stock. In Glendaruel, the valley where Black was born and where the population was dwindling to make way for sheep, this process was seen as beneficial, greening the grass and raising the value of the land; even the fate of departees to Glasgow's new industries was seen as to their advantage.[5] Such a parallel with the Aboriginal peoples of Australia would not have crossed Black's mind as he listened to the 'bouncers' in the Woolpack Inn; after all, the most impoverished farm labourer in Scotland had a soul, which could not be assured in an unchristianised 'black'. But if he could approve of one set of events – on the basis of which his own family had flourished – he could hardly disapprove of the other. He had been raised to believe that improving the productivity of land and stock was a religiously sanctioned cause, inexorably leading to the betterment of all. The improvement of the landscape by the judicious application of capital upon it was a core tenet of this creed. Indigenous populations of Australia or elsewhere had no role to play in this world view.

The lands of Australia Felix were claimed by the Crown as 'vacant'[6] though they were nothing of the kind. This designation was the basis for the incomers' presence in them, yet their emptiness was belied by the fight put up by the existing inhabitants against that presence. Officially, the land was 'wasteland', virgin bush. There was no respect for the Aboriginal system of land management – careful burning of vegetation, for example; the idea that there could be such a thing was inconceivable at the time. The colonial incomers were as one in assuming a God-given, Crown-sanctioned right to graze their sheep in a wilderness harbouring some groups of nomads without a settled life. They saw the main contest for grassland and settlement as being played out among themselves.

However, to graze flocks without serious loss required the settlers to have a strategy towards those being displaced by sheep. The alternatives were kill (by violence, poison or contagious disease), drive off, pacify, domesticate or accommodate, or some combination of these. Whatever strategy was adopted, it must succeed in leaving the incomers masters of 'their' domain. European settlers, including those sympathetic to Aboriginal peoples' plight, rarely doubted their own innate and Christianised superiority to the Indigenous population, including as exploiters and improvers of the environment. William Westgarth, for example, an enlightened contemporary commentator, deplored the way 'civilised man, in his irresistible progress' has 'either driven off the Aboriginal tribes, or subdued their native spirit and subverted their social policy';[7] but Westgarth was also a strong supporter of European settlement and 'improvement' of the bush.

Left to their own devices, the settlers would take the law into their own hands, with the result that the existing peoples of the Port Phillip district would be killed or die of sickness, displacement or deprivation, with a few individuals surviving as workers, domestics or 'pets' on certain runs. So the colonial authorities introduced a new arm of government to interpose between them and the graziers: the Aboriginal Protectorate. How this would stem their decline was not well articulated, but potentially it included establishing reserves for them to live on, with land to till, instruction in farming methods and the skills to become settled, God-worshipping members of the human race. In 1838,

George Augustus Robinson, who had tried and failed to arrest the extinction of Indigenous peoples in Van Diemen's Land, was recruited as Chief Protector for the Port Phillip district. He was to be aided by four Assistant Protectors, including Charles Sievwright for the section between Geelong and Portland Bay, a mere 15 500 square miles.

The Protectors began their work in early 1839 without being afforded the means – legal, administrative or budgetary – to carry out their mission effectively. Their main purpose was to reduce violence between settlers and the original occupiers of their lands, but their initial task was to conduct a census of the Aboriginal population – names, tribes, family size, customs, languages, locations.[8] This activity had merit, but the takeover of terrain was already far advanced and its accompanying violence meant that immediate conciliatory action was needed. Rivers, marshes and hunting grounds on which the original inhabitants' subsistence depended were being sequestered, and access to traditional camps and food sources cut off. When members of one tribal group were pushed out into land occupied by an unrelated other, hostilities broke out between them. Wildlife and edible plants would be insufficient for extra mouths, lives became increasingly vulnerable, and one way or another, the course of human devastation was accelerated.

Some of the worst affected were therefore open to the idea of aid and protection. In June 1839, members of the Barrabool people at Geelong helped Charles Sievwright to set up a home on the Barwon River, in return for a promise of food and clothing. But the necessary supplies were withheld by Robinson, who did not want an Assistant Protector usurping his privilege of making gifts.[9] So his Barrabool charges shivered and starved during the 1839 winter and were forced to return to the plains. Sievwright felt his whole operation had been revealed as a mockery. This was a portent of the inadequacy of future operations and of Chief Protector Robinson's capacity for vacillation.

On their side, most of the graziers pouring into Port Phillip disliked the Protectors, who were impeding their pursuit of their grazing business. While the landscape was 'vacant' and settlers few, Aboriginal groups might be kept away on the periphery of a run. But by late 1839, this was becoming less and less practicable. The Portland Bay district was rapidly filling up with Crown licensees. The Protectorate, an experiment never before attempted in Her Britannic Majesty's colonies, was seen by many of them as ill-conceived and its emissaries as inept. Its officers were shunned socially, and portrayed as abettors of sheep thieves and murderers whom they saved from punishment. That some graziers might lose 'their' land to make way for native reserves appeared incredible. How to reconcile their actions with the survival and well-being of Indigenous peoples was not a conundrum they were disposed to solve.

———————————

The reasons for Niel Black's lack of mention of the local Aboriginal inhabitants in the early pages of his journal can only be surmised. He wrote openly about his experiences, according to his own account, because he expected no-one other than his brother Walter and close family members to read it. However, what he wrote (and omitted) was also coloured, consciously or otherwise, by the need to reassure those at home of low risks to his person, his venture and his chances of success – especially as he hoped Walter might follow him to Port Phillip. He had no idea of conveying any view of the general policy towards 'blacks'

– other than that he thought all clashes between them and the settlers should be dealt with under the law, not by summary action. His attitudes towards Aboriginal people evolved over time as his experiences and the views of other squatters informed them. But there was one barrier that he personally would not cross: his vow of obedience to the Sixth Commandment, 'Thou shalt not kill'. He and his cousin Donald Black both believed that there was no circumstance other than extreme self-defence in which they would take a human life.[10]

The main problem he had to address in establishing a run was that local Aboriginal people were well known to have no qualms about 'stealing and spearing sheep in the folds at night, and even collecting in mobs and attacking the shepherd in day'.[11] This tendency had to be curbed. Black wanted to believe that the problem of violence was not as vexed as many settlers made out. 'They are in general a very timid race, and a man's life is in little danger from them',[12] he wrote. A few rounds of gunfire extinguished any instinct for aggression, and Black only expected to discharge his shot as a scare tactic, into the air. Disturbances between Aboriginal people and shepherds he blamed on the bad character and behaviour of ex-convict labourers. He had never heard of an attack on a homestead, nor did he know of cattle being speared in the Port Phillip district, while mounted horses – as with the conquistadors in South America – induced terror. He thought the original inhabitants had limited motives for aggression, no desire to cause bloodshed, and only injured settlers to acquire food or in retaliation for an injury to themselves.

To avoid clashes, he explained in his journal, it was best to take up a run where 'pacification' was already effected. A person 'may buy a run already occupied, and where the natives occasion as little annoyance, and I may with truth add less, than a party of three or four tinkers or Gypsies do at home'. Black thought that someone 'might live here in perfect safety in the middle of the worst of the natives'.[13] With such sentiments he tried to allay his own and his men's concerns, and any fears at home that he or his enterprise would come to grief at the hands of warlike braves, such as the Scots were used to hearing about from North America. He reacted with scepticism to the scaremongering and extravagant accusations rife in the district about Aboriginal cruelty and aggression, and despite later experiences of attacks on his sheep and incidents with his men, he persisted in his pacifist views. He thought that he and other squatters should lead by example – by not wounding or killing – and behave in such a way that good relations could be maintained.

On his first visit to his future run, Black was informed that, around Portland Bay, the 'natives are very troublesome'[14] – meaning that they violently resisted incomers. The further west a grazier went, the more shepherds would have to be hired to keep watch over flocks – an important cost consideration. At the extremities of settled territory there was a constant risk of 'affrays' between settlers (on horseback and armed with guns) and Aboriginal people (on foot and armed with spears). These were often provoked by settlers to give themselves an excuse for violent retaliation and murder. Having decided that he did not want to engage in 'affrays', Black was content to gain from others having given a 'serious check' to local inhabitants, and saw no moral ambiguity in this position.

This 'check' had been performed by Frederick Taylor, MacKillop and Smith's superintendent. In October 1839, Taylor, who was well known for his brutality against Aboriginal people,[15] had undertaken an extraordinary retaliation for sheep-stealing. Taylor did not worry about catching the actual culprits, but believed that a good dose of indiscriminate lead and some corpses would be sufficient deterrent to the rest. Hearing that around 50 members of the Jarcoort section of the Kirrae tribe were camping in a gully on Mount Emu Creek, he put together an armed party of local squatters and their men, led them down the gully with guns blazing, and killed almost all the men, women and children where they lay sleeping on the ground. This virtually wiped out one local clan, the Tarnpirr *gundidj* (Tarnpirr was the Aboriginal name for Mount Emu Creek). A few other Jarcoort people camping nearby escaped, including a woman, Bareetch Chuurneen, who swam across Lake Bullen Merri with her child on her back.[16]

The massacre was too extreme to be ignored, and in November 1839, Assistant Protector Sievwright arrived and set about taking witness statements from survivors. The news of Sievwright's investigation prompted Taylor to flee to Van Diemen's Land for fear of arrest. This was why his overseer, William Blackie, was standing in when Black bought the run. Blackie told the new occupier – as a reassurance – that 'about thirty-five to forty natives have been dispatched on this establishment and there are only two men left alive of the tribe'. Black added: 'He is certain we will never be troubled.'[17] Despite this, Black had difficulty persuading some of his own people that they were not at risk of attack.

However hard Black tried to convince himself that there would be no future 'trouble' (which turned out not to be the case), and of the need to chase the one-time occupiers of his run away for their own good as well as his own, there is an occasional touch of anguish concerning them in his correspondence. Taylor's scorched-earth policy had left its mark on Glenormiston, with burnt remnants of spears and artefacts in suddenly abandoned camps, and continuing discoveries of charred bones and bodies dumped in waterholes. When Black moved his home station in 1847, he selected a different part of the run. Ghosts at the original site and its waterhole lingered on.

------•◆•------

When Black began to encounter occasional hunting groups or figures in the branches of trees on certain parts of his run, he wrote of them as 'poor creatures' who would not hurt anyone unless provoked. His men came to believe him. Peter McIntyre, who made himself a bark canoe and spent his spare time shooting wildlife on Lake Terang, knew they camped there and was unconcerned.[18] Black put their resentments down to the worst type of station hand behaviour. 'Several of the men lately on this establishment are now very ill with the native pox ... Notwithstanding the bad name they had here, I am told it is not an uncommon thing for these rascals to sleep all night with a *lubra* [Aboriginal woman] and if she offend him, shoot her before twelve the next day. How can the father or husband avoid resenting such usage?'[19] He sacked Taylor's men and used ex-convict labour as little as possible, believing that good men and good management of men would minimise trouble and keep relations peaceful.[20] He was one of a handful of settlers noted by Chief Protector Robinson as having adopted this policy and making it work.[21] But he did not feel positive or kindly towards the men of the bush: few settlers did.

Black armed those of his shepherds who managed his out-stations, but they were instructed not to shoot to wound or kill, but only to fire their guns as a scare tactic or in extreme duress. Claud Farie, his neighbour to the west, wrote home to Scotland in

July 1840 describing in detail an Aboriginal attack in full daylight
– most were at night – at one of Black's outstations. Excitement
colours his account: '… grasping their spears as if they would
throw them at the men if they dared to interfere, they rushed
the flocks and drove off unharmed a number of sheep. The two
men were both well-armed, each having a double-barrelled gun
and a brace of pistols which ought to have brought four of the
black rascals to their bearings … and the rest would have taken
to their heels.' Farie was very surprised – even scathing – that
the shepherds had not used their firearms, and assumed that the
reason was that 'Mr. Black's men are afraid of the natives'.[22] But
they were simply obeying orders. Black's frighten-away policy
paid off: he only lost 27 sheep to theft in 1840.[23] This was far
fewer than most of his neighbours.

When Black encountered Aboriginal groups in the bush, he
sometimes gave chase, terrifying them by riding down at full
gallop, or discharged his gun into the air to scatter them and
show what damage he might do if he chose. If he found empty
camps, he did not torch them as other squatters sometimes did,
but left clear indications that their occupants should remove
themselves. He remained determined to keep them as far away as
possible, not trusting in ideas of domestication, as this led to them
'hanging around the stations, half-civilised'. To keep them at a
distance Black regarded as 'the greatest mercy that can possibly
be shown them'[24] so that they would 'keep to their ways' and
not steal from him. He must have known that he was stealing
their traditional springs and waterholes, especially when he cut
down vegetation and altered banks and water flows so that his
cattle and sheep could use them. The 6.4-kilogram black swan
he shot, the wildfowl that McIntyre went after in his canoe,
and the numerous 'cangaroos and emus' he saw as a threat to his

crops were an indication of the plentiful wildlife on which the local people had been used to thriving. But depriving them of the means for survival did not touch his conscience compared with the greater ill of physically harming them. Once driven off his run, their well-being was not his concern.

During his first year on Glenormiston, sheep-stealing and the occasional death of a shepherd or hutkeeper in the vicinity were more common occurrences than Black had anticipated. There were many local sites – Lake Keilambete, Mount Noorat, Lake Terang, Pejark Marsh, the Tarnpirr (Mount Emu) Creek – where certain tribal groups congregated at different seasons for hunting, fishing or trading. The closer density of white settlement was rendering their situation increasingly desperate, and they therefore retaliated more strongly against occupiers. In July 1840, Black wrote to Gladstone that 'the natives were worse in every part of the settlement' and had attacked two of his men in broad daylight (as described in Farie's letter). A few days later, a shepherd on a neighbouring run was murdered, and he felt he must temporarily close one of his own outstations as a safety measure. He regretted not having brought out more guns, and in July 1841 was still asking Gladstone to send a box of decent firearms. He remarked in the same letter that he had received the gift of an excellent 'carabine' from his other partner Alex Finlay, 'one of the best I have seen for a black hunt, an [sic] use to which I hope I may never have occasion to apply it'.

Although Black did not tolerate unprovoked assaults by settlers on Aboriginal people, the reactive 'hunt' for those who had killed a shepherd or stolen sheep, and the bringing of such 'criminals' to justice, was a different matter. The settlers had a genuine need of security for men and flocks. According to their view, if the Crown dictated a policy of 'Aboriginal protection', it must surely also provide 'settler protection'. In fact, it was difficult to draw a line between proactive and reactive violence, since it was often blurred deliberately by settlers spoiling for a fight. A settler known to perpetrate atrocities might talk of hot pursuit of sheep-stealers, and how in the turmoil 'the gun gaed off' and 'some puir creatures fell'.[25]

Black's journal gives an account of an 'affray' between the Whyte brothers and 'troublesome' occupants of land further west, at Konongwootong, near Wando Vale in March 1840. This was a case which failed to be treated as the massacre it was. John Whyte stayed at Glenormiston on his way to report his version of events to the authorities.[26] The account he gave Black, and had already given to Sievwright, who was in the vicinity investigating a similar atrocity, described a massacre of 25 people with only two survivors. But since they were all men and were with the sheep that the Whytes were trying to recover, the brothers regarded the full-scale slaughter as justifiable. The fact that no-one in their own party had been killed, or even wounded other than by the first spear to be hurled, was regarded as immaterial, as was the recovery of most of the sheep. Whyte told Black a large party of 'natives' had taken a flock of 900 breeding ewes.[27] A different squatter reported only 50 sheep cut off from the Whytes' flock. In this account, 51 people were killed, all the menfolk of the local tribe bar one, and the women and children were chased away up the Glenelg River.[28]

Black was sympathetic towards the Whytes. In his journal, he described 'the Blacks' drawing up in order of battle and standing 'feight' for an hour without hurting anyone after throwing the first spear. He offered no justification for the killing of 25 people other than that they were feasting on stolen roast mutton; but then, at that time, a British sheep-stealer might be transported for less. The Whytes might have to 'stand their trial for murder. But it will be a mere form. They must be acquitted.' Black apologised to his family audience for writing such a harrowing account, but this was to play down any sense of alarm. He felt strikingly little repugnance for the killings, given his earlier protestations and the rejection of violence on his own behalf. Being in the bush had begun to change his perceptions. Whyte, a guest, expressed perfect confidence in his own and his brothers' correctness in the matter, and Black, now incorporated into the squatter fraternity, accepted his view of it.[29]

The Whytes, as predicted, got away with their killings. James Croke, the Crown Prosecutor in Geelong, refused to accept Sievwright's sworn evidence and bring a case for murder against them. Instead a public hue and cry was got up against Sievwright. Since 'the natives' had thrown the first spear, the popular verdict was that they had invited their own execution. In common with almost everyone, Croke was antipathetic to the Protectorate and adept at finding technical reasons to avoid prosecuting squatters.[30]

A few months later, Black himself became involved in an expedition to hunt down 'natives', in this case as the result of the death of a shepherd on an adjoining run. John Thomson, the licensee, had arrived within a day of Black's takeover of Glenormiston. Thomson, also Scottish, had spent 19 years in Hobart helping his brother run a school. In 1839, reports of 'Australia Felix' summoned him across Bass Strait to invest their savings in sheep. His licence entitled him to a large tract between Mortlake and Terang, running down the western flank of Mount Noorat – land he had first viewed from the crater's rim. His home station was on the banks of a salt lake called Keilambete. He had found freshwater springs among clumps of tea-tree scrub, and his cattle had found fresh water within the lake, gushing out on the northern side.[31] Black, to his chagrin, could do nothing about Thomson's claim although Keilambete was part of 'Taylor's country'. With his Van Diemen's Land background and his ex-convict shepherds, Thomson was a hardened customer. Energetic and doggedly persevering, he was brusque of manner and blunt of speech.[32] He and Black were destined not to get on.

In late July 1840, Thomson waylaid Black on the Geelong road. Thomson was determined to go after those who had killed his shepherd – it was the third recent local murder. He recruited Black as one of a party of settlers, some from over 50 miles away, who met in Geelong and petitioned Superintendent La Trobe against the 'undeserved indifference' to their right to protection. They then accepted an offer from Captain Foster Fyans, newly appointed as Commissioner of Crown Lands for the area, to accompany them to the crime scene with his mounted police.[33] Fyans had a steely reputation, having put down a convict mutiny on Norfolk Island in a sufficiently brutal fashion to earn the nickname of 'Flogger' Fyans. La Trobe declared him 'a very rough hand'.[34] Fyans had no sympathy for the Aboriginal people he was supposed to protect, and put himself at the head of the expedition to hunt down the killers. Two of his police joined the party, and Fyans swore in some of the squatters as special constables. This was officially frowned on because it came close to letting squatters take the law into their own hands.

For several days this posse galloped about the country in search of the guilty parties. Black was sardonic: 'After riding around in the bush for a week, our zeal began to evaporate.' He thought the sight of 21 men thundering about on horseback must have a deterrent effect. But the quarry, or a quarry, was eventually found. 'We were all about to disperse when, on riding home one evening, I had the fortune to find them camped in one of their old haunts near my vacated station. At day break next day I guided the party to near the spot. We surrounded them and did not find it a very difficult task to take them without injury.'[35] A shepherd of Thomson's who had witnessed the murder swore that two of three men hiding in the trees were the culprits, and all three were taken off to Geelong in chains. To be dragged 90 miles by a man on horseback in the name of justice and then confined in a lock-up was indescribably harsh. But at least they were not shot on the spot.

Black credited himself with the prevention of bloodshed. This was the first attempt in the district to apprehend Aboriginal miscreants and take them into custody rather than kill them outright, 'and I believe I was mainly instrumental in getting the settlers to take these [men] without the least personal violence'. He believed it was essential that the accused were made subject to the law and its punishments, or 'this will become a scene of slaughter and bloodshed similar to what Van Diemen's Land was'. Settlers, he wrote to Gladstone, would not submit to being robbed and murdered without chance of redress. 'The Natives are (very properly) under the most rigorous protection of the laws ... But among the numerous outrages committed by them there has never been one instance of their being made sensible that they are amenable to the punishment the law accords. They are daily thus becoming more dangerous.' What, he asked, was the settler to do? 'He must take all the fearful risk of protecting himself'.[36] And if that became the norm, the settlers would do their worst.

Although Black wanted to avert this prospect, as time went on he became less inclined to criticise his fellows, and joined in the general disparagement of 'blacks'. Relations between squatters were complex: they were dependent on each other for friendship and for loans of stores and drays and assistance of various kinds, but also quarrelled over their boundaries and incursions of scabby sheep. As the economic depression of the early 1840s began to bite, contests over land and livestock safety became more bitter. But there was one subject on which they were universally agreed: the need for security against what were known as 'native depredations'. In this context, public opinion was on their side, and the issue was a glue that kept their comradeship intact.

In early 1842, the settlers from around Port Fairy – including Black – petitioned La Trobe for protection against 'enormous losses at the hands of aborigines whose numbers, ferocity and cunning render them particularly formidable'. La Trobe received this petition at the same time as the report of a murder of three Aboriginal women and a child sleeping at Muston's Creek north of Port Fairy. He was outraged by such an act, especially as it was committed on the run of two of the petitioners, Messrs Smith and Osbery. He therefore demanded that the murderers be exposed and brought to justice.[37] Black, who had occasional station dealings with Smith and Osbery, wrote to Gladstone: 'A correspondence has passed between the Settlers and the government in which the former is called upon to purge themselves and servants from all knowledge of or participation in this crime.' By this time he liked to think that those in his circle did not shoot people in cold blood and lie about it. He no longer saw these fellow squatters as 'bouncers' alluding to murder with a wink and a nudge, but as respectable men under duress. Squatters did not inform on one another, and it was unjust that all should be labelled complicit in a crime for showing solidarity.

The episode caused Black to expostulate that 'A Squatter here is worse off than the veriest serf in Russia.' His hyperbole stemmed from the belief that, at home, 'even the savage will excite the warmest sympathy on his behalf, but there is but little of it bestowed on the European whose fate it is to contend with that savage and to guard against a nature so treacherous, that it can never be won by any amount of kindness'.[38] In two years his views had undergone a transformation from previous talk of 'timid race' and 'poor creatures'. In fact, Black had put himself firmly in the wrong. Instead of cooperating with the government's request, some prominent settlers had produced a story for which there was no evidence. Black was one of those who put his name to this story. He chose to believe that the murders at Muston's Creek were not committed in cold blood on defenceless women, but as a result of an action on 'a marauding party of men and women in whose possession was found stolen property'. The suggestion that men had participated in the 'affray' was vouched for by AL Boursequot, a squatter and one of those involved.[39] Thus was the atrocity cast, as so often, as retribution for Aboriginal misdeeds.

This was clearly a trumped-up story, and La Trobe was furious. He informed Governor George Gipps, who reported it to London; Gipps thought this kind of cover-up would besmirch the colony's reputation. He threatened, if evidence as to who the murderers were did not come forward from those in the know, to consider extreme action: all squatter licences in the Port Fairy district would be revoked and the whole area made into a native reserve. His letter was passed on by La Trobe to the settlers. This elicited a mollifying response, signed by Niel Black and Claud Farie on behalf of the group, saying that their supposition was 'not stated as a fact, nor as a rumour, but merely as a probable supposition that the women killed were attached to a marauding party ... We can only regret now that your attention was ever called to it.'[40]

However, Black's defensive letter to Gladstone indicates that he felt the wrong was all on the side of the uncomprehending government – as did the squatters as a whole: 'The Governor's letter threw a stain upon every settler's name whose misfortune it is to be in our district.'[41] This attitude was echoed in the *Portland Mercury*, which described the Governor's threat to revoke the licences as 'tantamount to declaring every settler in the Port Fairy District accessory to an atrocious murder'. The risk that all their licences would be revoked was minimal and they knew it – they were the principal men of the Port Phillip District and bastions of the wool economy. But Gipps' threat played into the hands of Commissioner Fyans. Then embroiled in a quarrel with Black on other grounds, Fyans instructed the Treasury to withdraw his licence. Black was obliged to ride to Melbourne to remedy this.

Not until mid-1843, a year later, were the killers of the Aboriginal women and child at Muston's Creek finally apprehended. Farie wrote to Black, then away in Scotland: 'The murderers of the Lubras at Smith and Osbery's are at last said to be discovered.' The party of six included two settlers, Boursequot – who had clearly given false witness – and Robert Whitehead; and two overseers, one of whom – Beswick – was sent to Melbourne under police escort, handcuffed to a bullock driver. Beswick and the two working men were to stand trial. Whitehead fled abroad. Boursequot escaped prosecution.[42]

Although he shared the view that the Protectorate was an institution dreamed up by misguided visionaries and operated by incompetents, Black maintained cordial relations with Charles Sievwright. Sievwright had been an army officer but ran up debts and sold his commission. He obtained the Assistant Protector post in Port Phillip through influential contacts in London. His job put him in dispute with the Commissioner of Crown Lands and almost every settler in the district, cost him his marriage, and – in Black's epithet – turned him into 'the most unpopular man that ever breathed'.[43]

Black first met Sievwright a week after he took up his run. Sievwright had a camp at Keilambete, on the banks of the saltwater lake that was the Kirrae people's favourite place in the area. With its volcanic hills, fertile soils, lakes, waterholes, forests, rich wildlife and the creek they called Tarnpirr, the whole area was much valued by the Kirrae. Thus it was not as simple as Black had supposed to keep them off Glenormiston. Mount Noorat, on the western edge of his run, with a crater as deep as it was high, was a meeting place for local tribes. They went there in the summer to settle disputes and exchange goods – saplings for spears, red clay for ceremonial paint, and gum for fixing axe handles.[44]

In mid-1840, Gipps gave consent to the establishment of native reserves. Sievwright had petitioned for this as the only practicable way of providing security to the settlers and subsistence to his charges. He had hoped that each major tribe could have its own reserve, since relations between them were hostile. Instead, only one reserve per Protector was to be permitted. The site Sievwright had already identified was Keilambete; he had received Robinson's permission to form a camp there, and told Thomson that his run, including the lake and surrounding forest, might be needed as a reserve.[45] But Thomson ignored Sievwright's warning. He built a hut for his own residence on the banks of the lake, and a hut for his shepherds on his boundary. It was one of these shepherds who was killed in July 1840, prompting the posse of squatters that thundered about the country.

From Thomson's point of view, Sievwright was a menace not only because of the threat to his run, but also because Aboriginal people trailed him to shield themselves from 'justice' – a common interpretation of their presence at his camp. By contrast, Black decided to be friendly with Sievwright and not judge him prematurely. When he was short of supplies, needed flour to be ground or help with transport, Black lent him equipment or provided goods on credit.[46] He wrote to Gladstone: 'He is a man of Gentlemanly manners and address whatever he may be in other respects.' But Black's cordiality was not disinterested. He hoped to deflect Sievwright from any plan that would cost him part of his run. 'He says he will not trouble me although the natives wish him to take my place.'[47] Black did not entirely trust Sievwright's word and he knew that Thomson would play tough. For several months, a shadow contest took place between Black, Thomson and Sievwright, all using their influence with Robinson, La Trobe and Fyans to have the reserve put where the interests of each dictated.

As 1840 drew on, the threat of interracial violence continued. Gipps told La Trobe that he was prepared to sanction any expenditure necessary to reduce it. Sievwright clamoured to be allowed to establish the reserve at Keilambete to prevent his Aboriginal dependants from engaging in 'retaliation and revenge which must be a natural consequence of the rapid occupation of their country without either asylum or assistance being offered in return'.[48] Every time a planting season and potential harvest was lost, hunger would further induce them to attack the settlers' flocks. More than 2300 sheep had been reported stolen in the Portland Bay district during the winter months, and although most were recovered, this was not without further loss of Aboriginal lives. In one incident, Henry Gibb reconvened some of the squatters who had taken part in Thomson's posse to capture a youth who had wounded one of his shepherds with a spear. The boy was tied up in a woolshed at Black's station while his captors argued whether to dispense summary justice or follow due process via the law. In the night the problem was resolved: the boy got away.[49]

Because the settlers hid from the authorities much of what was going on, La Trobe was not fully aware of the scale of the clashes. Black wrote to Gladstone in early September of 'the natives daily robbing settlers at a most alarming rate', and of hidden reprisals against them. A few days back he had found 'a Grave into which about 20 must have been thrown'. Despite, or because of, what was happening, La Trobe wanted the Protectorate to try harder to establish friendly relations and 'proper influence' over those they were supposed to protect. In late 1840 he ordered Robinson – who had yet to leave his desk in Melbourne – out of his office and into the field, to go west and establish friendly relations with them.[50] Sievwright's existing efforts to do this, expressed in his reports and requests, were ignored. And he was becoming increasingly anxious about the threat of aggression from Thomson's men. He therefore appealed to Black, visiting the bush with him in search for alternative reserve sites.

In December, Black heard a rumour that Lake Terang, the freshwater lake on whose banks he had established his cattle station, would be taken for the reserve. Black rushed off to Melbourne to call on the Chief Protector, and on La Trobe. He threatened Robinson that he would write to England to complain – with his contacts, he was confident of his capacity to drum up official support.[51] La Trobe was cordial. 'He was indignant at the Powers the Protectorate body assume. Thanked me for the compliment paid him in applying for his protection. Other settlers in similar circumstances never applied to him but commenced a civil action against the Protector. He assured me of his assistance so far as he could.'[52]

Robinson finally arrived in the Western District in March 1841. Around 300 men, women and children were then at Sievwright's Protectorate camp at Keilambete, and had been clearing forest and starting to grow crops on the understanding that this was their future reserve. Thomson managed to turn Robinson against Sievwright's plans.[53] His litany of complaints against Sievwright included the accusation that he encouraged his charges to raid Thomson's sheep, or at the least turned a blind eye. Robinson ordered Sievwright to cease farming and move the camp to Lake Terang. This caused pandemonium. When some of the menfolk were moved there, fighting broke out among them.[54]

Black protested in very strong terms against the 'invasion' of his run and the arbitrary takeover of his freshwater lake. Robinson persuaded him to accept the situation, because he was seriously afraid that if the camp remained at Keilambete any longer, there would be violent confrontations between its occupants and Thomson's men.[55] Black then obtained a promise that if Keilambete was not taken for the reserve, neither would Robinson take Terang. He also hoped that the situation might be turned to his advantage. If part of his run was marked as a possible native reserve, this would deter squatter intruders. His main concern at this time was to keep new arrivals from nibbling off further sections of 'Taylor's country'.

Thomson and Black both had recourse to La Trobe and managed to plead successfully. Although the Kirrae people, and Sievwright on their behalf, appear to modern eyes to have been grievously wronged by the two men's protestations, it is not surprising that the 'hated protector' lost his case. Not only was his personal reputation dire, his wife having ruined any remaining shreds of goodwill towards him by quitting his camp and making complaints about his marital and fatherly conduct, but the territory around Keilambete, Terang and Mount Noorat was among the best in the whole Port Phillip district. It was far too rich to be sacrificed to people whose system of living lightly off the land was the antithesis of investing capital to 'improve' it and make it commercially productive.

Neither Black nor Thomson was the peripatetic type of squatter; both were there for the long haul. Black was already building dams, cultivating crops, clearing bush, experimenting with grasses, and undertaking 'improvements' of all sorts. He did this both to improve his profits and to fortify his claim to his licence on grounds of industry and commitment to the colony's economic health. He told Sievwright he would cease these 'improvements' if he was not given reassurance of not being removed, and no doubt he made much of them to La Trobe.

Over the next months, while the decision on the location of the reserve continued to be delayed, Black occasionally complained to Sievwright of thefts of his potatoes and stores, and told him to stop his charges coming up to his station to keep them from temptation. But these minor inconveniences seem to be all that marred good relations between the two men. In the spring, the decision was finally made: the reserve would be situated at Mount Rouse, over 50 miles to the north-west. Called Kolor by the local Aboriginal people, it was one of their venues, and the squatter there was newer and less able to promote his case. In October 1841, Black wrote home that 'the Aboriginal Protector and his sable tribe have been ordered to leave my run, but the place is to be kept as a Reserve, although not at present occupied by the Natives'. He represented this as a bulwark against new squatter intruders.

In January 1842, Sievwright began to organise the removal to the new reserve. Black lent bullocks and a dray to assist him, and supplied him with wheat and other stores. The departure of his 210 unwanted guests – 69 men, 65 women and 76 children – was a source of satisfaction to Black, and aiding their trek was the least he could do. His run had been definitively and peacefully cleared of Kirrae people. How they and their families would fare on the reserve was not his affair. As it happened, in the early weeks Sievwright was pleased with how things went there, even though food supplies were rarely sufficient, pulmonary diseases common, and blankets to ward off cold never appeared however many times he requested them. But Sievwright had acquired too many enemies. Local settlers complained that his reserve sowed disorder and provided a shelter for marauders. After he was removed from his post in late 1842, the state of the camp and its inhabitants rapidly deteriorated. Numbers dwindled, sickness and despair carried many lives away, children became a rarity. Gradually, the reserve failed.[56]

Immediately after Sievwright's extraordinary caravan set off in January 1842, Black began to reinstall his cattle yards at Lake Terang and, with the Protector's permission, took over Sievwright's hut. Black believed that his ten-month toleration of Protectorate occupation of a lake well known to be part of his run would make sure of no other claim being made upon Terang. But he had made a serious miscalculation. His worst antagonist would turn out to be no Aboriginal warrior or Protector, but a fellow squatter, Thomson of Keilambete. By contrast, Black's engagement with 'our sable friends' was over.[57]

Few references to 'natives' appear in his later correspondence. But when, in 1853, Black wrote about his early experiences, his retrospective view had hardened into a standard trope of flocks under threat from 'Aborigines lurking in bodies near our stations', stealing sheep and 'gorging themselves and their dogs on well fed mutton'[58] – a far cruder picture than his accounts in the moment. Either his attitude had changed, or he was deliberately guarded earlier on. By the late 1840s, in any case, this had become irrelevant. As contestants for land or livestock, the original lords of their soil had effectively disappeared from 'Taylor's country'. What the massacre at Mount Emu Creek had begun, his own and Thomson's protestations, and Sievwright's removal of his protégés, had completed. How and where the Kirrae's final fate might rest was well beyond his boundaries.

Chapter Three

'I SENT FOR A CHAIN TO MEASURE THE DISTANCE'

THE CRITICAL BATTLES over the early settlement of Port Phillip's Western District were not fought between Europeans and Aboriginal peoples. The outcome of those hostilities was, sadly, a foregone conclusion. From the pioneers' perspective, the serious battles, some of them long campaigns, took place between themselves, with the colonial authorities feebly trying to exert control over the unruly occupants of Crown lands.

The defence of 'Taylor's country' against others trying to carve out their own runs within his claim was the first of Niel Black's battles to gain dominion over 'his' lands, and one he waged ferociously. His weapons were force of personality, tactical alliance, flock manoeuvres, posting of outstations and the cultivation of official backing, including by riding to Melbourne and 'waiting on' Superintendent La Trobe himself. Black's relationships with other squatters – whether large or small, young and inexperienced or not-so-young and more formidable like himself – were conducted within this framework. Fellowship, and sometimes friendship, was cultivated with other settlers over 'black' troubles; wild dogs; traveller hospitality; labour; the care of souls; loans of tobacco, flour, bullocks and drays; and exchanges of stock for stud purposes. But over questions of territory no quarter was spared. As Black put it to Gladstone: 'Possession [is] the only acknowledged right to Crown Land.'[1] And possession of the fullest possible extent of his licensed terrain was his chief gladiatorial arena.

When Black arrived, most of the best land in the Western District was already occupied by Crown licensees.[2] A 'grass rush' of settlers was rapidly filling up the plains, forests and 'rises' between Melbourne and Portland. Fuelled by overconfidence, high prices for wool, speculation in Sydney, Hobart and Melbourne, and an inflow of capital from Britain, the rush was so headlong as to be chaotic. Some adventurers purchased sheep and simply set off. They stopped wherever they found grazing, hoping to hold their ground as first-comers, but moving on if a previous claimant could evict them. Borders of runs were vague – a plough line from a tree here to a rock over there, three miles due east along the bank of a dried-up creek, and so on. Such boundaries were fair game. Seizure of waterholes and destruction of marked trees were a normal part of pastoral life, all arrangements about whose land ended where depending on gentlemen's agreements.[3] Squatting regulations were introduced by act of Parliament in May 1839, and extensive powers were vested in the Commissioners of Crown Lands, not only to end violence between squatters and Aboriginal people but also to administer the licensing system and resolve disputes between squatters themselves. Later that year came the first official visit to runs in the west; on 23 December, Black met Commissioner Henry Gisborne camping at Mount Emu Creek on his way back to Melbourne.[4]

In February 1840, when Black took up his run, the battle of the boundaries was heating up. Any 'empty' grassland without visible stock on it was targeted. Most runs covered many square miles of untamed bush, and as every sheep needed at least three acres, and a cow many more, the land was not exactly teeming.[5] Many grass prospectors were young men with modest resources who aimed to cut out a small 'squattage' of a few thousand acres, make a quick buck and then get on with their lives.[6] Most large-scale graziers, such as the Henty brothers at Portland Bay and the Manifolds at Lake Purrumbete, had come over from Van Diemen's Land with considerable capital. To their ranks were now being added a few similarly endowed entrepreneurs direct from Scotland, such as Black, and the uncle–nephew partnership of Daniel Curdie and Daniel Mackinnon, who took up the run they called Jancourt to his south-east at roughly the same time. All the early settlers picked places with good water, but runs as well endowed as Glenormiston with creek, marsh and lake, were unusual.

Black's skirmishes with intruders on his boundaries began the day he arrived. Along the north-eastern bank of Mount

Emu Creek he found the camp of two impecunious young men, Nicholas Cole, a Cornishman, and Peter McArthur, a Scot, and some miles further down, that of Jean Duverney, 'the Frenchman'. These three adventurers had met on board ship coming down from Sydney in mid-1839 and joined forces. They encountered Peter Manifold in the Woolpack Inn at Geelong, and each purchased a flock of sheep from him at Purrumbete. They then jointly drove them west and sat down along the creek. They thought themselves first occupiers, but Fred Taylor told them that they were trespassing on country already claimed by his employers MacKillop and Smith. When they asked him to propose somewhere else, he took them to Lake Keilambete. They were dismayed by the number of Aboriginal people congregated there – this was before John Thomson asserted his claim – and thought occupation impracticable.[7]

When Protector Sievwright began enquiring into the massacre on Mount Emu Creek in November 1839 and Taylor disappeared, Cole, McArthur and Duverney took advantage of his absence to stay put, the two former along the creek, and Duverney further east at what became Frenchman's Marsh. McArthur, late in life, wrote vividly of the toughness of their early days, 'what with blacks stealing our sheep, wild dogs killing them, scab and foot-rot reducing them to skeletons, not to speak of the risk and hairbreadth escapes we had with our lives'. They camped in the bush, 'living on the commonest of food, such as mutton and damper one day, and the other day damper and mutton, and washed it down with a pannikin or two of either "post and rail" or "Jack the painter" [rough green tea]'.[8] McArthur built a wooden hut, but the first time he roasted a leg of mutton in the hearth, he set the chimney on fire and it burned to the ground.[9]

Black soon discovered Cole's and McArthur's presence. In order to move them on, he adopted a quasi-official approach, obtaining from Taylor's overseer a sworn statement that flocks under his management had grazed on both sides of the creek.[10] Cole and McArthur thereupon set off further north up the creek some distance beyond Black's outermost hut, and a new boundary line was agreed.[11]

Duverney had already built himself a decent hut and wanted to stay put. On 18 March, Black was 'honoured' to receive Duverney's call, visited his hut a few days later and was amazed by his set-up. He worked only with his wife, Rosine, who came from Paris: 'His wife is hut-keeper and he shepherd, and not another mortal to assist them.'[12] Duverney asked if his bullocks could roam with Black's because he did not want Mme Duverney left alone with the sheep if he was out following the cattle. Many marshes and lakes where game was to be found were still seasonally visited by their traditional occupants. Black, solicitous of the Parisian lady's safety, was happy to oblige.

The Duverneys were clearly not cut out for bush life. His eyesight was so bad that, when shepherding, he often came home without the full count. His wife would leave him to put up the night-time hurdles while she went out looking for the missing sheep, carrying in her belt two fully loaded pistols. She seems to have been fearless, but the closer crowding of squatters was leading to more risk of violence. Black and Duverney soon came to terms. The Frenchman promised to leave within 15 months if Black would buy his hut and improvements. The Duverneys left much sooner than this, for a place they named Cressy, after his birthplace, Crécy. Here, at a crossing point on the Woady Yaloak River north of Lake Corangamite, on what was becoming a well-travelled road, they opened a hostelry, the Frenchman's Inn.

Black lent them drays to move their goods and men to build their inn, having so played his hand that their patch of Taylor's country reverted to him painlessly.

———————

Cole, McArthur and Duverney were among those described by Black as 'persons having but small flocks [who] creep in on every corner near an extensive settler for the protection it affords them from the aggressions of the Natives'.[13] Not all such intruders were as easy to dismiss. A new arrival, the formidable Jeremiah Ware, set up opposite Cole and McArthur on the west of the creek. Ware refused to accept Black's view of the distance he had to keep from Black's furthest outstation.

A 'right of run' was understood to stretch for three miles from an existing squatter's pitch. Black believed this meant a distance of three miles from an outstation. Ware thought measurement started at the home station, and a mile from an outstation was sufficient. Such differences became critical as the squeeze on grassland and water became tighter. Black wrote: 'He [Ware] settled 30 miles off on another creek, but they were so crowded there that they were obliged to walk again and he came back upon me. Ware, Gibb and others were a fortnight or three weeks in the Bush lately in search of runs, and all of them are cramming their flocks upon other people's runs. Unless some new country is found we will soon feel crowded here.'[14] Ware was not to be dealt with lightly, and Black agreed to arbitration. This was one of many such disputes now filling the in-tray of the Commissioner of Crown Lands.

The nibbling away of his run caused Black serious anxiety. 'I have scarcely time to eat my food, but flying from one part to another to keep off the enemy – civilised man. He is much more troublesome to me than the savage.' He took personal charge of these boundary battles: no-one else could be depended on to fight them satisfactorily – or, rather, win them. He wrote Gladstone that he was 'dreadfully annoyed and put to a very serious expense' on account of the need to hold country.[15] This was incurred in erecting extra outstations every three to four miles, subdividing his flocks to cover more land, and therefore having to hire extra shepherds and hutkeepers – the latter costing 15 or even 20 shillings a week for doing very little. He also made extra watch-boxes and hurdles for yarding the sheep against night-time wild dog or Aboriginal attack.

Black's problem was that he had barely enough sheep to occupy the area he claimed. The £10 annual squatting licence could in principle be for any amount of land, but the grazier must not claim more land than needed to pasture his stock. Black's first official statement of his holding was 16 000 acres or 25 square miles (he probably understated it),[16] an area on which a minimum of 5000 sheep should be depastured. Black did not have enough money to afford anything like this number at the current prices. The run had been advertised with 7000–8000 sheep. Captain Eddington had agreed to buy 1000, a flock for Donald Black to manage separately. The rest were split with John Riddell, who left them with Black until he had a place of his own. But at the final count, there turned out to be only around 5500 sheep. Eddington received a one-sixth share rather than the promised 1000, leaving Black and Riddell with 2300 each. The total was only just enough technically, and too few strategically, until the flocks increased. This was a real challenge to Black's ambition. 'This is the most princely place I ever saw', he wrote in his journal. 'I am delighted every time I ride round it. Had

I money enough to buy 500 head of cattle and 5000 sheep to keep possession of the country, I believe it unequalled in the colonies.'[17]

Within a week, new interlopers threatened. These were Donald Craig and Stephen Ewen, travelling with a small herd of cattle and a flock of sheep brought across from Van Diemen's Land in August 1839. Black deployed his own men and flocks in a carefully orchestrated manoeuvre to prevent them from taking two important wetlands: an area of tea-tree scrub and marsh known as Pejark, and Lake Terang just further south. Craig actually carried a letter of introduction to Niel Black signed by the Duke of Argyll's factor, Lorne Campbell, Black's landlord in Scotland.[18] But Black was relentless. He moved a small flock down the creek and set up two new outstations. When, defeated by this device, Craig and Ewen called on him to say that they had found a run further south, he still told them that he would apply to have them removed. They went off 'grumbling that I meant to take a whole country to myself', and sat down on the other side of Mount Emu Creek where Black had to admit that his claim was not so good.[19]

Niel and Donald Black then carefully measured the distance from Ewen's camp to Black's most southerly outstation and reckoned it at less than two miles. On this basis he regarded their claim as too close to him. Whatever Black may have thought were his rights over territory, he was on thin legal ground, and Craig and Ewen would not give way. Their complaint that he had more than enough country for his needs was reinforced when, on 25 March 1840, Riddell reappeared with news that he had taken up a place near Mount Macedon and needed his flock. This was a serious blow. Black was now reduced to well below the number of stock required by his licence. Drastic action was needed.

Early in April, armed with a map of his run, he set off for the first time since his arrival to ride the four-day, 130-mile journey to Melbourne to enlist officialdom on his side. Gisborne, the Commissioner of Crown Lands, had gone to New Zealand on sick leave, so Black called upon La Trobe. La Trobe obligingly wrote and advised Craig and Ewen to remove their stock from Black's run, but said the final decision was the Commissioner's.[20] Until Gisborne returned, Black's only leverage against Craig and Ewen was this letter, which failed to dislodge them. The other purpose of his trip was to buy stock to replace Riddell's flocks. He rode to Mount Macedon for rams, then up the Goulburn Valley for cattle – 122 miles in two days, followed by 40 miles up the Yarra Valley. The cattle were destined for the station he had prepared for them at Lake Terang, where his men were busy clearing the dense scrub from the banks to allow access to the water.

To his chagrin, he could only afford 200 head of cattle, prices still being extraordinarily high. He had intended to buy twice as many, half on credit, but was forbidden by his deed of partnership, and the idea of breaching it so tortured his mind that he could not bring himself to the act.[21] He was deeply frustrated to have double the land he needed for his stock, knowing that if he could only buy more cattle he would have no extra expense in grazing them and would correspondingly increase company profits; and for the same reason of not being able to buy stock, he was at serious risk of forfeiting land. If this happened, he would not have enough grazing to conduct operations on the extensive scale he envisaged when his flocks increased. This was the conundrum he was trying to finesse. 'I will struggle to keep all the land I can with what I have, but it would be an advantage to all partners to have the capital increased', he wrote to Gladstone, lamenting the advice which brought him to Port Phillip at the height of a boom with too little money.

Thus began his clamour to his partners at home to invest further in Niel Black & Company so that he could take full advantage of the beautiful stretch of country he had acquired. It would be around four months before the request reached them and a similar period for any response to arrive. He knew he was stymied, but his sense of honour and religious faith did not allow him to break a promise to his partners. He would have to rely on his wits and resourcefulness to minimise territorial losses.

———•◆•———

The rules governing land occupation outside the formally settled areas of New South Wales were ambiguous in relation to the squatters. Sheep and wool were the basis of colonial wealth and revenue, and the graziers the backbone of prosperity. But they could not indefinitely be allowed to take up large expanses of Crown land without controls. They had a tendency to act as if they were beyond the law – which, in a literal sense, they were. Encouragement to settle should be limited: the authorities did not want them to think a grazing licence, coupled with 'improvements', would entitle them to future tenancy or ownership rights. To maintain their insecurity of tenure, the licence was supposed to be renewed every year. But until the 'grass rush' really took hold and the Commissioners of Crown Lands became properly active, the £10 fee was often neglected. MacKillop and Smith, like many early Port Phillip squatters, never bothered to pay up.[22] The authorities did not initially come down on recalcitrant graziers, knowing that they oiled the wheels of the colonial economy, and were 'the real discoverers of the Country and … the Pioneers of Civilisation'.[23]

Although the Colonial Office in London might wish to rein in the frontiersmen – one official described them as equivalent to 'the Nomadic Tribes of Russia and Tartary' – the authorities on the spot were more realistic. In mid-1839, Governor Gipps wrote to Lord Glenelg, Secretary of State for the Colonies in London, that: 'All the power of Government, aided even by a Military force ten times greater than that which is maintained in the Colony, would not suffice to bring back within [the designated limits] the Flocks and Herds which now stray hundreds of miles beyond them.'[24] Gipps was only too aware that a state of near lawlessness existed in more distant areas. He also knew that, in relation to aggression against Aboriginal peoples and whatever else stood in their way, it would be hard to submit a mob of such independent-minded men to regular forms of restraint.

On their side, the settlers had strong views about the Crown's duty to protect them from attack and facilitate their opening up of lands. Their opinion of the government's ability to smooth their productive lives was very low. On the contrary, the authorities wasted licence fee income on ineffective schemes such as the Aboriginal Protectorate, and did far too little for Her Majesty's pioneering subjects. They neither secured the graziers' investments by giving them physical protection, nor fulfilled their promise to bring in sufficient immigrant labour. By 1840, Port Phillip's speculative bubble had burst, depression was setting in, and many of the more debonair squatter-adventurers were in trouble. The government was failing them, including where it hurt the most – in their pocketbooks. It was not proving adept at settling disputes, and nor was it solving issues such as containment of flocks with contagious diseases. In the absence of other means of keeping the peace, the settlers themselves administered justice and controlled crime and immorality on their stations, and took steps to protect their interests, including defending them against marauders of every gentlemanly, criminal and 'savage' hue.

Along with the squatting regulations of 1839, Gipps had introduced a system of levying livestock per head, and strengthened the powers of the Commissioners of Crown Lands to impose on settlers and 'Nomadic Tribes' a greater degree of governance. Commissioners were expected to register runs, collect licence fees and livestock taxes, keeping an oversight of stock, labour and pasturage tallies per licensee; they were also to settle boundary disputes and deal with 'affrays'. Since the Commissioners were backed by a force of mounted Border Police, the squatters were prepared to pay their dues as the price of improved protection. However, their security over their territory was otherwise rendered more fragile. They were now vulnerable to the cancellation of their licences if they failed to fulfil the letter of the law, or if they upset the Commissioner in such a way that he could accuse them of so doing. He had been granted such extensive powers that he could – at least in theory – become a dictator over the 'Tribes of Tartary', acting as judge, jury and enforcer, and holding the future of every settler in the palm of his arbitrary hand.[25] To confer such powers on any official, given the nature of the grassland barons he ruled, was a serious risk. Indeed, he was guaranteed to be almost as universally loathed by them as were the Protectors.

In May 1840, Gisborne, the first Commissioner of Crown Lands for Port Phillip, resigned after less than a year, his health broken. On 1 July 1840, the district was subdivided at the Werribee River, and Captain Foster 'Flogger' Fyans was appointed for the Portland Bay section. This was greeted positively by most of the squatters, who hoped not only that the Commissioner and his mounted police would deal with Aboriginal 'collisions' but also that he would supply a trustworthy arbitration service between themselves. Before he had even taken up his job, Fyans found himself summoned all over his vast parish by squatters disputing their boundaries. The question of whether he would be fair, just, neutral, and free from prejudice or inducement in the exercise of his very considerable powers was to be thoroughly tested.

Captain Fyans, however rough a fellow, was seen as a man of honour and a zealous public official. But his reputation was primarily as a military officer and a hard man in circumstances where fearlessness and decisive action were what counted. In a role requiring steadiness of judgment and acumen of a more cerebral kind, he was a misfit. He did not grasp the concept that remaking existing decisions in a way that played topsy-turvy with individual settlers' fortunes would earn him derision and provoke their wrath. Fyans' imperious exercise of his office caused problems both for his superiors and for those obliged to accept his erratic judgments. Niel Black described him as having 'an ill-defined but very despotic power which he is not over-scrupulous of exercising'.[26] Fyans' pride was also easily bruised. He boasted that he carried a loaded holster to protect his dignity, and was assiduous in seeking out any discernible insult. His choleric outbursts were bywords in the colony, the *Portland Guardian* complaining that his decisions depended on 'the proportion of bile in his worshipful stomach'.[27] He was quite up to countermanding his own previous boundary decisions on a whim or as a favour, 'depriving a Settler of what he had granted him six months before', according to Black. He may not have been guilty of outright corruption, but gifts, flatteries or any slight to his vanity worked miracles of contradiction.

John Robertson of Wando Vale was kinder in his verdict on Fyans than most. 'There was no possibility of his seeing the boundary of the different lands, and if he had, it was through thick forest where each tried to lead him astray. The most conflicting evidence was given by unprincipled men, so that there was no getting at the truth who was the first to occupy the land.' However, Robertson's generous assessment was contained in a story that perfectly illustrated Fyans' lack of objectivity. Robertson had been cheated out of land by a finagled decision in favour of Edward Henty, and only succeeded in having his claim restored by careful wooing of the Commissioner. 'I waited on him about twenty miles off, invited him to my place, and held out the bait of hay and corn to his horses; I did not forget the man as well. It had the desired effect. He promised my place the site I had chosen, told me I had been misrepresented to him, and after seeing his horses next morning, offered to extend my boundary in order to put my place in the middle of my run, which offer, to his astonishment, I declined.'[28] Robertson wanted his site restored to him, not a clearly prejudiced and provocative decision calculated to renew problems with Henty.

To addresses of this nature, as well as to other quirks and seductions of spurious kinds, Fyans was eminently susceptible. As a result, enraged squatters besieged the offices of Gipps and La Trobe and threatened civil actions in the courts. Both Governor and Superintendent were driven to distraction by Fyans, but neither seemed able to bring him to conduct his duties in a more balanced and convivial way. 'Men on becoming Crown Commissioner seem to take leave of their senses', Gipps wrote. 'There is scarcely an officer in the public service whose want of discretion and whose loose manner of transacting public business I have had so frequent occasion to censure.' La Trobe was equally irritated: 'His behaviour has secured the chance of a duel once at least in the week as long as he may live.' Gipps also deplored Fyans' uncontrollable urge for letter writing. 'I wish there was a clause in the Squatting Act to fine Commissioners for writing foolish letters.'[29] That Fyans' writing was impossible to read and his grammar and sense uncertain cannot have assisted his case.

Niel Black knew well how important the favour of the Commissioner would be and did his best to make a good impression. He first met Fyans when reconnoitring in December 1839, having breakfast at his house in Geelong when Fyans was still Police Magistrate. They were both men of energy and principle, disinclined to affect social pretensions, and in the early months of their acquaintance there was no sign of the problems to come. As far as licence fees and stock taxes were concerned, Black expected to pay and did not neglect his dues. But in the matter of his shortage of stock, a little wool-spinning was in order.

When the Commissioner toured the district, Black rode out with Fyans to one part of the run, where they would inspect the flocks. He then took him back to his well-appointed hut for a fine and leisurely lunch served by his cook and housekeeper, Mrs Swan. In the afternoon, Black would take him out to a different part of the run and inspect the flocks there. These were in fact the same flocks, pressed into a forced march during the interlude.[30] Thus the whole run would be inspected, with continual movements of stock behind the scenes. Perhaps Fyans was initially convinced by the subterfuge and became resentful once he realised he had been fooled. More than likely, Stephen Ewen informed Fyans what was going on. For whenever Black subsequently requested a licence for more grazing land to carry his increased flocks, Fyans was persistently obstructive.

From the earliest moment, Fyans was drawn into Black's dispute with Craig and Ewen. On the eve of his appointment, in April 1840, La Trobe had called him in to meet Black in Melbourne, and Fyans told Black he would not only send Ewen and Craig packing but also fine them.[31] Nothing happened. In June 1840, Black found there was a problem with his licence. Accordingly, he rode 90 miles to Geelong to sort this out. After a discussion with Fyans, the licence was reissued and Black renewed his request to Fyans to come and settle the dispute with Craig and Ewen. By July, he had been 'waiting day and night' for the Commissioner to appear. 'I dare not quarrel with the Commissioner as he may recant, and find against me', he wrote to Gladstone. When Fyans eventually showed up, he took the same line as Ewen, that Black had too much fine country and was inclined to guard it over-jealously: Ewen was proving a match for Black in the 'possession' stakes. Fyans did not throw the pair off or fine them, but he did tell them to keep to the southern side of Mount Emu Creek and cease intruding on Black's run as far as Lake Terang.[32] Black reported this to his partners in a positive tone, but years later, the loss of this part of 'Taylor's country' still rankled. After Craig went elsewhere, Ewen named the run Marida Yallock, built a homestead in a clearing in the gum forest and began to improve the pasture. In 1853, he sold his licence for 17 300 acres to Daniel Mackinnon.

After the settlement in 1840, relations between Black and Fyans were unruffled for a while. But a year later, in August 1841, they erupted. Cole and McArthur, dissatisfied with the run they called Wooriwyrite, decided to trade it to Jeremiah Ware for a team of bullocks. They then moved across to the eastern bank of the creek onto an area later divided into two runs: Meningoort and West Cloven Hills. But they positioned themselves too close to Eddington's station. Captain Eddington had taken out a licence on 5000 acres on the north-eastern corner of Black's run. A home station had been built, and Donald Black installed there with Eddington's flocks as Eddington's manager. This was in keeping with usual absentee licensee–manager arrangements, but in reality it was another of Niel Black's devices for gaining a firm hold over a northern stretch of 'Taylor's country'. All instructions to Donald Black came from himself. When his own flocks increased sufficiently, Eddington would remove his sheep, making way for Black's, who would thereby gain the right to possession and buy out Eddington's licence.

Niel Black regarded Cole and McArthur as young men he had helped, thinking their flocks so small and their situation so impoverished that he had been gracious in allowing them to take up land on his border. Now he saw himself abused by their intrusion on Eddington's run, putting their hut a half-mile within a boundary that Fyans had settled. 'I sent for a chain to measure the distance', he told Fyans grandly, pointing out that the Commissioner had been duped by Cole and McArthur into redefining a boundary he had already fixed. 'I cannot for one moment doubt you have been induced to do so on misrepresentation.' If Fyans was unwilling to reconsider the matter, 'I shall have the ground surveyed at my own expense, and I shall ascertain the opinion of every respectable Settler I know.'[33] Black's wrath was overwrought, and the challenge to Fyans' authority enraged the Commissioner. He saw it as a gross insult to his dignity and office. Black's threat that he would recruit other settlers to his side touched Fyans at his sorest point. He hated to be friendless among the settlers – to be 'proclaimed throughout the country with every odium which can be cast on him'.[34] Black wrote an apology, but his tone was insufficiently abject. Fyans refused to accept that Niel Black had any role in a dispute over Eddington's boundary, especially as Donald Black, who was ostensibly in charge, had not raised any objection.[35] As their exchanges continued, the Commissioner whipped himself into a fury. 'If you do not withdraw your letter of the 16th August last in a proper manner, I shall submit it to His Excellency the Governor through his Honour the Superintendent, with my recommendation of your removal from the run you hold, and your licence cancelled … I need make no comment on the unbounded indulgence which you have received in retaining so large a tract of fine country on so limited stock, and which should have been occupied long before this only for the claims of the Chief Protector.' The native reserve was now established elsewhere, so Black must put more stock on his run: 'It will be out of my power to permit the ground to be kept in idleness by you to the prejudice of others.'[36]

Black was not naturally given to contrition and was familiar with Fyans' habit of threatening to cancel licences on the most trivial pretext. When in Melbourne, he called on La Trobe with copies of the correspondence to explain what had happened in case the Commissioner attempted to carry out his threat. His stock had increased considerably by now. When he submitted his returns in December 1841, he did so in person to Fyans at his Geelong office. He had made a substantial purchase of cattle, horses and sheep and was also importing valuable breeding animals, and asked if there was any outstanding problem. When Fyans answered in the negative, Black assumed that the matter of the insult had been laid to rest. But it had not. Fyans nursed the grievance and waited to get his revenge.

Where Black challenged the Commissioner's erratic decisions, John Thomson at Keilambete adopted a policy akin to that of John Robertson at Wando Vale. He had wooed Chief Protector Robinson, and he wooed Fyans too. The Commissioner's quarrel with Black was an opportunity not to be resisted. Thomson built on Craig and Ewen's complaint against Black by suggesting that he had an unfair command of the area's fresh water. His own land was 'badly' watered.[37] Whereas Black, with his marshes and his lake, in addition to a good stretch of Mount Emu Creek, had a cornucopia. Surely Thomson should be allowed to get hold of a piece of this watery abundance?

Ten months previously, Black had acceded to the move of Sievwright's 'native camp' from Keilambete to Lake Terang. Although this meant that his cattle had to be moved, Black had given in to pressure to avoid a collision between the Aboriginal occupants of Sievwright's camp and Thomson's men, on the understanding that the permanent reserve would be placed elsewhere. In January 1842, when Sievwright moved to Mount Rouse, he told Black that he was welcome to his hut at Lake Terang. But Thomson had another plan, in which he had enlisted Fyans. Sievwright wrote to Black from Mount Rouse: 'I was very much astonished to learn from your neighbour at Keilambete on our way here that he had obtained permission to occupy the Lake and intended to do so. What will the world come to? I pray let me know what you are doing regarding it.'[38] By the time this letter arrived, Black had been actively trying to undo what was clearly a prearranged coup to deprive him of country previously acknowledged as his. The boundary had been set by Fyans in July 1840 when he resolved the dispute with Craig and Ewen.

As the deportees began leaving their campsites on Pejark Marsh, Thomson drove flocks of sheep onto the ground they were vacating. Black protested to Fyans: 'He feeds his sheep actually into the very heart of the ground you on a former occasion declared to be my Run – and this is done coolly, as if on purpose to convince me that he may but walk his sheep into my cabbage garden or wheat paddock if he felt so inclined.'[39] He reminded the Commissioner that he had increased his cattle, horses and sheep and had waited on him in person in December when he brought in his stock returns and been assured that nothing was wrong. While Black expostulated about the flagrant breach of his rights, Fyans was equally high-handed. He 'begged leave to decline his offices' in relation to Black's complaint against Thomson, not having received adequate repentance for Black's disrespectful letter of the previous August. Instead, he would send his papers to His Honour the Superintendent. Black immediately presented himself before Fyans in Geelong and made a complete spoken and written retraction of all offending statements.[40] He then rode on to Melbourne.

Black had an interview with La Trobe two days later. He then wrote to him, recapitulating the course of events. He repeated that he had fully retracted whatever had caused Fyans such offence, and that the Commissioner still refused to take up his complaint against Thomson. 'I can do nothing further. I have paid his assessment, conformed to his wishes, and must I now go home to sit down quietly and see my stock wandering over the country, unable to keep them together.'[41] A day later, further news arrived. Thomson, having had his sheep mess up the marsh, had now moved them to Lake Terang. Informing Black's men that this territory was now his, he had told them to remove the cattle, dismantle the yards, and not to enter the hut left by

Sievwright. Black learned this news on his way back home, and instantly turned back to Melbourne to report this new outrage to La Trobe.[42]

Black called on friends to support him. John Riddell went to see La Trobe on his behalf, then wrote to Black: 'His Honour suggested you should get Mr Robinson to forward to him a statement as to your *previous* occupation of the Lake and the understanding between you as to his *temporary* occupation of it as a Black Reserve. I reminded His Honour … [that] nothing was further from your intention than disrespect to [Captain Fyans] or the office he holds.'[43] Black, once back on his run, steadfastly refused to move his cattle or stockyard. 'On 29 July 1840 you decided this to be my run, and as such it is well known all over the district', he wrote to Fyans. 'Mr Thomson now says he has your permission to occupy it but I cannot think you would give any person such permission without giving me notice first. I maintain my right to it and shall do so until I have contrary instructions.'[44] In pencil, in the margin of the copy of this letter, Black wrote: 'not answered'. And so things, for the time being, remained. For several months, Thomson left Black and his cattle in peace.

But Fyans could not give up his grievance. In July 1842, despite all Black's retractions, he was still referring to the letter of 16 August 1841 as 'a most insulting and improper production, for which he had yet to receive Mr. Black's account. Until he does this no Licence shall be granted to him by my recommendation.'[45] A new problem arose in December 1842 when Claud Farie sold Black a flock of sheep on The Sisters, a run to Black's west. The economic downturn was becoming a nosedive and many squatters were in difficulties. Black, meanwhile, was in possession of new capital from his partners, and could afford to buy flocks that

Farie needed to offload. Farie had already obtained Fyans' verbal agreement to hand over to his friend the station as well.

The minute Black left on a trip to Scotland in January 1843, leaving Farie in charge of his affairs, the problem of the licence to The Sisters re-emerged. Another squatter, James Hamilton, lodged a complaint intended to secure the cancellation of Black's claim to The Sisters. However, Farie kept a cool head, and pointed out to Fyans in temperate prose that whoever had a claim to the run, it was certainly not Hamilton.[46] After more delays and on-the-spot visits by the Commissioner, Farie finally wrote to Black: 'Fyans has given everything I wanted and fined Hamilton £5 for an ill-grounded complaint.' The matter must at last be fixed as Fyans 'has now settled it in four different ways. He was most oppressively civil and polite the last time I saw him and has again taken to inviting me to his house. I think I must condescend, in case the old fellow should take the strunts again.' Farie did go and dine with him on his way to Melbourne a few days later, and found him 'as gracious as ever'.[47]

If the transfer of The Sisters cleared its final hurdle, that of Eddington's run did not. By early 1843, Eddington, who had lived in Melbourne with his family since his arrival in 1839, was in financial difficulties and could no longer afford town life. So he removed to a run called Ballangeich on the Hopkins River. Writing to Niel Black, now 'tumbling off the Cape of Good Hope', with his gossipy news about the lamentable state of affairs in Melbourne, he reported that Fyans still had it in for him. The Commissioner had raised no objection to Eddington moving his sheep and leaving his old run, 'at the same time giving it as his opinion I could not better myself as my run is really a good one … with a *quiet hint* that Mr Niel Black *has too much ground* and could I not get part of it? This is hardly fair from your kind friend the Commissioner as soon as he got your back turned.' Farie, Eddington suggested, would need to 'meet the old Boy with his own weapons'.[48] Farie, on Black's behalf, asked Fyans for permission to put Black's sheep on Eddington's run once the ground had had time to clean, his sheep having been scabby.[49] Everyone knew that there had been a longstanding deal between Black and Eddington. But in this case all Farie's tact and bon-homie could make no impression. Fyans was not going to allow Black a licence on Eddington's run, however many sheep he had – and they were now so cheap, with ruined squatters offloading them for almost nothing, that Glenormiston was overstocked. To rub Black's nose in it, the successful applicant for Eddington's run was Donald Craig, the young man who had arrived with Stephen Ewen in 1840 with an introduction to Niel Black signed by the factor of the Duke of Argyll and gained nothing by it. But Black, away in Glasgow, was impotent.

Black's battles with Fyans were far from over, including more rounds of land grab and displacement at Lake Terang in 1848–49 – out of which Black did not emerge a happy man. Thomson's shepherds continued to graze scabby sheep over Black's boun-daries, and Black's cattle trespassed over his, leading to irate expostulations and letters back and forth. After more attempts to take up new land for his expanding flocks, in 1845 Niel Black reached the conclusion that Fyans' prejudice against him would never dim. No licence over new country would ever be granted to him by the Commissioner, however strong his claim. If he was to extend his grazing interests, he would have to look in areas beyond Fyans' reach.

By this time, Fyans' arbitrary behaviour was catching up with him. In March 1845, Alexander Sprot, a squatter from a wealthy Glaswegian family and victim of one of Fyans' more grotesque decisions, brought a court case against him. So wide were the Commissioner's powers, it was a daring course of action which eventually cost Sprot £1000. Fyans lost the case and was reviled on all sides, but the judge refused to award Sprot his costs – to discourage other squatters from similar actions.

This experience finally pulled Fyans' sting. Black wrote: 'My old friend Fyans, from being the greatest tyrant on earth has become as timorous as the cowering hare. He is beset on all sides with his own snares, devices, and wicked practices and cannot move but in fear and trembling lest he should get into some new pitfall. I am sure his reign is near a close.'[50] In this expectation, Black was premature. La Trobe did not wish to hand the squatters such a triumph. Finally, in 1849, Fyans' ten-year tenure ended and he was reappointed Police Magistrate at Geelong – to the relief of everyone, including himself. He had made enough from squatting and other 'practices' to establish a well-known herd of Shorthorn cattle, give his name to a mountain and a ford, and live comfortably to a distinguished old age.

Chapter Four

'ABOVE ALL, I AM ANXIOUS FOR MEN'

IF HOLDING HIS RUN was Niel Black's top priority, number two was the state of his workforce. Shortage of labour was a perennial problem for the early Port Phillip squatters, and Black's laments on the high cost, poor performance, drunkenness and immorality of local workers began soon after he landed.

Most were ex-convicts from Van Diemen's Land. The Port Phillip District was far larger than the island colony, and only the roughest men were willing to work deep in the wilderness of the interior, miles from any outpost of society. 'The servants in this country are actually more savage than the natives', Black wrote.

'To manage the men well and keep them sweet (in harmony) is the whole secret of sheep farming according to the colonial idea, and really it is no easy task to do. It requires the boldness of the lion, the patience of Job and the wisdom of Solomon to accomplish it successfully.'[1]

Black became ever more appreciative of the 'good Scotch shepherds' he brought with him. These had been indentured for three years, in return for their passage, yearly pay, basic rations and shelter, with married couples being entitled to extras.[2] On arrival, many were offered inducements to transfer to other employers – and resisted. Black removed them from further temptation by lending them to Archibald Yuille at Ballarat until he took up his run. He showed his own mettle as their guardian by his determination to get Peter McIntyre released from the grip of the law, including hiring a lawyer, standing bail and pleading for him in court. His people must have thought him a good master, because they stuck to him.

Like others who came directly from the home country, Black observed that the typical ex-convict or 'ticket-of-leave' worker – used to, and used and abused by, a penal colony and its slave drivers – was unwilling to serve an employer with any dedication. The graziers were at the mercy of such men, a situation Black, with his experience of collegial if status-conscious Scottish working life, found repellent. 'What would you think of seeing a nobleman's son (no uncommon commodity here) courting popularity among a parcel of emancipated convicts, the veriest blackguards that move upon the earth and, I believe, the most independent of any class of labouring men alive', he wrote to Alex Finlay. 'Let anyone get a bad name as a master he will get none to serve him. His sheep have scab, but he can get none to dress them. His lambs are to wean but he cannot get hands to do it.'[3] He believed Niel Black & Company's squatting enterprise would depend on the skills, loyalty and sobriety of his own people, and he nurtured and rewarded them accordingly.

Black was used to managing men in Scotland, but not in such circumstances as these, marooned in the distant interior of strange country, thousands of miles from home. Even Geelong, the nearest town, was several days away by dray, and his men and their wives and children were dependent on him for everything – food, clothing, protection, spiritual sustenance and medical care. Many spoke little English, being more used to Gaelic, the language of hearth and field in their native Argyll. Acclimatisation cannot have been easy.

During the first weeks at Glenormiston, all hands other than shepherds worked as a team, Black himself included. The sheep were in poor condition, and food crops and tobacco needed harvesting. His participation in daily work, and leadership in the face of bushfires and lesser crises, boosted the men's flaky morale. The scene was of bustle, 'some employed at the tobacco, others at sheep folds, making hurdles for sheep washing, Donald Black and self making a stall in the woolshed for putting in the young mare'. One night he found the harvest maiden hanging in his room. 'Having only two bottles of rum, I did not intend giving the reapers any of it, but the hint was so neatly given that I thought it too bad to shut my eyes. I therefore gave them one bottle. They seemed highly pleased with the scanty allowance of my first *kirn* [feast for the harvest home] in Australia.'[4]

Under the influence of good food – daily portions of vegetables 'and as much fine wether mutton as they can eat' – his men began to settle down, even the perennially anxious Donald Black becoming more confident. At this stage, everyone including Niel ate the same meals together, as at home. Every day he was up at

5 am and into the saddle to ride around inspecting the flocks and country and talk to the shepherds. He needed to know – and map – the terrain thoroughly, especially the water sources and woodland tracks, and work out the best regime for the flocks, including their strategic positioning for boundary-holding.

The sheep were divided into four flocks of around 600 and each entrusted to a shepherd. The morose Duncan McNicol was persuaded to remove himself to one of four outstations. 'Yesterday [he] was asking for his freedom', Black recorded on 29 February 1840, a refrain in station journals of the next few years. 'Both he and his wife are disappointed as she is not made my housekeeper.' Instead Jane McNicol took her infant Christina to the bush and became her husband's hutkeeper.[5] She acted as nightwatchman, cooked the meals and kept the hut clean.

Black described the grazing system: 'Soon after sunset the flock is put into a yard made of movable hurdles, which are shifted every day to clear ground for the sheep to bed on. The watchman relieves the shepherd and takes charge for the night, having first chained up his dog and examined his carabine. He turns into bed in a box hut large enough for that purpose (6 ft x 2½ ft), which is carried about with the yards. Here he sleeps comfortably all night unless the sheep are disturbed.' If the sheep were set into a panic by a wild dog or 'visitors' and trampled down the hurdles, it was vital to get them back into their enclosure straightaway. 'By sunrise the shepherd has his breakfast on board, he bundles up a flagon of tea, a piece of damper and a slice of beef and follows his flock.'[6]

Black's shepherds were expected to shoot wild dogs and occasional game, but against human marauders, they were instructed to shoot only into the air. They were extremely proficient flock guardians, as Black lost few sheep during his first year, despite all the alarms and the cavalier posse got up by John Thomson. In his stock returns for December 1840, Black recorded in his own hand that 133 sheep had been slaughtered for food and 27 taken by 'natives'; 81 sheep had died from disease or its treatment.[7] By then, the ewes' condition had vastly improved, and the flock numbers began increasing rapidly. Shearing started in October, early so as to avoid grass seed getting into the wool. Each flock was washed a few days before being shorn, in a place where a stream entered Lake Terang. Donald McNicol, brother of Duncan, was in charge of the sheep wash; in 1840 he built a hut on the east bank of the lake and moved his family there.[8] 'There are pens made in the water into which the sheep are dropped from a platform raised two feet above it. They are then kept swimming in the soaking pen for some time before being passed into the washing pen where 5 or 6 hands are standing in a line. The first catches a sheep and after washing it for some time passes it to his neighbour who does his share of the work and passes it on also. In this way each sheep is passed through all the hands. The Overseer being the last in the line, he gives it the finishing touch and passes it out to a long swim fenced in on both sides to guide the sheep to the proper landing place, but if he finds it not properly washed he returns it to the men until he is satisfied.'[9]

Controlling disease was critical. Catarrh was common in sheep from the north. 'One man from Sydney left with 7,000 sheep and arrived with 400 in life': Black bought sheep from Van Diemen's Land to avoid this risk.[10] But scab was as bad a scourge, 'a herald of ruin and loss, of endless torment to all concerned, of medicated drippings, dressings, deaths and destructions innumerable'.[11] Scab was caused by a mite boring into the sheep's skin. Skin discolouration was followed by pustules which broke and ran together, forming a scab with a sore underneath. Infected sheep were restless, scratching themselves, biting off their wool, and gradually going bald as they rubbed their sores against tree stumps and rocks.[12] Unless treated – and some of the treatments involved arsenic or corrosive sublimates, which killed off weakened animals and played havoc with the dressers' hands – the animals' health rapidly declined. Weakened and dewoolled sheep were also vulnerable to cold.

Scab was highly contagious, and could be contracted from country over which infected sheep had moved. Clean sheep could not be put safely onto an area where scabby sheep had grazed until several weeks had passed. Scab Acts made it illegal to move diseased flocks except during the month of February, and imposed penalties on any squatter who allowed scabby sheep to graze near a boundary or avoided reporting scab by pushing his infected sheep onto someone else's land.[13] The Commissioner of Crown Lands was responsible for enforcement of the Scab Acts. Foster Fyans was under frequent request from Niel Black for 'orders' on neighbouring squatters to keep their scabby flocks away from his boundaries. 'I verily believe', he wrote to Gladstone, 'a man can never have peace, pleasure or profit so long as he has scabby sheep.'[14]

Thomson at Keilambete was Black's most complained-about spreader of disease. Black's ripostes against his neighbour were frequent: 'Sir,' he wrote to Fyans in October 1842. 'Some weeks ago I wrote you to acquaint you that I was under the necessity of abandoning the Hill Station on account of the encroachment of Mr John Thomson's Scabby flocks on my Runs. Since that time my men have been living under a tarpaulin in the edge of the forest, but even there my sheep are not safe from infection as his shepherd rambles with his flocks over more than half that

Station ... I feel myself under the necessity of requesting you to grant an order for the removal of his flocks.'[15] Such letters became routine, the 'scoundrel's' sheep being perennially scabby and straying where they should not. Black's annoyance was fortified by his success in rendering his own flocks scab-free by June 1842. 'Our flocks are now clean and they are the only sheep on the Portland Bay district that has [sic] yet been *entirely* cleaned – although many have been trying it for five years back. My success must be entirely attributed to my men as it is their faithful and trustworthy service that has accomplished it.'[16]

As flock numbers increased, and the risk of losses to wild dogs and hungry marauders declined, there was less need to employ so many men or yard the sheep every night. During the economic depression, squatters began to increase the size of their flocks. In December 1842, Black increased his flock size to between 800 and 1500, and even experimented with larger flocks, 'being strong in the belief that it is better to put a large number together and let them spread at pleasure'. By late 1844, he had managed to expand his flocks nine-fold despite the depression years.[17] His improver's instinct paid dividends at a time when many squatters were going to the wall. Black wished everything on his run to excel: the condition of the sheep, the wool-washing, the 'getting-up' of the wool, the pressing – he ordered the most up-to-date iron screw press from home – and the men's well-being. The belief that his stock was the healthiest, his run the best cared for, his men the most hard-working, strengthened his sense of being an asset to the district, whatever Foster Fyans' opinion. On one occasion, he told his adversary: 'I am much mistaken if it will tend to promote the interest of the colony to sacrifice any enterprising improver of stock without a very good cause.'[18]

Black expected his superintendent to keep a station journal on a daily basis.

On 24 September 1842, Captain Fyans visited to settle a boundary.

Niel Black papers, Box 43, MS 8996, State Library of Victoria

Black expected his men to become squatters in their own right in due course. He let them run their own small herds and flocks, and encouraged those with a skill to make boots, ropes and whips from kangaroo hide, as well as household goods and clothing, and sell them through the company store to build up their savings.[19] He also paid them bounties for dead dingoes. At the end of their three-year indentures, the Scots all signed up again, some at £35 to £45 a year.[20] This was £10 to £20 more than was typical for European labour at the time.

Black wanted Port Phillip to offer the struggling rural classes of Britain a new life. 'There certainly is not a better place than this in the World for curing that very common complaint among the labouring classes, POVERTY',[21] he declared. In 1842, he wrote: 'The men I brought out with me will be masters in less than three years, and if they remained at home none of them would ever have £50 of his own.'[22] To persuade men without prospects at home to emigrate and become 'improvers' was, to him, a patriotic endeavour that he did his best to promote.

Black thought that immigration was the issue that would make or break the fledgling colony. Accordingly, he frequently begged Gladstone to send him more workers. His agreement with the authorities allowed him to claim a bounty for bringing out, within two years, ten more married men with wives and families, and 20 single men. He preferred single men at £25 a year. 'A sprinkling of married men is useful but I have enough', and they were 'fearfully expensive, each woman's rations costing £20 a year'.[23] But it was not easy to persuade men to go to Australia. His brothers were not able to get him more shepherds. Walter wrote: 'I engaged one on Loch Awe-side, but I cannot get him to go. I came from there yesterday, having failed to prevail on him.'[24]

Gladstone did manage to recruit for him a number of men in Liverpool, two of whom arrived on the *Frankfield* in June 1841.[25] Black liked James Doig and John McCabe, and thought they would do well. They had misbehaved during the voyage, but he made sure that grog was inaccessible up-country. When Gladstone wrote saying that Doig had been accused of stealing a shirt, Black temporised, saying he could not check out the story 'till his box was brought up to the station, and his linen put out to be aired; but it has been raining ever since'. The rain and Black's good opinion kept Doig's shirts from washing-line scrutiny: 'He is incomparably the best man sent me and such an enquiry would destroy his humour.' Doig turned out to be an asset, working out his three-year term as a hutkeeper.[26] Not all 'blackguards' were irredeemable, apparently.

Seven more men arrived on the *England* in July 1841. These were men 'down on their luck' on whom Gladstone had taken pity. Most turned out to be unsuited to minding flocks in the bush. In one flock several sheep were killed and ten severely bitten by native dogs. Two nights later the same flock was rushed out of the yards and the watchman lost sight of them. 'Most of these men are yet very stupid and ignorant respecting the business at which they are employed and unless they improve I fear they will be no great acquisition.'[27] The question of their usefulness became academic when, one by one, they bolted. By the end of 1841, seven out of Gladstone's nine 'unfortunates' had run away, including the saddest case, Frederick Treveranns. 'The mother that sent her son to this country in so weak a state of mind has much to account for and had he not bolted from me I would think myself morally bound to provide for his safe return.'[28] Black had to ride to Melbourne several times to hire replacements, and resented the money lost on their outfits; to recoup on Treveranns, he auctioned off the – quite extensive – contents of his box to the other men. Treveranns later reappeared and was rehired as a kindness.

Gladstone's experience of recruiting men in Liverpool was so discouraging that he gave it up. But the general principle that the mother country ought to promote the emigration of men who desperately needed work, to colonial settlements that desperately needed workers, was not lost on the man whose first cousin, WE Gladstone, was now politically prominent. Black was fully aware of his partner's connection and sometimes wrote passages in his letters that were clearly meant for a wider audience. 'I must return to a subject I am most anxious to press upon the attention of every person of influence I know at home. I allude to Emigration. We never had and can never have too much labor. We want men out here to make ourselves and them independent. You keep them at home to starve them. Every man that wishes to become a benefactor to his country, he has only to use all his influence to promote emigration here. We will be ruined very soon for want of it.'[29]

Black also stressed the need for free emigration to Alex Finlay, a man with ambitions in public life. He spelled out the horror of being forced to employ ex-convict workers, 'scoundrels [who] can on any day find at least six new masters ready to engage at £40 to £60 a year. That this sum is all spent on brandy and champagne is as uniform and certain as that the sun succeeds the moon.'[30] With no better men to employ than those whose reason for taking on work was the prospect of squandering their wages on a 'bright flare up' at the grog shop, everyone was at risk. Even when wages dropped – by 1843 they had fallen to £15 to £20 a year – this did not ease the squatter's problems, given the plunge in prices for wool, and the unsaleability of his assets. In March 1843, Eddington wrote to Black, then on his way to Scotland: 'Sheep were heard of being sold last week at the amazing price of 9d [nine pence], run etc. given in. Alas for Australia, we are all going to Pot at a hard gallop!'[31]

Black had yearned to take a run home almost from the day he landed, and eventually left for Scotland in February 1843. Officially, he went to renew the terms of his partnership, but his main purpose was to get himself a wife – a quest that had failed before he left in 1839 when his chosen bride, Captain McKellar's daughter Mary, unaccountably turned out to be already engaged.[32] By 1843, many of his neighbours had recruited helpmates from Van Diemen's Land, bush life was becoming more settled, and at 38 years old, his bachelor state oppressed him. However, before going wife-hunting in Scotland, he used the visit to take up the issue of emigration in London. William Campbell of Dunmore, a well-known squatter from a well-known run in the Portland Bay direction, had encouraged Black – staying at the Melbourne Club pending departure – to lobby hard with the Colonial Office. 'Emigration is the grand desideration, and surely when thousands are starving at home, a patriotic government will not allow the consideration of passage money (and even that might be repaid somehow) to interfere with their emigrating to a country where they can rely on the best feeding in the world, and at least £15 of yearly wages. But the emigration must be steady.'[33] Black took with him a 'memorial' on this and other grievances signed by several Port Phillip squatters.

In June, Black did the rounds in London. He pushed for an interview with Lord Stanley, Colonial Secretary, and eventually succeeded. When it was reported in August 1843 that the government would be sending out labourers from Ireland, one acquaintance congratulated Black as responsible.[34] Meanwhile, Lord Stanley took up a different approach. A new model prison had been opened at Pentonville in London, where the inmates were treated to a medicinal dose of moral instruction in keeping with the most advanced theories of criminal reform. After serving two years, they could be released, as long as they went overseas as 'exiles' and did not return to England until their original sentences had expired.[35]

In 1844, the first group of 'Pentonvillians' was ready for shipment to Port Phillip. William Yaldwyn, another Port Phillip colonist who had also been in touch with the authorities, agreed to a year's employment for 21 'exiles'.[36] He and they shipped back to Australia on the same ship as Niel Black. The *Royal George*, with her assortment of deportees – carpenters, engineers, grooms, a shoemaker, tailor and coachman – raised her anchor off Portsmouth on 29 July 1844. During the voyage, there was no sign of ill-behaviour.

When the *Royal George* arrived on 16 November, a hue and cry was instantly raised against the importation of 'convicts': the *Port Phillip Patriot* denounced the arrivals as 'cargoes of felons palmed off on us as genuine immigrants'.[37] Port Phillip had never been a convict destination and no-one wanted 'transportation' in another guise. It was feared the 'exiles' would undersell immigrant workers at a time when jobs were desperately short. Despite Black's earlier expostulations against 'blackguard ex-convicts', he put his backing behind the Pentonville experiment. After all, James Doig the shirt-stealer had turned out well. Three of the *Royal George* arrivals were hired by Niel Black & Company. One, Thomas Higgins, a carpenter, stayed for six years. Despite political agitation in Melbourne, the scheme continued. Black hired two more – a shepherd and a general labourer – landed at Geelong in March 1845, but although over 1700 Pentonville exiles were shipped to Port Phillip between 1844 and 1849, that was his limit.

Other labour schemes were mooted. In early 1845, some Geelong pastoralists formed a society to bring over men from Van Diemen's Land. Most of these squatters had come across the strait originally, and the hire of ex-convicts did not appal them in the way that it did Black. He contributed a £5 subscription to the society in solidarity, with no intention of hiring any. He wrote to Gladstone that the want of labour 'is so severely felt that we have formed an association and subscribed funds for the introduction of labour from Van Diemen's Land, where we find and give free passages to the most immoral men on the face of the earth'. Everyone agreed that the quality of these men was abysmal. Black continued with gusto: 'We entrust [them] with a large amount of valuable property, while we know that their whole boast and study is in the exercise of such ingenuity as will expose their employers' property to the greatest risk, loss and injury.'[38] His protestations were purely rhetorical. He was anxious that Gladstone should have first-hand information to circulate about the need for immigrants wherever policy might be influenced, and as it happened, in December 1845 WE Gladstone was asked by Prime Minister Robert Peel to replace Lord Stanley as Secretary of State for the Colonies.

Emigration began to recover when the depression eased, from 1846 onwards. For Black, this was just in time. In December 1844, after he returned from Scotland, his men all signed on again; but he knew that this would not be repeated year on year. Donald Black had already established his own station, taking a small flock on loan and setting up on the Hopkins River, four miles from one of Claud Farie's outstations.[39] Gradually, the key members of Black's original 'band of Gypsies' who had trekked westwards across the plains in February 1840 towards the great unknown were graduating from the ranks of shepherds and stockmen and moving on to pastures of their own.

—————

The quality of his livestock mattered deeply to Niel Black, and it was his policy to improve his animals by breeding as well as good management. From the start he carefully studied the existing colonial livestock. With its relatively well-watered soil, Glenormiston was really 'too luxuriant for sheep, better suited for cattle'.[40] This played to Black's prejudice – he preferred cattle. But beef prospects were low for the time being, given that there was no way to preserve meat for the journey home and only a small market for its local consumption.

However, he did not neglect the sheep, importing rams from the famous flocks of Lord Western, which he thought might do better on his land than merinos. Western had crossed merinos with hardier breeds to create a larger sheep with a heavier fleece and coarser wool, also good for mutton. Black brought in not only the part-merinos, but also other crossbred rams and ewes.[41] Good breeding bulls would be much more expensive, but almost immediately he asked for them to be sent, although this required adding to the company's capital. 'I would wish you to send me without the least delay two or three Pure-Bred Durham Bulls of first rate quality. If very expensive, two may do and young ones sent, but with my present means I cannot afford to pay for them',[42] he wrote to Gladstone. Durham was a premier Short-horn breed developed earlier in the century.

A brother of Peter Serjeantson, Gladstone's business partner in Liverpool, had gone out to Port Phillip as a squatter at the same time as Black. The two men had little to do with each other – snobbery on Serjeantson's side, lack of respect on Black's – and this contact dwindled further after Serjeantson sneered privately at Black's tenant farmer's caution. Everyone known to anyone was the subject of gossip in letters going back and forth between the colony and home. Black was aware of this and did his best to be discreet. Serjeantson lost his horse in a similar accident to the one that nearly cost Black his, and he did not flourish as a squatter. But his requests for livestock reinforced Black's pleas for pedigree stock, and the Liverpool partnership acted accordingly.[43] In February 1841, four Durham bulls were purchased in Yorkshire, of which two were for Black, one white, one red, both with good pedigrees. The cost with shipping was £398 altogether, and they arrived on the *Frankfield* in June, along with some rams from Lord Western's flock.[44] Also on board, apart from some Gladstone 'unfortunates', was an expert in 'getting-up' the wool, a Mr Prescott, whom Black hired for £25 a year.

Black recorded the successful arrival of the stock. The only casualty was 'Mr Serjeantson's boar, who died on shipboard'. Sending such animals by sail through some of the stormiest waters on the globe was a risky affair. Special stalls had to be constructed, usually on deck. Slings were made to cradle the bull's or horse's belly and keep the animal on its feet if the ship rolled about precipitously in a storm. Feed for over 100 days had to be provided, and arrangements made to care for the beasts throughout the journey. Animals were often landed in poor condition. Once ashore, their strength had to be built up by weeks of exercise in preparation for the 130-mile walk to the station. On one occasion, Black sent full instructions as to how to proceed upon landing a bull at Melbourne. 'He should be put into an open yard where he can move about freely for a fortnight, and fed partly on grass and partly on dry food. Great care should be taken to change his food gradually. He will thus be prepared by food and exercise for the journey. He should then be placed under charge of a very careful man who should *lead him on foot* by very short journeys to the station. He can be led like a horse by a rope and halter.'[45]

In October 1841, the Durham bulls reached Glenormiston, and Black pronounced himself well pleased. However, they had been shipped too young, and never fully recovered from the voyage. In future, better provision for care on board would have to be organised. Only the sheep had not suffered, thanks to the ministrations of Mr Prescott. The Durham bulls' good blood made 'a wave in the colonial eye',[46] but the animals did not flourish. In 1843, one dislocated a hip, and was never able to be used for 'family duties' again; another died suddenly with no warning, from a ruptured blood vessel close to the heart. Fortunately, by this time they had sired enough progeny to found the NB-branded Shorthorn herd that later became Black's pride and joy. Gladstone did not appreciate Black's enthusiasm for cattle: 'We think sheep will pay us the best. How are you to get rid of your surplus cattle? Do you sell to the butcher? I fear it will never pay us to cure the meat or bring home hides.'[47]

In 1842, Cotswold rams were sent and these turned out to be the best suited for Black's ground. As for horses, in September 1842 he purchased Black Prince, a stallion originally sent to Serjeantson, to improve his bloodstock. He needed good horses for the station, especially when his cattle herd increased and mounts were needed for stockmen. Although he sold horses, and charged a good stud fee for Black Prince in his prime, he did not think horses a good business proposition. But he regretted the lack of big work horses. In early 1842, at the height of the depression, he wrote: 'A Clydesdale Horse would suit us, but I have not courage to wish for more money invested in stock at present. Things here are in a dreadful state, daily getting worse.'[48] Not until 1853 while again in Britain did Black finally purchase two Clydesdales. One, Mary Matchless, was a splendid three-year-old mare of 16.2 hands with an impeccable pedigree. Gladstone's brother Adam supervised the shipment of the horses from Liverpool. Boxes large enough to enable them to turn around at sea had to be built, and the bill for their travel, feed and water, and £10 for the passage of a groom, came to £260 altogether.[49] Although their ship, the *Matilda Wallenbach*, was dismasted by a storm and had to put in at Lisbon for three weeks of repairs, Mary Matchless and her companion survived unscathed. 'Our horses are all safe though much frightened by the rolling of the ship.'[50]

By early 1843, all the various efforts – breeding, disease control, good management of flocks and herds – had led to very significant increases in Black's livestock. His mature ewes returned 161 per cent increase in that year, and cattle, 89 per cent. Unfortunately, the drop in values more than kept pace with output, and there was as yet no upturn in the economy. 'We must for some time to come estimate our wealth like the Patriarchs of old according to the number of our herds of "cattle and she asses"', he wrote to Gladstone. By this time he was running very large flocks, 1200 or 2000 together. It was necessary to make 'the wool pay our expenses, and this is the only way at present I can think of'.[51]

Gradually, though, the corner was turned. In December 1844, after returning from Scotland, Black encountered a heartening sight on the road between Geelong and Camperdown: a file of ten Niel Black & Company drays, laden with Glenormiston wool on its way to shipment. He found that 20 000 sheep had been shorn, producing 24 950 kilograms of wool. He wrote to Gladstone: 'the quantity of our wool will this year far surpass your expectations. Sheep-holders are all in high spirits now, with just cause.'[52]

By now the Glenormiston community was well established, with many of Black's men being promoted into new responsibilities. The usual circumstances on pastoral runs – that it was very difficult to rise unless employed as an overseer or superintendent[53] – did not apply at Glenormiston. As his cattle increased, some of his shepherds graduated to stockmen, mustering and droving on horseback. Some bought their own mounts from him on credit, as they had cattle. Those with wives and children were offered a cow or two to supply fresh milk. The McNicol brothers became overseers, and in 1845, William Swan was promoted to superintendent. His wife, Margaret, continued as Black's housekeeper and cook.

Black's station, with its original 'sprinkling of married men', was something unusual: a family place. The couples raised children, and many of the single men married and did likewise. By July 1843, there were 12 children at Glenormiston under ten years old. During the first 12 years, 24 children were born there, including the first white child native to the district, Mary McDonald, at Glenormiston in August 1840. The presence of families gave the station a unique status: women about to deliver would come from elsewhere knowing they would receive support.[54]

Under Black's direction, the Scots maintained the habit of prayers on Sundays. In 1843, he requested Alexander Laurie, the Presbyterian minister at Port Fairy, to visit Glenormiston to conduct baptisms. Laurie responded: 'I admire the spirit with which your people have been animated on this occasion. It is rarely the case that servants in this country spend their money in promoting the interests of religion. You may let them know I shall see them shortly.'[55] He baptised five children on that visit, and in 1846, four more. In 1847, when the squatters were finally granted some security of tenure, with support from Black and others, a manse was built at Kilnoorat, a spot within reach of several neighbouring runs. The Reverend William Hamilton took up residence and was paid a modest stipend. He rode around the stations and held services in barns and woolsheds, according to a rota.[56] In 1848, Black appointed a master and opened a school for the growing number of school-aged children on Glenormiston.

The moral and spiritual health of his people was close to Black's heart. Although he could not prevent men having 'a flare up' on visits to town, Black disallowed drinking on the station, except for the traditional ration of grog for the sheep-washer and 'footrotter' teams. In the mid-1840s, an inn was opened on the road to the east of Glenormiston. In September 1846, just before the shearing season was due to start, Black wrote to Thomas Storey, the proprietor, insisting that he not sell spirits to his shearers for consumption anywhere but on his premises. 'Last year spirits was [sic] carried from your place for the use of my sheep shearers, on receiving which their work was exchanged for the pleasures of the Sup, and all control was soon thereafter at an end. I had to sit up a whole night to watch and protect the establishment, and was thus necessitated to witness a scene of Riot and drunkenness I never saw equalled.'[57] If his injunction was ignored, Black would make it his business to have Storey's establishment closed down.

Bullock drivers also had a reputation for hard drinking. Temptation came when they were away from the station for days, taking wool bales to Geelong or picking up stores. One of Black's bullockies, William Kirkwood, often succumbed. Kirkwood, a Scot transported to Sydney for house robbery, worked for Black between 1842 and 1847 and was one of only two ticket-of-leave men he employed long-term. On 13 March 1845, William Swan noted in the station journal: 'Started Wm Kirkwood with a dray to Geelong.' The following day: 'Found William Kirkwood at Murray's Public House where he had remained all day with the Team yoked to the Dray and he was that stupid with drink that he did not know what he was about. I got the Bullocks put to rights myself and sent them home.' The next day a curt entry records: 'William Kirkwood left Mr. Black's employment.'[58] However, he was soon back at Glenormiston, a good worker and well liked despite his lapses.

One of Niel Black's early hopes was that a township would be built on his land. He mentioned the idea to Gladstone several times: 'I am quite satisfied that this is the best site for a township between Melbourne and Portland, and if the latter becomes a place of importance, a thriving village will spring up somewhere here.'[59] The question of how this would happen, and the investment required, became embroiled in issues of land tenure and proprietorship. Not until the mid-1850s was a township laid out at Lake Terang, on the land originally used for an Aboriginal camp in 1841 and made a reserve at that time. In 1845, the idea was fomenting in his busy mind: 'If we got the right of pre-emption to our runs, I once had some thought of making this a village ourselves, as there is no doubt the situation is suitable.'[60] He pictured a thriving community of Scots spreading out from Glenormiston to build the new pastoral world.

That dream is echoed in the *Old Melbourne Memories* of Rolf Boldrewood, writing decades later of his first droving excursion in 1844. 'Next day saw us at Mr Niel Black's Basin Banks [Lake Gnotuk] station. Here we saw the heifers of the NB herd. And a fine well-grown well-bred lot they were. The overseer was either Donald or Angus "to be sure whateffer", one of a draft of stalwart Highlanders which Mr Black used to import annually. Very desirable colonists they were, and as soon as they "got the English", they commenced to save money at a noticeable rate. A fair-sized section of the Western District is now populated by these Glenormiston clansmen and their descendants, and no man was better served than their worthy chief, Niel of that ilk.'[61]

If Black had lived long enough to read that passage, what quiet satisfaction it would have given him.

Chapter Five

'I THOUGHT IT BEST TO BUILD A STONE HOUSE'

WHEN BLACK LEFT PORT PHILLIP for his 'run home' in February 1843 carrying the memorial from his fellow squatters to the Colonial Office in London, their grievances focused not only on the lack of immigrant labour but also on the insecurity of their licensed occupation of Crown lands. During his interview with Lord Stanley, Black talked about the high minimum fixed price of land. This most affected those squatters whose runs near 'settled' areas might soon go up for sale.

In 1842, the price per acre below which no Crown land could be sold was raised from 12 shillings – for bush grazing land a price already inflated way beyond any realistic market value – to £1. This had been greeted by the graziers with outrage.[1] While easily surpassed at auctions for plots close to town, it was absurd to think of a would-be proprietor of bush pasturage paying such a sum. Just over three acres were needed to feed one sheep,[2] so an investment of at least £3 would be required to feed an animal worth – in the depths of depression – a few shillings at most. Grazing land's only value was contained in the feeding matter upon it, and since stock was almost valueless, so was pasturage.

The Colonial Office was in thrall to the political philosopher Edward Gibbon Wakefield's idea of 'concentrated settlement' as the way to develop its territories.[3] This envisaged a land of ploughing and sowing agriculturalists, not of sheep and cattle graziers whose flocks and herds fed over huge areas. Australian geography and conditions were uniquely suited to the livestock industry, not to villages and tidy patchworks of crops. But the colonial authorities persisted in regarding the squatters as merely an interim population, whose wandering herds must soon make way for far greater numbers of farmers tilling the soil. The price of land was deliberately set at a level that kept the alienation of Crown lands in check against the day when farming settlement could proceed, by making it unaffordable to those who were using it 'merely' – by implication, wastefully – as pasturage.[4] The high price was also supposed to augment the land revenues and thereby pay for immigration. In fact, because of the disincentive effect on purchasers and the depression (some saw the two as cause and effect), in 1842 both land sales and the land revenue collapsed. Without the means to pay for it, immigration dried up.

Thus, it was not surprising that the squatters were opposed to the £1 minimum price: it upset the applecart of colonial economics. On top of this, it was galling. Purchase as a way of securing permanent occupation of land to which many had committed their all had been intentionally put beyond their reach. What this told them was that, at the Colonial Office and in the mind of Lord Stanley, the idea lingered that they were not respectable men, the backbone of the wool industry and guarantors of colonial prosperity, but parasitical invader-exploiters of lands where they had no right to be. For reasons of ideology, they were to be prevented from gaining any security over their licensed lands, against the apocryphal day when a yeomanry of small-scale cultivators would appear over the horizon and take their proper place. In the interests of an unrealisable dream, and in the name of the Crown's preservation of the imperial patrimony, *their* rights and contributions to colonial development were to be ignored.

The fact was that, after several years of grazing their sheep, increasing their flocks, damming 'their' streams, erecting heifer stations, dairies and stockyards, sowing crops, creating vegetable gardens, and building woolsheds, sheep washes, and living quarters for their men, squatters such as Black did – inevitably – feel that they had a right to 'their' land. This right was not necessarily to own it, but to have security of tenure and not be at risk from year to year of being thrown off, especially when a vain, arbitrary and irascible Commissioner of Crown Lands might, out of pique, revoke their licence. They also wanted a 'pre-emptive right': the right, if land they had squatted on for many years was put up for auction, to purchase it ahead of some other buyer with larger means who could outbid them well beyond any justifiable value, purely for speculation. In such a case, the pasturage would be removed from under their stock, leaving them with no choice but to destroy their unsaleable flocks and herds. And finally, they wanted the right to compensation for the 'improvements' – buildings, homes, stockyards, dams, forest clearing – that represented the work of years. What motivation did they have to 'improve' if money spent was at risk of being wasted or of benefiting the person who, by questionable means, managed to displace them?

Governor Gipps had seen for some time that a confrontation between government and squatters was imminent and that delay would only make the clash more vehement. Every passing year tied the 'squatter' – a term implying transitory occupation – more intimately to his lands and his station. This station was now fast becoming not just a ramshackle set of buildings but a homestead. By 1844, squatters had begun to marry, and Black's neighbour at Mount Shadwell, Captain James Webster, begged him to do the same, to increase their local society: 'We shall then have within visiting distance Mrs Manifold and Mrs Peter ditto, and I suppose Mrs John Ed[dington], Mrs Thomson, Mrs [Lauchlan] Mackinnon, Mrs C[ole] and Mrs W[ebster]. Then we can muster a quadrille already.'[5] Gipps wanted to introduce a system which acknowledged the justice of claims for homesteads and supported the domestication of the bush. He believed it his duty to resolve the irregularities concerning squatter holdings before he left office in 1846. But he was utterly opposed to the squatters' more extreme assertions – such as that thanks to the 'improvements' they had made in the landscape they had become its rightful custodians and should be allowed to metamorphose seamlessly into landowners of areas the size of shires.

In April 1844, Gipps published a first set of proposals, the occupation regulations, revising the terms for licences. He wanted to raise the charges, reinvigorate the revenues, and end the injustice whereby a squatter-magnate could hold 186 000 acres (nearly 300 square miles) on two £10 licences. 'Small occupiers get only 22 acres for one shilling per annum, [whereas] the large occupiers get 510 acres', Gipps wrote to London.[6] In future, no station was to be larger than 20 square miles; neither could one licence cover a station capable of depasturing more than 4000 sheep or 500 head of cattle, or some equivalent mixture, without incurring additional charges. In the case of a squatter of medium size such as Black (43 000 acres), this would mean several licences instead of one.

Gipps' occupation proposals provoked a furore – one that eclipsed, by some margin, the grievance about the £1 upset price. A campaign began in Sydney and spread throughout New South Wales, and an emissary was despatched to London. In Melbourne, the *Port Phillip Patriot* published the proposed regulations surrounded by a black mourning border. Gipps had timed his bombshell poorly, appearing to ignore the devastating impact of the depression on the squatters, and the difficulty – for some, impossibility – of paying extra charges. Instead of acknowledging their need for security of tenure, Gipps seemed determined to penalise the squatters further. They saw the extra fees not as a rise in rent, but as a form of arbitrary taxation – the kind of imposition that provoked armed rebellion in British colonies, and some spoke freely in those terms.

In early May, Gipps tried to allay popular discontent by publishing his proposed purchase regulations, to be taken in tandem with the occupation ones. These appeared to give the squatters the security of tenure they demanded, but in a curious way. A squatter could purchase, at the £1 minimum price, an area of 320 acres (half a square mile) on his run for his homestead. This 'homestead right' would entitle him to five-year licences for the rest of his grazing land, in multiples of 20 square miles, as per the occupation regulations. At the end of five years, he could purchase a further 320 acres, and again renew the licence(s) for his grazing lands. At first sight this seemed to answer the case for the pre-emptive right, and extended the duration of tenure. But the security of this tenure was an illusion. If the squatter did not exercise his right to buy another 320 acres after five years, someone else could buy this new section at auction, and the original occupier would lose the entire run, including the homestead previously purchased, only receiving compensation for 'improvements'.

The Port Phillip squatters were even more incensed by these proposals than by the earlier ones. A grand protest meeting was convened in Melbourne in June, with cavalcades of squatters on horseback, bands and a Scottish piper. Among the speakers to the large open-air crowd was Claud Farie, along with Edward Curr, AF Mollison and other leading squatters. The main grievances were the expense, the lack of long-term security and arbitrary gubernatorial behaviour. Port Phillip also lacked effective representation in the Legislative Council in Sydney: Gipps had inadvertently managed to fuel Port Phillip's call to become a separate colony.

Beyond this, his proposals were complicated and obscure. What the squatters needed above all, according to one speaker, Archibald Cuninghame, was 'the concession of long leases on equitable terms'.[7] The demand for long leases, which crystallised the issue, was to echo for years to come.

Gipps was totally opposed to long leases, which he saw as tantamount to conceding property rights. What Gipps was trying to do was to satisfy the squatter's legitimate right to a homestead, and encourage him to build a proper house, marry, raise a family, and transform social life in the backwoods, but prevent him from establishing dominion. This could only be done by denying him long-term security. Gipps was trying to maintain the power of the Crown over all 'wastelands' as a sacred trust for the generality of colonisers, against the claims of the most active and economically powerful men throughout the whole of New South Wales. Whatever the moral justice of Gipps' attempt to keep the lands out of the maw of upstart livestock barons, the squatters were having none of it.

------ • ------

In April 1844, when Gipps' proposals were first aired, Claud Farie – in charge at Glenormiston during Black's Scottish pilgrimage for a wife – wrote to his friend TS Gladstone about the government's contemplated change in the squatting regulations. 'Several schemes are under consideration', he explained. The squatter's right to his run would be converted 'into something more of the nature of a lease for a given number of years. Some have proposed that every settler should get a five-year lease of all the land he has now in occupation for £50 a year.' To Farie, bearing in mind current licence fees and the £1-per-acre minimum price, the sums sounded alarmingly high. 'It would press very unequally on different individuals when you consider the difference in the value of runs, which is of course regulated by extent, quality of pasture and the distance from market.' Farie went on: 'I'm sure any change will be to the bad. Nothing can be devised which will make the settler better off than he is at present when he can feed an unlimited number of stock for the payment of £10 a year.'[8]

Farie had put his finger on the issue. Nothing that could be devised would favour the squatter better than the existing arrangement, and the squatter being the bloody-minded creature he was – and, in the face of rock-bottom wool prices, one currently avoiding ruin only by boiling down his assets to sell as solidified fat (tallow) – he was not going to welcome any worsening of his situation. Grazier anger touched a popular chord, feeding the growing demand throughout Port Phillip for full-scale colony status and 'separation' from the rest of New South Wales. Thus was the squatter – for a rare historical moment – cast politically as an underdog deserving the sympathetic rally of all true colonials to his cause.

By November 1844, when Black – still wifeless after his failed courtship in Scotland – returned to Port Phillip, the initial thunderous hue and cry had muted, and it took him some time to catch up with the debates on the various regulations. He had to put aside the emotional disappointments of his trip, tidy up the company books and get things back on track. He was not impressed with Farie's management – he was rarely impressed with anyone's – and felt things had slipped in his absence. 'We used to have the best cattle in Port Phillip, others may now get ahead of us, but I do not entirely despair of keeping the lead', he wrote to Gladstone.[9] More importantly, he was now facing a shortage of pasturage for his increased flocks. He blamed the capricious Foster Fyans. The Commissioner had disallowed the long-planned reversion to him of Eddington's run, and so much time had elapsed since the ruling that it was now too late to try to redeem this via the courts.[10] Although Black had done favours for Fyans in London, their relations experienced no improvement. Within no time, Black was sucked back into battles over runs, intruders and scabby sheep trespassing across his boundaries – battles in which Fyans invariably backed his opponents.

Once he realised that Fyans would never grant him a new squatting licence ahead of any competitor, Black began to look for pasturage elsewhere. He and his overseer, William Swan, reconnoitred for a month in the bush towards the Murray River, but gave up when 'we could scarcely get feed to keep our horses alive'.[11] He then turned south towards the Glenelg River and found a place near the South Australian border. At the outer edge of the Portland Bay district, this was beyond Fyans' remit. Assigning the boundary-marking and map-drawing to a young Scot he was mentoring, Black obtained a licence from Charles Bonney, Commissioner of Crown Lands in Adelaide.

The new run, Warreanga, would carry a further 14 000 sheep. But the expenses of setting up a new station were considerable. 'I shall sell no stock this year, my object being to secure run by placing stock on it.' His two remaining partners – the elderly William Steuart had withdrawn – groaned when they read this, as it meant less cash for them. Black was determined to build up the company and expand its potential, rather than provide Gladstone and Finlay back home with the entire annual surplus in cash – which was really what they wanted. The slow pace of communication between Britain and Australia was a useful aid in this regard: by the time the partners heard of the new investment in Warreanga there was little they could do. 'As long as I continue extending the business here it cannot be expected that I can make larger remittances to the partners at home, and I cannot suppose any of them are in need of an income from here', he wrote defensively. 'Indeed, it would be a very great pity to interrupt a concern that has gone on so rapidly. When it began it was so small I was almost ashamed to sign Niel Black & Co;

it is now, if not the very largest, about the most extensive stock-holding concern in Port Phillip, and it ought to increase with five-fold rapidity.'[12] And the company was indeed flourishing. Even in the depression he had multiplied sheep numbers and assets. Now bad times were receding, things were on the up.

Gradually, Black began to immerse himself in the 'land question'. That he might have to purchase his homestead did not now worry him. He had a rich tract of country, a good homestead setting, and the necessary resources. He was less animated against Gipps than many of his fellows. 'He is firm, perhaps obstinate, but not able to withstand the overwhelming torrent of opinion opposing him. Consequently he has been explaining, altering and amending the proposed Regulations until no-one can say what they are intended to be, but the last version which proposes to give us right of pre-emption is the most favourable.' Black's ire was reserved for the London end of things. 'Lord Stanley seems very warm and decided in his views respecting the rebellious squatters, but he ought to be certain he understands the subject before putting his veto upon the voice of a whole people crying out.'[13] Black told Gladstone he would revert to this subject 'so soon as I get time to settle quietly at home'.[14] Gladstone had been invited by others with Australian interests to swell the ranks of home-based opposition to the regulations and was eager to know Black's views.

In November 1845, Black gave him a considered response. A young man named Gideon Scott Lang had been canvassing the views of squatters on the land question, and Black had entertained him at Glenormiston and spent time helping Lang to develop his ideas – and vice versa. Lang's treatise was to be published, and Black told Gladstone that the views contained in the publication coincided with his own. Lang's vivid account of the challenges faced by the squatter was clearly based on Black's colourful narrative: the months of acute anxiety and exertion in finding a run, the threats from 'the prowling savage', the incessant dangers to person and property, and so on. In this version of the settlement myth, the squatter's role as frontiersman-conqueror conjures images of the pioneering story first elaborated from the Americas.

The thrust of Lang's exposition was that any value 'wasteland' acquired was entirely due to the efforts of capitalists to make it productive. The logic of a belief in the worthlessness of land in a 'state of nature' was that it lacked any value to government or the human race – Aboriginal people were excluded from this account – until such time as the squatter appeared. This meant that to confer it on the squatter was essentially to hand it over to its rightful 'owner'. Alienating it to the squatter therefore did not entail sacrificing to him the resources of the colony, but entrusting the land's future to the one who would invest in it and do whatever necessary to add value to it.[15] Labour, too, played an essential role. Whatever had occurred in the past, settlers today had to pay high wages to free, hard-to-obtain immigrant workers. Capital, labour and hardship were thus the three necessities required to enable stock to occupy the land in a productive manner. 'In the limited number of parties possessed of the requisite capital, and of energy and self-denial to undergo the hardships and deprivations necessarily endured by the first occupiers of a wild and uninhabited country, lies the only *artificial limit* to the naturally rapid increase of stock, and the extension of the Colony.'[16]

In discussion with Lang, Black had worked up no insignificant thesis of political economy to suit his view of the matter. 'If the Crown will not alienate the land of the colony – subject to such taxes as may be necessary for the Government to impose – to those who have the best claim to it, then the next best thing they can do is make the present holder tenant at a low rent.' In return for this low rent, the squatter would be obliged every eight years to purchase 320 acres of every 20 square miles he leased. Black accepted the anomaly that it would take 320 years for the whole 20 square miles to be bought, regarding the long credit term and the right to pre-emption as necessary 'to enable many to get on. But if the leases are exposed to auction at the end of eight years, Woe be to the colony for many will be ruined, and Government will then, when too late, grant better terms than ever to the few remaining in a solvent state.'[17] The government would thereby achieve the opposite of its intention: a few huge proprietors would end with everything. His perspective on the issue conveys a palpable sense of how hard it had been to pioneer the settlement of a wilderness and survive the depression at the same time. Over five years, squatterdom had been turned upside down, so many of the early clan had gone to the wall. The less able or less well resourced Faries and Eddingtons, and young Scottish squatters Black had helped to get started, as well as his cousin Donald Black and his own ex-workers the McNicols and McDonalds, might well follow suit if these regulations came in.

According to Black's calculations, the real value of grazing land was no more than one shilling an acre. The major evil, in his view, was still therefore the £1 upset price. Too many of the squatters would never be able to find this sum, and without tenured security would be forced to give up when the first, second or subsequent purchasing period fell due. The government had taken for granted, and now presumed to capitalise upon, all the risk and hazard the squatter had taken upon himself. 'In attending to his own interest, [the squatter] has found employment and sustenance for hundreds of his fellow beings. But Government, lest he should employ too many and do too much good, steps in and tells him "You must pay 20 shillings for your land".'[18]

Black obviously hoped his partner would send Lang's publication to WE Gladstone, then serving as President of the Board of Trade in Sir Robert Peel's ministry. He believed that the principles it laid down – purchase after eight years' occupation of as much land as a squatter needed for his stock, at a price proportionate to the stock the land would carry, payable in 15 annual instalments – 'to be sound and based upon truth unalienable truth'. But, realistically, 'I do not expect to see them ever applied in this colony'. He did not blame Gipps: 'He is a very talented man and a very able ruler, and would have wielded the power committed to him of a despotic sovereign of NS Wales with great wisdom, were it not that he was the servile agent of Downing Street at the same time.'[19] In Black's mind, the government's hostility towards the squatters could only be explained by the arrogance, and social prejudice, of English imperial power.

On 28 May 1845, the *Geelong Advertiser* announced that it had changed its name to the *Geelong Advertiser and Squatters' Advocate*. The leading article stated: 'Our journal has been established nearly five years in the natural centre of the most extensive Squatting District of New South Wales – a district peopled by a class of men, who for wealth and intelligence will proudly stand comparison with any other society on the face of the globe; men, too, who are excluded from all means of making their grievances known except through the medium of the public press.' The campaign on behalf of the Port Phillip squatters – and therefore on behalf of Port Phillip itself – was up and running.

Among the squatters' grievances were the benefits Sydney derived from taxes they paid, and the continuing difficulty of meaningful representation in the Sydney-based NSW Legislative Council. A compounding grievance was that squatters, as unsettled vagrants, were disenfranchised and denied the vote. Not only did this encourage them to use the press to express their ills, but it eventually pushed some of them – those who had purchased land in or near town and were thus qualified to stand for election – into active political life.

When elections for the newly established NSW Legislative Council were held in 1843, of the six representatives returned for Port Phillip only three were residents; few men were prepared to spend months travelling to and from Sydney to attend sittings. These three all resigned in 1844. One of those elected in their place was Benjamin Boyd, leader of the campaign against Gipps' proposals. In September 1845, Boyd too resigned. Edward Curr, a one-time squatter and a fiery political champion of separation, put himself up as a replacement candidate. But prejudice against Curr, an Irishman, among the Scots and Port Phillip 'gentry' was considerable.[20] The squatting question was at a critical juncture, and if Curr represented them in Sydney, Black wrote to Gladstone, 'our interest must necessarily sustain injury, through Mr. Curr's captious, quarrelsome, ungovernable temper disgusting those members who are at present favourable to the interests of Port Phillip, besides stirring up Sir George Gipps' bile against us'.

To Black's dismay, some of the squatters decided that he should represent them instead: 'How they came to fix upon me as a more fit person I can't tell, but I was waited upon by

Mr James Atkinson of Sydney, a great personal friend of Sir Geo Gipps, Major Firebrace, John C Riddell, Archibald McLachlan, Mr James Ross solicitor, all of them very extensive resident squatters in Port Phillip district.' Black was eligible to stand as he owned land, having bought 785 acres at Moonee Ponds in Tullamarine for the company in 1842.

He continued: 'Every argument was made use of that ability, zeal and ingenuity could devise to induce me to stand. In reply I stated that I was not a free agent therefore that I could not do it, and that it would be difficult to make partners at 16,000 miles understand why I had yielded to their solicitations.' They ignored his refusal and gave his name to the press, insisting they would nominate him even without his consent. To make his position crystal clear he wrote them a letter: 'I would not go to Sydney nor take a seat in the Legislative Council even if elected. This is my final statement and hope you will not mistake me.' He still found his name had been put forward at the hustings, so he withdrew it. Black ended his long account of this 'exceedingly disagreeable affair' to Gladstone: 'None was more strenuous in his endeavours to send me to Sydney than my friend Farie.'[21]

Despite his protestations, Black was clearly flattered by the confidence expressed in him, if not by the assumption that he would obligingly fall in with whatever plans these 'leading men' proposed. Gladstone applauded his actions: 'I am very glad both on your account and ours that you have kept clear. The public is a bad and generally an ungrateful master and you will be much more happily, as well as profitably, employed in looking after your own affairs.'[22]

Niel Black was not a willing politician, nor was he well endowed for the role. Whatever his prolixity with the pen, he was not a natural speaker. But from this time onward he was drawn into the political life of Port Phillip, developing his views in private. Given how rapidly the district was rushing towards fully fledged colony status, it was difficult for anyone with a stake in the future not to get caught up. William Westgarth described Port Phillip under La Trobe's administration as 'a small body as yet, but making an ominously loud noise upon the far southern skirts of the vast colonial expanse of which Sydney was then the official and business centre'.[23] Black was very much the archetypal Scot who never took a subject of deep interest to himself quietly. But a discussion among friends was one thing, to stand on a public stage and become an audible part of that noise quite another. He pleaded the obligations of company affairs partly as reason, partly as excuse. Unlike those who ran stock as a means to gain wealth and open the way to something else, the land was his life. He expected to forward a vision of 'improvement' on his run and in his neighbourhood, not champion policies or proposals at the broader level of public affairs. He thought this task was fitting only for those with education, breeding and social standing – in which class he had only a toehold.

Soon after his refusal to stand for the Legislative Council, Black was again approached to take up a political role: 'I was applied to yesterday to allow my name to be brought forward as Agent to go to England for two years with £500 a year of pay, to get the Cause of Port Phillip advocated there.' Again, he refused. Instead, Archibald Cuninghame, a Scots barrister with squatting interests, was recruited. 'He is the best we can get to agree to go, and he will devote himself to the subject of his mission.'[24] This mission was to argue for separation, long leases, the pre-emptive right, labour emigration – all the usual causes. Cuninghame was indeed assiduous, and remained in London for many years snapping at the Colonial Office's heels.

From May 1846, Cuninghame made himself thoroughly known to Lord Stanley, and to the new Colonial Secretary, WE Gladstone, writing so many detailed proposals and commentaries that his efforts could not be ignored. TS Gladstone, by contrast, was loath to petition his cousin. Alex Finlay wrote to Black: 'He [WE Gladstone] is cautious and will not do much till he understands what he is about. We have not therefore thought it prudent to make direct application to him, but shall not hesitate if he seems to be taking a wrong course.'[25] Cuninghame felt no such compunction. WE Gladstone wrote back that his 'proposals have often been put forward before but have been thoroughly condemned by all the authorities'.[26] Cuninghame was not dissuaded. Gladstone's stint at the Colonial Office was much briefer than Cuninghame's mission to harass its servants.

The political pot continued to boil during the next year or so, but Black stayed below the parapet. To Finlay, he decried his ability to argue a case in print. Lang the pamphleteer became a squatter neighbour on the South Australia border, and at the end of a letter to Black in 1847 added: 'What about your political letter? Have you not mustered courage to appear in print yet? I suppose you feel like a young lady going to her first ball, or a boy about to don his first pair o' breeks. What a modest man you are to be sure. I think, for public interest, you and such as you should make it a duty to overcome such feelings.'[27] Black was still unwilling to put himself forward, but active in trying to find others who might relish a stab at public life. In 1848, together with Colin Campbell from Mount Cole, he suggested to a friend at Mount Fyans, Lauchlan Mackinnon, that he might stand as a candidate for the Legislative Council.

By this time, the cause of separation was entering its home straight. But Edward Curr, ever quarrelsome, was trying to force the issue along by populist tactics. Curr had also caused an outcry by backing the reintroduction of transportation to New South Wales as a way of solving the labour shortage. As the Pentonvillian experiment had shown, anything that smacked of bringing in convicts as workers was strenuously opposed by working men in Melbourne. Many squatters were in favour, however, viewing any labour as better than no labour.

Niel Black, Colin Campbell and Lauchlan Mackinnon were among the minority of squatters implacably opposed to transportation. This group, who had sent Cuninghame to London and were dubbed the Constitutional party, preferred to maintain non-confrontational relationships with the authorities in Melbourne and Sydney, distrusted the 'democrats' and disliked the rabble-rousing that Curr engaged in, instead aiming to achieve separation in a circumspect and orderly way. These were troubled times, with every mail reminding the colonists that Europe was in the grip of revolutionary fervour. His neighbour Dr Daniel Curdie wrote to Black in July 1848: 'Every post nowadays brings us sad news from Melbourne. Events as sudden and extraordinary as those in Paris seem to take place there and I hope the country may not be compromised by the acts of a few demagogues.'[28] Such men viewed the prospect of an influx of convicts as likely to ruin the social and moral fabric settlers such as themselves were carefully weaving, compromising the Christian, law-abiding communities they were creating around their stations. They also believed that a successful agricultural tenantry had to be peopled by free farmer-immigrants, not ex-prisoners.

Lauchlan Mackinnon, whose future lay in journalism and ideas, was receptive to the prospect of the political fray. He wrote to Black: 'I am the more easily led to form this determination from the proposal having originated with one for whom I entertain a warm friendship and on whose judgement I fully rely.' He set out his platform: 'I would not enter on the responsible duties of a representative of this splendid province as the supporter of the interests of any particular class, the advancement of the general good would be the sole object of my energies.' In addition to supporting agricultural and pastoral interests, his concern was his 'zealous and devoted advocacy' of a non-denominational system of education: 'The ignorance in which the rising generation is suffered to grow up is the most lamentable grievance of which we have to complain, for it is not ourselves but succeeding generations that will have cause to deplore the culpable neglect on our part of that without which Religion and Morals must give place to every species of public and private depravity.'[29] Improvement, not only of the land but also of the colonial human being, was the Mackinnon lodestar – as was the case for Black. Thus were some squatters committed to liberal ideals in the dawn of Victorian political life before ideological identities had crystallised.

Mackinnon was soon in the thick of the political battle, recruiting friends and establishing committees at Portland and Port Fairy. At the hustings in October 1848, Mackinnon won. He then went home to Mount Fyans to relax. In due course he wrote to Black: 'I send home your gig for the *very long loan of which I beg to thank you most cordially.* I know it should have gone home long before this, but it is not my fault – the ladies professing a knowledge of Mr Black's gallantry insisted that he would feel annoyance if his gig being sent home would deprive them of any pleasure. The ladies beg me to assure you that they will have very great pleasure in visiting Glenormiston soon.'[30] Regrettably, Black was still without his own 'lady' to receive them.

By this time, the squatting regulations had been settled by a new Australian Land Act, passed in 1846. Business houses in London, Glasgow and Liverpool wanted their interests protected, and the squatters' representations had made their mark.

By 1846, Gipps was about to be replaced as Governor, his health and spirits broken. Although the Colonial Office had shifted to the squatters' side and was preparing to concede their demand for leases, Gipps was still trying to fight a rearguard action against their being granted long-term security of tenure. A bill had been tabled by Lord Stanley in 1845, and resubmitted in May 1846 with virtually no alteration by WE Gladstone; but when Peel's ministry fell in mid-1846, all was again to play for. The terms of the latest bill, while reasonably favourable towards the squatters, still bore the marks of Gipps' resistance to rights over 'their' lands. Insecurity of tenure was now to be brought about by the use of auctions – effectively cancelling the 'pre-emptive right'. Black gloomily tried to explain to Gladstone the problems they had with the proposed provisions. 'By this Bill we are to have 7 years leases of our runs, if we bid highest for them at auction. If we are outbid, we must shift for a run, as we best may. If we have been 5 years on our run, and [have made] improvements on it, the Governor if he chooses, may give us a 7 years lease of the improvements [i.e. the buildings] but not of the rest of the run. If we think the rent fixed by him too much, he cuts short the discussion by putting up the run to auction. Such are the pleasant prospects of the Squatter under this Bill.'[31]

In July 1846, the old Squatting Act of 1839 expired. A few days later, Black wrote to Gladstone: 'We have at present no Squatting Regulations. The Legislative Council opposed the measure brought forward by Sir Geo Gipps. It was thrown out

and we are at present beyond the pale of the law, paying neither licence nor assessment. The question at issue was taxation
without representation, the Governor claiming a right to the
Crown Lands on behalf of Her Majesty as if they were his private and personal property, the Council contending that these
lands were vested in Her only as trustee acting for behoof of the
interest of the people, whose property they contend the lands to
be.'[32] A few days later he again took up his pen. 'The alternative
repletion and difficult supply in the labour market gives rise to
fearful fluctuations in the value of everything produced in the
colony. This speedily brings a capitalist into difficulties, renders
property unsaleable, shakes public confidence, checks progress
and for a time ruins the prosperity of the colony.' Little could
anyone have realised for how many long years insecurity and
volatility were to punctuate Victorian development.

Black embellished his descriptions in the hope they would
find their way to influential audiences. 'You cannot conceive
the miserable bankrupt-like appearance [the land] presents. The
once noble forests stript of their solitary grandeur, the rich soil
freed from its luxuriant herbage now beaten and trodden. Here
and there a miserable bark or slab hut surrounded by desolating
shepherds sometimes having an attempt at a garden in front of it.
This is generally the visible extent of improvements in the bush
and even these are effected at very considerable expense to the
first occupant. The land regulations operate against any further
attempt at improvements. So in this way, men of family and
education spend many years of their lives in this country vainly
hoping that a more favourable change may enable them to make a
settled existence and permanent home where they are.

'The hut in which I now write has stood for eight years. It is
built of "wattle and daub" or a very coarse basket work plastered

over with mud or clay. I employ 60–100 men exclusive of women and children accompanying them and not one of those in our employ have had the opportunity of being to church since I came here. I have made an attempt at collecting subscriptions sufficient to pay a salary to a clergyman to itinerate in this neighbourhood and have nearly succeeded. But what home can we offer – who may be said to have no home of our own – or what settlement in life can we make suitable to the habits of a respectable clergyman? … In short, the whole of this system is most impolitic. It would benefit the mother country as well as this colony much more to grant a right in fee simple to every acre of wasteland *made productive*, subject to the payment of an annual assessment in the produce of the soil – whether horses, cattle, sheep, pigs or cows. This would be a more equal tax and bear a proportion to our estimated wants. If this system were adopted, the face of the country would be changed. Bark huts would speedily give place to substantial comfortable houses, fences would be erected, roads formed, churches would spring up, schools would be established and the whole face of the country so far occupied would soon assume the characteristics of a settled civilized Christian land.'[33]

The battle of the squatters versus Sir George Gipps has been passed down by history as one in which a coterie of rapacious land-grabbers managed to defeat the defender of the people's patrimony, a valiant man who destroyed his health and reputation by trying in the name of his Queen to prevent the alienation of the great 'wastelands' of the interior to a few hundred 'shepherd-kings'.[34] This picture is not borne out by Black's more nuanced version of contemporary concerns and their interwoven complexities. Black accepted that his own proposals for granting rights over land to those who had made it productive would be met with opposition. 'I am aware that it will be objected to this plan that it would be placing great tracts of country in the hands of a few individuals. True! But how long would they retain this land, as abundant labour is scarce? Until they become equalized, the law of supply and demand would soon reduce the extent of the landed possessions, and the certain tendency of this country would be to an immense number of small, petty proprietors in place of a wealthy landed aristocracy.'[35] The encouragement and financial help he gave to several of his employees, especially his Scottish shepherds, to take up their own runs and look to a future as 'petty proprietors' in their own right was a practical manifestation of his ideals. 'The first overseer I had in this country was here this day and told me that he has this year shorn 5200 sheep of his own', he wrote to Gladstone in December 1846. This was the solid citizen entrepreneur that Black wished to encourage; not those with 'low character and prodigal habits', elevated by 'too rapid a tendency to democracy'.[36]

By this time, although Black did not know it, the Land Act had been passed in London. The new Colonial Secretary, Earl Grey, wanted to support the sheep and cattle industries, and he could see that the yearly licence system was seriously inhibiting 'improvements' and the growth of a stable agrarian society. So he accepted the argument for leases of long duration. The squatters gained all their key demands. The new Act classified the land into three types: 'unsettled' land, in which leases could be given for 14 years; 'intermediate' lands where settlement was more organised, and where leases could be given for eight years; and 'settled' land close to town, where leases would run for one year only. In Port Phillip, relatively few areas were designated 'intermediate', and these did not yet include the Western or Portland Bay district. The Order-in-Council containing the new provisions was sent out in March 1847. By then, the news had already arrived that the squatters' long battle for security over 'their' lands had been won.

Black had been waiting for the outcome of these negotiations to decide whether to build a more solid house in place of his dilapidated hut. The desire for a better house had to do not only with durability, but also with status and comfort. The success of Niel Black & Company meant that it was no longer suitable for the company's managing partner to live like a cottager. A decent house would also, incidentally, have to be built before the wife he imagined for himself could be persuaded to live in the bush. But, like everyone else, he postponed building 'until I felt secure of compensation in the event of our being sold out'. Premature investment in permanent homesteads might also have compromised the squatters' arguments. That they could not build proper homes, thus delaying the advance of civilisation, was one of their points of leverage.

The moment it became clear, at the beginning of 1847, that the battle over leases was won, Black's plans for a new homestead at Glenormiston went ahead. In February he wrote: 'I thought it best to build a stone house though it will cost a little more money, and I am now building a neat little place having two front rooms and a back skillion [kitchen area], the whole to consist of five apartments. It will cost about £300.'[37] His partners did not object to the company's expenditure on Black's new dwelling or on his more comfortable establishment – including the arrival of a butler, Mr Prout. But they had become worried about the shape his venture was taking. The development of a Glenormiston 'settlement', with its large permanent workforce plus wives and families, its school, the church and manse at Kilnoorat, and its reputation for entertaining Lauchlan Mackinnon and the ladies of the neighbourhood, was far from their idea of itinerant flocks and herds browsing through a grassy wilderness and rangeland to fill their pockets year by year.

Black met their reservations coolly. To be granted leases for 14 years, as they had now been promised, 'shall unquestionably end in fee simple [ownership]. We can never again be disturbed in our possession, this opinion is now almost universal.' So why were Gladstone and Finlay objecting to this major success – even talking of selling up and ending the partnership? He was more than a little scathing, not to mention offended. 'Is this then a time to reduce our possessions considering we occupy some of the finest land in this colony? If, for every twenty square miles we occupy, we must buy 320 acres of land, I must not forego our claim', and he would do this with his own money or theirs or whosesoever he could muster. 'I may say that the chief end of my life for years past has been to see the affairs of Niel Black & Co in their rise and progress equal the expectation of those who first framed the scheme.'

But those who had first framed the scheme had not thought at all in terms of purchasing land. Again and again Gladstone counselled less expansion, insisting on money being sent home, and asking how Black viewed his future. 'I sometimes think it might perhaps suit you to take the whole concern off our hands, if you wish to be a large proprietor in that quarter of the Globe.'[38] Black was judicious in response. 'When the Concern is brought to a close I cannot say that I have formed even a faint outline of any future course of action for myself. But it is very probable I may wish to continue to nurture the plant I have myself planted in the wilderness and called Glenormiston.'[39]

With such a declaration, they were, for the moment, silenced.

Chapter Six

'A DAY WE HOPE
NEVER TO SEE THE
LIKE OF AGAIN'

IN MID-JULY 1850, Niel Black again set sail from Melbourne destined for Scotland and home. This time, he intended to travel at a more leisurely pace, so he went first to Sydney as a staging post for the northerly route. On 30 July he took passage on the *Bank of England* bound for Calcutta. She was 'a crack ship, Commodore of a fleet of five and expected to make a good passage', and the living on board was 'better than the best hotel in Melbourne'. The company also pleased him, the five first-class passengers happening to include the 20-year-old Prince Frederick (Christian) of Schleswig-Holstein, returning incognito from a visit to the Antipodes.[1] Black was even paid the compliment of being asked by Captain Stanley Carr, the prince's guardian, to act as his substitute during the voyage: Carr was staying behind in Australia.[2] But the *Bank of England* nearly sailed no further than the dreaded Torres Strait.

As the fleet entered the strait they encountered a great storm, in which – Black believed – they were saved from shipwreck only by the intervention of Providence. 'We entered in safety and dropped anchor 15 miles inside. Another ship dropped anchor right ahead of us and then drifted down upon our prow and to save both ships we had to slip our cable chain and set sail again. We dropped our second anchor at a short distance but soon lost hold, and drifted at the rate of about a mile an hour continuously. At 11 pm we were within two miles of the coral reef. We could not set sail as we were in a channel and drifting onto an island which we could not see at night. We thus paid away our last link of chain, being 145 fathoms, and with this she began to hold for the first time. 'On taking up the anchor yesterday we were within a quarter mile of the rocks and minus the "fluke" or hook of the anchor. How the ship could have held with a broken anchor is what I can't understand. Five anchors have been lost out of four ships and at present the fate of one ship is altogether unknown to us but we still hope she may make her appearance.'[3] In the many sea passages Niel Black took during his lifetime, this was the closest he came to foundering.

The same quest carried him westward as had taken him to Scotland in 1843. The failure to recruit that elusive companion – Mrs Black – was again troubling him deeply. It was common knowledge throughout the district that he was in want of a wife, and his inability to find one was a subject of speculation. Claud Farie and others had wooed successfully in Van Diemen's Land, or else at parties or racecourses closer to home. Promising candidates were introduced to Black by neighbours who entertained. James Blair wrote to him from Portland with a keen invitation to visit: 'There will be a ball and supper graced by an amount of beauty as embarrassing to me to describe as it will be to you to contemplate.'[4] Captain Eddington, now living on the Hopkins River at Ballangeich, could no longer matchmake in Melbourne. But others did. During 1848–49, Black spent a great deal of time in town.

No intimations of his pursuit of love exist in his surviving letters, but occasional giveaways appear in letters he received. His romantic failures mystified his friends. One had the boldness to write: 'You know, "it is not meet that man should be alone", especially a man like you so open to the sympathy of women and to all the kindnesses of domestic life.' He told Black that a helpmate would 'keep you out of *scrapes*. I have no doubt all your misdemeanours arise from the want of the guiding hand of such a personage'.[5] What scrapes and misdemeanours?

In 1839, Black had left behind in Scotland several fluttering female hearts. During his trip home in 1843, his brother Walter had disapproved of his courtship behaviour: apparently, he led on and then abandoned.[6] Maybe a similar proclivity blighted his romantic adventures in the colony. A neighbour, William Adams, wrote in April 1849: 'I suppose you will have returned by this time from Melbourne, but whether with a hole bored through your heart, or a sound one, is doubtful. "Oh, these women, these women" as the song says.' If Black had gone to Melbourne to propose to his latest flame, expectations were not high. Clearly, nothing came of it.

In 1847, Black rehired William Swan as his manager at Glenormiston. In 1845, from overseer, Swan had been promoted to superintendent. This job would normally be reserved for someone from a more elevated social background, a man of the managerial class educated well beyond the parish school. But Black preferred to promote his original Scottish shepherds, 'men with a thorough knowledge of stock [who] were proud – not ashamed – of their new position'. He wanted an overseer who would *lead* those under him out to work, not men of a superior breed that would *send* them there.[7] Under this policy, Swan had become 'the best overseer in Port Phillip'. Swan's letters to Black during 1848–49, when his master was often in Melbourne, show both how completely Black felt able to rely on him, and how keenly Black stuck to principles of merit, not class, in managing a large and fluctuating workforce. But whatever principles of social equity he applied in his employment practices, it was a different story in his romantic skirmishes. Here the bar remained high. He wanted a wife of gentle birth. But it seemed there was none such willing, or acceptable, in Melbourne.

The closing years of the 1840s were not easy ones, despite the general view that, since the 1847 Order-in-Council, the squatters had nothing further to complain about. Labour was still desperately short, and men whose performance was abysmal had often to be employed at high wages. Black described to his partners losses of strayed sheep and deaths from wild dogs far greater than in previous years. In addition, after all the pains taken to keep the flocks clean of scab, a new scourge – footrot – appeared and ran riot through the sheep of Port Phillip. Footrot was bacterial, and if infected animals were not instantly removed, the disease spread fast. Extra hands had to be taken on to dress the sheep's feet to contain infection and relieve the distress that eventually led to their destruction. 'I always think it best to meet any evil boldly and at once', wrote Black to Gladstone. 'On this principle we have gone to much expense, the season being very wet, in addition to which good labour cannot be had at any cost.'[8] The effort would have paid off if the price of wool had been high, but it was not.

This was not the only health disaster to affect Black's flocks. Early in 1847, sheep at Warreanga sickened and died from a mysterious blight. Black's expectations of his new run were dashed. From one day to the next, the sheep dropped like flies: 680 altogether. The cause turned out to be their consumption of a poisonous plant that grew on sand hummocks near the coast.[9] Here Black also took drastic action. He bought rights and obtained a licence on a small station just to Warreanga's north, to which he moved the sheep as a stopgap, before selling them off as fast as he could. He then turned Warreanga into a cattle run. He remained bullish, assuring his partners that he could purchase the necessary cattle with what the sheep would fetch. But in the meantime there was new outlay and less remittance home. Black lamented 'the frequent extreme and violent changes that affect the value of everything in this country'.[10] He felt hard-pressed to keep the company afloat in such an unpredictable sea and to convince his partners that all must come well.

The low price wool was fetching meant that many graziers depended heavily on the 'steaming vat' to boil down their animals for tallow. But fattening up stock for such a purpose – there was no point in boiling down an animal that was not fat – was deeply depressing. Swan did his best to persuade Black not to sell off the sheep at Warreanga prematurely, but to keep them on pasture away from the coast. 'I think it's a great pity to see such fine sheep sold at boiling prices, if any shift could be made for keeping them', he wrote.[11] But Black refused to entertain any scheme for keeping them alive. They were disappointing 'boilers' anyway, bringing in far less than anticipated. Tallow was not an easy way to compensate for low wool prices, but this alternative 'crop' kept many – including the ever-struggling Captain Eddington – from going under as prices in UK wool markets kept plunging to ever more disastrous lows.[12]

Black remained preoccupied with the forthcoming leases. Before the provisions of the Order-in-Council could be carried out, runs had to be properly mapped. In late 1847, Black hired Henry Bourne Foot to survey his run for £25, 'to include a fair map and two copies, and a written description of the boundaries'.[13] Such a survey reprised old grievances about boundary lines fixed years back by marked trees and plough lines long since disappeared. Black had final settlements to make with John Thomson of Keilambete, and with Jeremiah Ware and Peter McArthur to the north, Stephen Ewen at Marida Yallock, Donald Craig at Eddington's, and others to the south and south-west. He put potential clients in touch with Henry Foot, supplied him with a horse from Geelong, organised joint days of boundary reckoning, and offered every courtesy. Black, more in hope than expectation, wished his neighbours to agree among each other rather than call in his nemesis, Foster Fyans. On 7 April 1848, he wrote to Gladstone from Melbourne: 'All the squatters are in town at present as this is the last day for applying for our leases', adding: 'Goodness knows what trouble we may have before they are granted. I expect it will take a whole year.' A year turned out to be wildly optimistic.

The earlier sense of relief that the Order-in-Council had finally done right by the squatters had gradually dissipated. It was not only a question of delays due to surveys and boundary disputes. The Order's provisions were loosely cast and needed interpretation – over which legal experts differed. Were the provisions to be put into operation automatically and unconditionally, or did the Governor and his officers have some discretion? In the all-important matter of the 14-year leases in unsettled lands and eight-year leases in intermediate lands, did they *have* to be issued to the squatters or was it simply that they *could* be issued with caveats of various kinds? And could they be revoked? The most vexed issue was the wording in the Order – seized on by the squatters – that land in the unsettled areas, now subject to tenure for 14 years, could only be sold to an existing leaseholder.[14] How this extreme expression of the squatters' pre-emptive right ever came to be articulated in the Order is a mystery. But the words were there in black and white and they caused a major problem. Very few squatters – Colin Campbell, Black's friend at Mount Cole, being one of them,[15] and Lauchlan Mackinnon another – were prepared to accept that the establishment of such a complete stranglehold on land by the squatters was never intended and could not be wise or acceptable to the majority of people. Most squatters took the contrary, literal, view.

Gipps had approved the provisions of the Order from his deathbed, which meant that he did not believe they granted the squatters inalienable rights over 'their' land; and nor did Earl Grey, now Colonial Secretary. Long leases that could not be curtailed and that conferred exclusive purchasing rights on their holders would inhibit the creation of townships, public amenities, reserves, roads and railways, not to mention settled agriculture in suitable locations as markets and transport developed. Neither Governor FitzRoy in Sydney nor Superintendent La Trobe in Melbourne was prepared to issue the leases on a basis which would compromise planned development of the country.[16] Every year from 1848 on, special Commissioners would sit and lawyers wrangle, and the *Government Gazette* in Sydney would announce that the leases were not yet ready. As the process dragged on, Niel Black – who had earlier written to Gladstone that he could not leave Port Phillip until the issue was settled – decided after all that he would undertake a visit home. It seemed unlikely that the landholding question would be fixed before Victoria was created as a separate colony in 1851. And with separation, all the issues – leases, compensation and pre-emptive rights – would again be thrown open while Victoria's new institutions cut their teeth on them.

If he went back to Scotland now, Black could return soon after separation. Apart from a renewed marital quest, a run home would give him the opportunity of clarifying his policies for managing 'our Concern' to his disgruntled partners. Only face-to-face persuasion would enable TS Gladstone and Alex Finlay to see that things were going in the right direction.

The circumstance that made Black feel that an absence of a year or so was manageable was the presence at Glenormiston of a new arrival: his nephew Archie, his brother Walter's elder son.

In 1848, Niel Black's sister-in-law Jessie had sent Archie out to Port Phillip as an apprentice to his uncle. She and her 19-year-old firstborn were both strong-willed and had begun to clash. She hoped Niel would check the young man's over-heated temperament and inclination to excess, as well as offer the opportunity in life his father was too ill to provide. Thus began Black's long career of receiving into his guardianship the next generation of would-be gentlemen-colonists, sent out to him by ambitious or disaffected parents. His nephew was the first candidate to be enrolled in what he later called his 'College for Squatters'. The experience was a trial in unanticipated ways.

Archie's father, Walter, had entered a lunatic asylum in 1844. His first major collapse took place while Niel was in Scotland in 1843, and his angry, censorious tongue – not understood by Niel at the time as stemming from mental illness – destroyed the deep mutual support which had characterised their relations since Niel was a boy. The arrival of Archie represented a chance to mend divided hearts, and for Niel to repay Walter the debt he owed him for being the only father he ever knew, of having raised him, educated him, taught him his grazier and stock-breeding trade, and – along with Jessie and their children – given him a home. Walter, delusional and manic Walter, would never now visit Australia, but his sons might have a good start in life thanks to Niel's success. Niel looked on Archie's arrival with hopeful expectation.

Archie Black arrived by the *Martin Luther* in January 1849 and proceeded up-country. His uncle received him at Glenormiston enthusiastically, and wrote home to Jessie: 'Your letter of 1 September reached me safely. It is weakness to say that its pages, while reading them, were well moistened by the dew of keen feelings filtered freely from my brain. I can conceal such feelings but I cannot control them when unforeseen and unexpected causes recall the associations of earlier days.' He was inclined to dismiss her criticisms of her son. 'I think that sensible and judicious kindness may yet soften down those rougher aspects of which you complain',[17] he continued. Jessie was loathed by Niel's other siblings back in Cowal, and her recriminatory tongue was blamed for Walter's mental disintegration. Niel took a more forgiving view. He treasured the reawakening of family ties, and tried to make up for the 'cold chill that many years of neglect has thrown over our former friendship'.

The Blacks' story of misunderstandings and jealousies would have resonated with many families sundered by the colonial diasporas of those years with their long distances, lack of pictorial records and infrequency of communication. 'The time has been when I knew no higher enjoyment than this [writing letters home]. In those bygone days, my pen carelessly traced the rambling thoughts of my own fancy and feelings as they occurred. My spirit was then wont, when freed of the cares and turmoil of a busy life, to spring triumphant, roaming "to the uttermost ends of the earth" – there to commune with the spirits of those I loved so well. Half the circumference of the globe was the distance between us, the diameter of the whole earth intervened. Yet this was counted as nothing, distance and space were annihilated by the power of strong feelings. In thought I sat at your fireside for hours each day, so strong was the force of imagination, that this enjoyment did not fall short, for the time, of what the reality would have been. How changed and now, the weary world of waters that intervenes between us oppresses the imagination, so that my own thoughts do not seem to me seaworthy and it is like presumption to expect that they can outline so far a journey.'

Niel wrote with sincerity of the love he had once borne his sister-in-law – an innocent love, given his strict Presbyterian code. But 'that which was once my home and the home of my affection is not now the scene to call forth the voice of gladness in my heart. I can never realise in my own mind that Walter is so helpless, this belief can never become a living active principle in my mind until I see him. Is it too much to cherish the hope that he will yet be well?' He finished his letter, one of the most eloquent he ever wrote: 'It was the love of serving my family that sent me to this country, and the harvest I reaped was a personal quarrel with them. This was a disappointment rather hard to be borne, but it is past.'[18] In reality, such ties could never be recovered. Not only could they not survive the long separations, but there was a growing gulf of lifestyle and aspiration, opposing fortunes and misfortunes, social elevation and personal collapse. In western Scotland, the years 1848–50 were famine years. Within every family, the story of emigration brought its quotas of shame, pride and jealousy which ate away at old affections and turned friendships sour.

His uncle maintained his high hopes of Archie, whom he found to be 'as obedient and gentle with me as I could wish'. However, he admitted that he could be strong-willed and impetuous. 'I believe his principles are very good and upright and he has a sharp and penetrating wit about him. If left to himself, I am inclined to think he would be expensive, but a little time will correct this.'[19] He wrote to Gladstone: 'My nephew is with me but not employed by us. He will receive no wages except his living for many a day to come. I think he promises to turn out well. At the same time I would wish to have him under my immediate eye for a few years until he gets a little older and more acquainted in the Colony.'[20]

Such caution was soon thrown to the winds. Within months Niel began to think of his young nephew as being capable, with the assistance of Farie and William Bell, his agent in Melbourne, of running the company's affairs for a while. His letters provide glimpses of Archie, dashing and strikingly handsome, riding over to Warreanga, driving fat cattle to market, and cultivating friendships at the Faries' and Eddingtons'. Black himself seems disenchanted and restless at the time – perhaps because of the mysterious 'scrapes' and failed romantic attachments. There may also have been some social competition between himself and the good-looking younger man to put him out of sorts. New disputes erupted with John Thomson of Keilambete over intrusions on his sheep wash and cattle station at Lake Terang: the fresh water there was under increasing pressure. He also picked unnecessary quarrels with other local squatters, dragging in friends such as Dr Daniel Curdie at Tandarook.[21] He was inclined to become enraged over minor matters and refused to put grievances aside.

By December 1849 he had made up his mind to go to Scotland. Whatever his earlier views about Archie's need for years of training, he had convinced himself that his nephew could manage. Archie himself opposed any idea of a superintendent being appointed above him, and Niel did not intend to be away long. As in 1843, he imagined himself gone and back within not much more than a year, accompanied by a carefully won, affectionate and suitable Mrs Black. He forgot his earlier courtship difficulties and that, at 46, age was no longer on his side. On 9 July 1850, he wrote to Gladstone from Melbourne that he had been 'hanging on from day to day here for a ship to carry me to Sydney. In the meantime I have stopped my salary and put my nephew in charge.'

———————

Archie Black thoroughly enjoyed his new-found vocation and immediately began to imitate his uncle's voice of command. While Niel was near drowning in the 'Terror Straits', Archie revelled in a splendid degree of personal authority for a young man of only 20. By this time, Niel Black & Company represented a significant capital enterprise: the estate was valued at £27 600 in February 1850,[22] and it employed around 150 workers in two locations. This was a business in a very different league from the one Black had nursed into being a decade before. If young Archie was daunted, he gave no sign. His uncle's friends Claud Farie and his partner, George Rodger, went over to see him at shearing time and wrote reassuringly to Niel.[23]

However, he soon felt under pressure. The bush was still a lonely place. His nearest friendly neighbours – Daniel and Mrs Mackinnon at Marida Yallock – were five miles away and he had no regular companion of his own age or kind in whom to confide. So he failed to maintain the social distance from the Glenormiston workforce that his seniority as his uncle's representative required. He fell out with Donald Swan, William's brother who had come out from Scotland to take his place, and fired him. His uncle was furious: 'You have been made a fool of by Crawford and others, they have managed to turn the overseer off the station and thus far encouraged you will soon find that many other schemes will be attempted in smooth and plausible language.'[24] Archie also quarrelled with William Swan, now a squatter in his own right, unjustly accusing him of selling NB cattle on his own behalf, and with Alexander Mitchell, superintendent at Warreanga – all men whose goodwill he could not do without. His actions were over-hasty, those of an inexperienced young man with a firecracker temperament, determined to prove his mettle. This was a fear his uncle had harboured, and he spared nothing in writing him to this effect.

In September 1850, two months after his uncle's departure, came the first major crisis. By this time, forward-looking squatters with ample means were beginning to think of purchasing land or stations, even at the price of £1 an acre. This would become possible as soon as the leases were issued. Black himself, aware of the importance of holding on to the 'best run in the country', intended to recommend this – diplomatically – to his partners, and was preparing to purchase at the earliest opportunity. However, one land-buying operator in Port Phillip was ahead of the game. This was WJT 'Big' or 'Long' Clarke, a 'shepherd king' on a voracious scale. Clarke was a man feared, hated and admired for his abilities, particularly his talents at 'money-breeding', to which he was notoriously devoted, as well as for his lack of scruples.[25] His rapacious eye had lighted on Glenormiston.

William Bell wrote away to Black, his friend and client, still on the high seas: 'That great Van Diemen's Land Leviathan, commonly yclept "Long Clarke", has taken advantage of an unrepealed clause in an act of the Imperial Parliament and has purchased at the minimum price of £1 per acre, 26,000 acres of land next Greenhill [north-west of Melbourne], thereby acquiring right of pre-emption for grazing purposes over 78,000 acres of Crown Lands at 10 shillings per Section.' The clause to which he was referring allowed for a 'special survey', whereby a person could claim 5120 acres (8 square miles) at £1 an acre, so long as it was 5 miles from a town (settled area). 'This has caused a great commotion among the squatters who are either bought out or whose runs are interfered with under the pre-emptive right.' One of the dispossessed was Black's old friend John Riddell, much of whose run, including his woolshed and sheep wash, Clarke bought from under him by this device.

This was the sort of questionable deal that made squatters with less expansive pockets defensive and damaged the reputation of all. Bell was alarmed that Clarke would engineer the same fate for Black. 'On dit says, and I believe truly, that he has £100,000 ready for next January and that he intends applying for 20,000 acres of Glenormiston.'[26] This would have given Clarke rights of pasturage over an additional 60 000 acres: Niel Black &

Company's empire would have collapsed. Bell had spent the previous three days engaged in negotiations between Clarke and Riddell and the other dispossessed squatters, and rushed to his writing desk at the first opportunity to send Black a warning.

When he disembarked in England in January 1851 and received this news, Black was seriously alarmed. But after some days he wrote to Farie: 'The more I reflect on this, the less I am apprehensive.' He studied the 1847 Order-in-Council in detail: 'No-one can obtain a pre-emption to land *placed beyond the settled districts*. This appears to me to set the matter quite at rest.' He forgot the tendency of government to interpret rules contrarily, depending on who was exerting *force majeure*. There were now many thousands of miles between Black and his antipodean lands, and his preoccupations had changed, thanks to an extensive Mediterranean tour in company with 'the Prince' – Prince Frederick of Schleswig-Holstein – with whose care he had been charged on the voyage from Sydney. But if his uncle was sanguine about Clarke's scheming, Archie at Glenormiston was not. 'Clarke is well known to have large sums of money at command and only waits for the issues of the leases to pounce upon this run. The "special survey" near Melbourne only serves to whet his desire to become a more extensive landowner. Beware!'[27]

The colonial authorities were still unwilling to confer the leases authorised by the 1947 Order-in-Council. To the squatters – whose more extravagant demands La Trobe was trying to resist – it seemed as if, after winning the argument over their insecurity of tenure, settling their boundaries, and doing things by the book, they might yet be dispossessed on a whim. Squatters in 'settled' areas were purchasing lots on their runs; by mid-1851, land-buying beyond the outskirts of town had become something of 'a mania'.[28] Clarke was eventually refused any further 'special surveys' – having sought them at several places, including Dandenong and Port Fairy – on the grounds that it was 'not considered for the good of the public to give such a large quantity of land to one individual'.[29] The clamour from all sides, high and low, against such purchases managed to put some steel into La Trobe's pliant backbone, and no more 'special surveys' were granted.

By then the seminal year of separation, 1851, was already searing itself into colonial consciousness for other reasons. This was the year of 'Black Thursday', the day of the worst bushfires in Victoria's history, of catastrophic floods following in their wake, and of the start of the Victorian gold rush. Niel Black was far away and, at Glenormiston, the weight of all these extreme events fell on Archie's slim shoulders.

The New Year was savagely hot and dry. In mid-January, disaster struck. Archie wrote to Niel: 'My Dear Uncle, It is my duty to tell you that a number of sheep have been destroyed here a few days ago by fire. It originated in the Stony Rises and broke out into the plain in spite of our exertions to keep it within bounds. When our efforts proved quite useless in the attempt to stop the progress of the flames, we went with all possible speed to see whether the flock was in a place of safety. We arrived there only a few score yards in advance of the fire. About 500 were either destroyed on the spot or rendered useless.' Flocks under other shepherds then demanded attention. 'Crawford's sheep seemed to be in imminent danger and we made all haste towards them. A small spot to leeward of the flock had scarcely been burnt [as a preventive action] when the furious flames reached them on the other side and about fifty died on the spot. A good many have been so seriously scorched that they cannot live.'[30]

This was only the prelude of much worse to come. On 5 February, Archie again sat down to write to his uncle. For weeks all the squatters in the neighbourhood had been threatened by fires, 'and have spent days and nights in the attempt to extinguish them'. Glenormiston and The Sisters were relatively unscathed, or so he implied. 'We have succeeded in saving the whole of the cattle run and the greatest part of the heifer station', but others had fared less well: 'Ware, McArthur, Craig, Cole, Montgomery, Stevens, Thomson, Gray have been burnt out, many of them losing their woolsheds and flocks of sheep. And with difficulty saving their dwellings.' Archie's worry now was water. 'I am very much afraid we are to be in great want of water as already we have been taking horses and bullocks out of the water-holes.' These deep pools were left when seasonal streams retreated, and their steep sides were a hazard for stock, who fell in and could not get out unaided. Archie ended his letter with an appeal: 'I wish you were here for such a season is new to me and who knows how we may get on.'[31]

The following day, Black Thursday itself, was 'one we hope never to see the like of again'.[32] The lurid sky and the roaring wind, the smoke and darkness that many thought the harbinger of Judgment Day, instilled terror from one end of Port Phillip to the other. Mount Macedon was swathed in flame and the whole Portland Bay district seemed to be ablaze. The thermometer rose to over 110°F (43°C), and in Melbourne, people took shelter from the whirling dust and unprecedented heat, fearing that the town would burst into flames at any moment. Out at sea, Dr Daniel Curdie, sailing home to Scotland on the ship

Constance, observed the dense black cloud hanging over the land and the burnt leaves and showers of ash blown far out to sea in the upward rush of scalding winds from the north. Hundreds of scorched birds desperate to escape perched in the rigging of the ship, many falling dead onto the deck below. Curdie, whose station was near Glenormiston, could not know what ruin his run, men or stock had suffered nor expect to learn of their fate until he reached Britain. On the plains, animals stampeded before the onrush of the flames, and livestock losses were heavy. The fire was mercifully extinguished when the wind changed direction, blowing up from the south-west and forcing the fire back over land it had already consumed. In some places for 15 miles at a stretch there was nothing but blackened land, charred trunks – and carcasses.

News of Black Thursday did not arrive in Britain until May. Archie wrote, but gave the impression that Niel Black & Company had sustained few, if any, losses on Black Thursday itself – that the 550 sheep burned in January were the total. To his horror and bemusement, however, Niel Black gradually discovered from accounts in the newspapers and from reports brought by those arriving from Port Phillip that the company had lost at least 2000, maybe many more, sheep to the flames.[33] Gladstone soothed Black's anger, pointing out that Glenormiston could not be immune from such a disaster and that it was not his nephew's fault. But Archie, having endured the trauma of watching thousands of animals burn before his eyes, could not bring himself to write an account of what had happened. Instead of detailing the devastation of the company's flocks, he described how he let the neighbours move their sheep onto his remaining pasture until the new grass came. He even wrote positively: within days it had rained heavily and bright green shoots showed quickly through the ash-laden surface. By late March, Archie was requesting Craig to remove 'his flocks from the honeysuckle station'. Glenormiston's temporary role as a refugee resort for Black Thursday flocks was over, but the drama was far from done.

By early April, severe drought had set in. Archie wrote: 'Thousands of sheep have died of starvation and thirst and thousands will yet perish if rain does not fall more copiously than it has done. Many people in our neighbourhood are destroying the lambs, the increase of the season, in the hope of saving the sheep. I have been told by people who know the country and who would scorn to tell an untruth that there is scarcely a blade of grass between this place and the Murray River.' However, on the better-watered pastures of Glenormiston, the sheep still had feed enough to stay in reasonable condition – for the moment. How many sheep they now had Archie did not say.[34] By early May, hundreds of thousands of lambs were expected to be slaughtered in the district. 'The water at The Sisters is almost done. Many of the cattle have stuck in the mud while attempting to reach it.' But Archie's reports were without statistics or assessments of stock or feed. Gladstone complained that accounts in the newspapers were fuller.

During this drought came the first intimation of the havoc that was to be caused by the discovery of gold. The first strike was at Bathurst in New South Wales, at a site named Ophir by Edward Hargraves, a prospector from the California goldfields. The news, reported in the *Geelong Advertiser* on 26 May 1851, had a heady effect in Port Phillip too. '*Gold* is as abundant as water in our colonies at present', wrote Archie. 'The people are perfectly mad and are flocking in hundreds to the land of Ophir. Wages are rising and if the precious metals continue to be found in any quantity I am at a loss to know what the squatters are to do.'[35] The first gold strikes in Victoria came in July, first at Clunes and Warrandyte, then a few weeks later at Buninyong, just south of Ballarat. By August, Archie was becoming increasingly anxious as the discoveries multiplied, and wrote again to his uncle. 'Gold at Bathurst, Gold at the Pyrenees, Gold at the deep Creek, and Gold on the Lodden. One man Sydney side got £2000 for one piece of gold. What we are to do during the approaching shearing time no-one seems to know. Some settlers are offering shearers £1 per hundred sheep, thus making matters worse ... I hope you will be here before the first of February as I am sick of this life of constant anxiety.'[36]

Archie's next letter brought news of another tragedy – this time due to floods. 'I have just returned from Warreanga after a most disastrous journey. The rivers are many feet higher than they have ever been known to be before. It was impossible to muster cattle so I made up my mind to come home. Two men accompanied me, Peter McEwen and Henry Windsor, *both of whom are no more*. We got into a water-hole, our horses would not swim as they had fallen in suddenly. The horses ridden by the men rolled over and were free. I was still in the water and was only saved by being perfectly calm and collected.'[37] Peter McEwen was from the Blacks' home community of Glendaruel in Argyll. He had arrived on the same ship as Archie in January 1849 and had been employed as a stockman and drover. He was therefore someone from home whose future had been entrusted to the Blacks, and he had done well. Niel later gave the struggling McEwen family some money as compensation. Archie rode back to Glenormiston alone with the horses. He returned with some men a few days later, and they 'recovered the bodies and buried them near the fatal spot'.[38]

145

Meanwhile, in Scotland, Niel was still awaiting a full account of what the company had suffered in the Black Thursday conflagration. Nothing came. Finally, in October, he wrote to his nephew that in reviewing the returns, he could find no account of the losses in stock or the decreases (or increases) month by month. 'You once stated that 500 sheep were burned but you never since thought the matter of sufficient importance to return to the subject. The newspapers stated the loss at 4000 and the information of persons who left the colony subsequent to the loss represent it as about 2000. My partners apply to me for information which I am unable to bestow and they ask "Why does Archie not inform you on such a matter?"' What Niel Black hated most was the sense that Archie was deliberately withholding information. 'Confidence can only be gained by telling the truth and concealing nothing.' He insisted he was attempting 'to assist and direct your judgment' and was without 'any wish to incriminate or find fault'.[39] But find fault he never failed to do, on this occasion and many others.

This homily reached Archie exactly a year after Black Thursday. He overreacted angrily and refused to do as asked, writing that the event was now long past and the estimated losses had been recorded in the accounts.[40] Distress, not subterfuge, accounted for his obfuscating behaviour. But to Black, distress was an inadequate, even an improper, motivation for failing to deliver an accurate account of an important business matter. In December 1851, he went over from Glasgow to Ardentraive, where he kept all his papers at Walter and Jessie's home. He there worked out that the decrease for February had been 5000 sheep, and that since there was no sign of a gain from melting for tallow, the fires were the only feasible explanation. The loss in cattle he never discovered.

The matter of Archie's refusal to enumerate, or even acknowledge, the burned sheep cast a permanent cloud over future relations between uncle and nephew.

Chapter Seven

'YOUR UNCLE IS GOING TO BE MARRIED, AS USUAL'

COMING DOWN TO EARTH from his European tour in company with 'the Prince', Niel Black took up squatter concerns in London and Glasgow 'to stir up emigration, especially from the Highlands', and badgered the Colonial Office over the long-sought leases.[1] He then travelled relentlessly about the British Isles, visiting TS Gladstone and his family near Liverpool, Alex

Finlay at Castle Toward, and Jessie and Walter at Ardentraive. But apart from an odd glimpse in a letter here or there, no record exists of the social calls he undertook to seek prospective candidates for the role of Mrs Niel Black. At all events, his marital hunt yielded no immediate catch.

He was avid for news from Port Phillip. Worry concerning Big Clarke's intentions caused him to write to Claud Farie: 'Why have you laid your pen on the shelf wherefore it is covered with cobweb when distant friends are sighing – if not dying – to hear from you?' He told him that Gladstone was retiring to Dumfries to 'play the Laird' on the Capenoch estate he had recently purchased. 'The mountain streams of my native land wear their channels wider and deeper as they roll their course along towards the ocean, and such is the effect which I find time has on Gladstone's friendship. He made many proposals to me for remaining in this country, but I am now more fit for Port Phillip than for any other sort of life.'[2] Farie, like everyone else, was preoccupied with saving his run, and did not reply.

The crises thrown up by the discovery of gold were so acute as to eclipse the fires, drought and floods of that extraordinary year. The world was turned upside down in ways that no-one not a witness to the popular frenzy could comprehend. In May 1851, people from Port Phillip rushed northwards to Bathurst in New South Wales, and business began to slump. In July – just as the new colony of Victoria came into being with La Trobe as Governor – came the first gold strike in Victoria, and fears about the scale of departures eased. In August, strikes around Ballarat set everyone rushing again in that direction, but with little initial success.

Then, on 20 September, a party arrived in Geelong with 27 kilograms of gold. With the price at £3 an ounce, mayhem ensued.[3] There was a run on the banks in Melbourne and people sold all their assets to make up a 'swag', leaving for the goldfields as fast as they could. 'Not only have idlers and day-labourers in town and country, but shop-men, artisans and mechanics of every description thrown up their employments, leaving their employers, their wives and families and run off to the workings, but responsible tradesmen, farmers, clerks of every grade, and not a few of the superior classes', wrote Governor La Trobe in a despatch of early October. 'Some [are] unable to withstand the mania and force of the stream, or [are] really disposed to venture time and money on the chance, but others [go] because they were as employers left in the lurch. Cottages are deserted, houses to let, business is at a stand-still and even schools are closed. In some of the suburbs not a man is left.'[4]

Geelong, a town of 8000, was the departure point for Ballarat. Its fluctuation in population was dramatic. During one week in late September, 500 newcomers arrived, and 1500 people left for the diggings.[5] The mayor, our old friend Captain Foster Fyans, found it very unsettling. Employers, including the government, were forced to double wages to retain any workers at all. Out on the sheep runs, hutkeepers deserted, and flocks were left untended. Not only from 'the hearth and the workshop, the labourer's hut and the merchant's warehouse' did the tide of humanity stream out, but 'from the field ready for the plough, and the corn ready for the sickle'.[6] La Trobe believed the mania must work itself out. Only a small proportion could endure the slog of gold-digging and the discomforts of camping in the bush. But even if they stayed only a few weeks, the disruption to social and economic life was immense.

When news of the chaos arrived in Britain, many absentee squatters took the first ship back.[7] Black, too, stood at the ready.

A letter from Niel Black to his mentor and partner, TS Gladstone, one of hundreds written to him between 1840 and 1880. This letter is a furious reaction to one from Gladstone apparently giving credence to his nephew Archie's view of how to run the company, when Black is certain Archie's pilotage would wreck it. He records at the bottom that his wife persuaded him not to send it, as it repeats a previous tirade.

Niel Black papers, Box 28, MS 8996, State Library of Victoria

'Bridge at Woorawyrite', early landscape photo (1850s).
Wooriwyrite (correct spelling) is a run bordering Glenormiston to the north.
The bridge crosses Mount Emu Creek.

Thomas Hannay, photographer; H2013.345/86, State Library of Victoria

Sheep - Wash

Niel Black's first sheep wash in the stream entering Lake Terang
would have looked like this – it might even be this one,
photographed around 1859.

Thomas Hannay, photographer; H2013.345/82, State Library of Victoria

Theil des Kratersaufschnitt Noorat
26 März 1857.

ABOVE Eugene von Guérard, *Krater of Mount Noorat*: a pencil sketch drawn from the western lip of Mount Noorat crater on 26 March 1857. *Volume 05: Sketchbook XXVI; DGB 16/vol5 a3328, Dixson Galleries, State Library of New South Wales*

LEFT Eugene von Guérard, *Lake Bullen Merri*: oil painting, 1858, sent by Niel Black to TS Gladstone in Scotland in 1859 as a gift. The western banks of Lake Bullen Merri and Lake Gnotuk (just visible in the distance) were part of Niel Black & Company's pastoral run. *Private collection, Robert Gladstone, descendant of TS Gladstone; image courtesy of National Gallery of Victoria, from* Eugene von Guérard: Nature revealed *(Ruth Pullin, 2011)*

Glenormiston *Mep*

'I thought it best to build a stone house.'
The first solid house on the homestead site, built in 1847; photo taken
around 1859. In the right foreground a man with a horse is just
discernible; this is Archie Black, Niel's nephew.
Thomas Hannay, photographer; H2013.345/87, State Library of Victoria

'One bull branded NB on horn.' A bill of lading for a pedigree Shorthorn bull, and an iron gate and fitments, shipped from London on the *Copenhagen* bound for Port Phillip, 30 July 1860. 'The Captain to have (£5) five pounds if the Bull is landed alive.'

Niel Black papers, Box 31, MS 8996, State Library of Victoria

'The best feather in my wing.'
Claud Farie was Niel Black's first and closest friend in Victoria. He died in 1870 aged 53, a widower and almost penniless; Black took in his children.

Print from wood engraving, Illustrated Australian News, 10 September 1870;
IAN10/09/70/157, State Library of Victoria

RIGHT Tinted photograph of Niel Black in kilt and regalia, taken in a Scottish studio c. 1856, when he was seeking a wife.
Private collection; image courtesy of Art Gallery of Ballarat, from For Auld Lang Syne: Images of Scottish Australia from First Fleet to Federation (Alison Inglis and Patricia Tryon Macdonald, 2014)

LEFT Niel Black of Glenormiston, sketch by Nicholas Chevalier, 5 December 1867, when Prince Alfred the Duke of Edinburgh stayed at Glenormiston House.
Chevalier collection, 1999.23.19, Art Gallery of Ballarat

OPPOSITE Photograph of Niel Black by Batchelder & O'Neill for Legislative Council, c. 1859.
Victorian Parliamentary Library

'The far-famed Glenormiston', c. 1866. There are visitors at the homestead,
and small children – possibly Niel Black's sons – on the drive.
Collection of descendants of SG Black

The residence of Niel Black Esq., wood engraving by Frederick Grosse,
based on drawings by Nicholas Chevalier, undertaken during the visit of
Prince Alfred the Duke of Edinburgh in 1867.
Illustrated Australian News, *4 February 1868; IAN04/02/68/SUPP/5, State Library of Victoria*

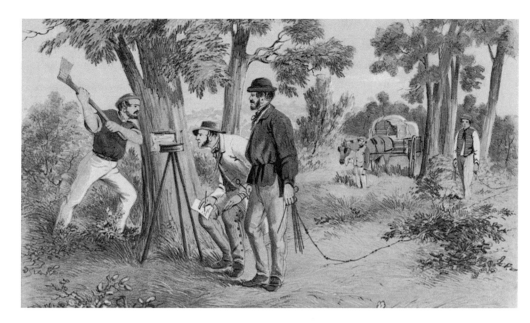

ST Gill, *Surveyors* (detail). Before land could be sold or put up for selection, it had to be surveyed and mapped. The lines – especially boundary lines between runs – set by the government surveyor were of vital importance to a squatter. From the 1850s, surveyors were busy and important men.
Colour lithograph from The Australian Sketchbook *(Hamel & Ferguson, Melbourne, 1864); H4977, State Library of Victoria*

ST Gill, *Splitters*. Clearing woodland, and turning trees into posts and rails for fencing, was an ongoing job for many years on runs such as Glenormiston. Teams such as this would have been a common sight.
Colour lithograph from The Australian Sketchbook *(Hamel & Ferguson, Melbourne, 1864); H4977/a, State Library of Victoria*

LEFT Map of land purchases on Glenormiston, 1864. Niel Black's clerk, John Buys, prepared detailed maps of all sections and allotments of land sold from the 1850s, in Glenormiston and adjoining parishes. Many small sections were mapped out for 'villages', which were absorbed into the squatters' purchased freehold: such a level of smallholder settlement was hopelessly unrealistic. Buys coloured the map according to purchaser: pink = Niel Black & Company; blue-green (east of Mount Emu Creek) = Daniel Mackinnon; yellow (east) = Archie Black; blue (west) = John Thomson; orange (north-west) = Donald Craig.

John Buys, 'Statistical Report of All the Land bought by Niel Black & Co in the Australian Colonies down to August 1863', Niel Black papers, Box 43, MS 8996, State Library of Victoria

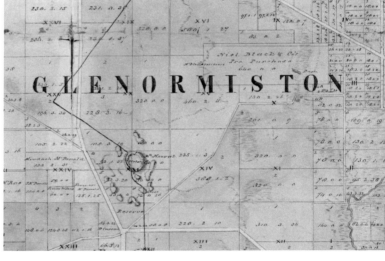

ABOVE This detail of the map shows how Mount Noorat was originally divided between Black and Thomson of Keilambete; Black later bought Thomson's allotments. The names of selectors and occupation licensees can be seen along the road; so can Black's pre-emptive homestead purchase, containing Glenormiston House. The later Mount Noorat House was built just east of the Mount.

RIGHT Mount Noorat
House, the main hall.
Private collection

BELOW Mount Noorat House,
'the crowning folly of my life':
an Italianate mansion with
an English flower garden,
in the heart of the pastoral
Western District.
Private collection

ABOVE WM Boyes, *Lakeview, Keilambete, looking towards Mount Noorat*, watercolour, 1882. Commissioned by James Armstrong, the original selector on the site (1861). Owned by his descendant, Andrew Boyle.
Private collection

LEFT Hon Niel Black MLC, squatter number 341, from a shield containing portraits of 713 old colonists, by Thomas Foster Chuck, photographer, completed December 1872.
H5056/341, State Library of Victoria

LEFT Norman Macbeth, *Niel Black*, portrait commissioned in Scotland by Niel's widow, based on a photograph, c. 1883. *Private collection*

BELOW Artist unknown, *Grace Black née Leadbetter*. *Private collection*

At first Alex Finlay thought that he should return immediately, but Black wrote to Archie: 'he has changed his mind and says it will be best for me to stay until we hear from you and Farie'.[8] Niel himself doubted what good his departure would do; in any case, early reactions in Melbourne's business community were positive. William Bell wrote that gold would attract free emigrants, expectations at the diggings would far outstrip success, and the end result would be cheaper labour.[9] So Black sat tight. He had already sent out six men contracted to work for the company, advancing their passages and expenses.[10] Until early January 1852, the news suggested that – despite Archie's anxieties – the gold discoveries had not much affected company affairs and fears of labour decamping wholesale were unrealised.

In Port Phillip, the view was less sanguine. In late September 1851, all the squatters became truly alarmed. Within days of the drowning of Archie's companions returning from Warreanga, a number of men left Glenormiston for the diggings. As October began, and the weather cleared, shearing was due to start. 'I am very much afraid that it will be a work of great difficulty in consequence of the discovery of a very rich *Gold* field near Buninyong', wrote Archie. 'Three thousand men are on the spot and are finding gold on average to the value of 15 shillings to three pounds a day. I am at a loss what ought to be done. Some men "bolt", and others then follow. *The fact is that men cannot be got for love or money.* Surely you have taken warning and are now on your way here again.'[11] A week later, he wrote again: 'My Dear Uncle, I hope most sincerely that you are at this moment on your way here again. The country is in a most alarming state. I believe the number of people now at the "Diggings" is about four thousand, and three hundred are daily added. All bonds are thrown aside for the sake of Gold dust. I have got a few shearers but find it impossible to get a bullock driver. How the wool is to be sent to town is difficult to find out.'

For graziers within easy distance of the goldfields, the loss of station hands was a recurring nightmare. A few struck lucky at the early workings, but many returned to their employers after failing – and left again on news of another find. Archie's fears about the shearing were not borne out. In late October, enough shearers showed up. 'We have this day begun our shearing operating under very favourable circumstances. It seems rather strange but we have got our own complement of men while our neighbours give higher wages and are without half the required number.'[12] But things were again thrown into pandemonium by new strikes, the richest yet, at Mount Alexander (Castlemaine) and Bendigo, in November and December. The men sent from Scotland, met off the boat by Bell and despatched up-country, miraculously appeared at Glenormiston. 'The two men from the *Indus* have arrived, to my surprise. The quantity of gold found is now so great that the temptation to bolt must have been very powerful.' Archie upped their wages to £25 a year to quieten their grumbles. Every letter to his uncle contained a plea to return. 'Lose not a single day in leaving home and all its pleasures, as God only knows how your affairs may prosper here. All our best men are going to the "diggings" when their engagements are concluded, even old John Crawford.'[13]

In late January, after a visit to Melbourne – then in a state of gold-fuelled excess – Archie wrote to his uncle in the most persuasive tones he could muster. 'My Dear Uncle, I returned from town about the beginning of this month and have been since occupied in preparing for the coming storm that threatens to sweep all hands away from tending flocks and herds. *The danger is indeed imminent* and the remedy difficult to find out. The scarcity of labour is sorely felt. Wages are double what they were six months ago and many employers are glad to get men even at that increased rate. It is quite common now for a man to refuse one hundred a year who, a few months ago, would gladly accept one third of that sum.

'When you consider that such is the case now when water is scarce and the small quantity that exists is green; when the labour of procuring gold is so great and the danger of losing health is imminent; what will be the result when the rainy season sets in, when there will be plenty of water to *drink* and *wash gold with*, to moisten the soil and render the labours of the diggers easy? *We cannot get men to hire for more than three months.* All are determined to try what fortune will do for them at our El Dorado.' He exhorted his uncle to recruit more workers. 'Yesterday a hut-keeper demanded £40 for another year's service. Surely it is better to send men here than to give such wages to ruffians? If you have not already left home you will not surely do me the *injustice* to remain a single hour which you can avoid. I cannot any longer support this responsibility I now labour under, so that your own interest calls more loudly than ever for your presence. I remain, Your affectionate nephew, Archie Black.'[14]

This is the last letter that Archie copied into the outgoing letterbook. At 21 years old, shouldering a burden beyond his capacity, he was at the end of his tether. On his side, Niel Black seemed remarkably uncaring about his nephew's plight – on the contrary, he deplored Archie's indulgence in agonised forebodings: 'Do not become too anxious, for that only unfits a man for his duty.' Archie must harden his mettle. Everyone reported that he was doing well. Each situation he cried up was three months out of date when his uncle learned of it, and had been resolved by the next letter to arrive. Even if he set off at once, it would take him three months to get there. So far, he had not accomplished his critical mission, the gathering of a wife – and there was now a candidate in the offing. Niel Black was not to be moved.

———•◆•———

With the discovery of gold, the battle over the lands changed direction. In the previous five years, enough land – over 100 000 acres – in the settled areas had been put up for sale to meet existing demand from farmers. The squatters' distant flocks and their licensed control of remote and 'unimproved' lands had not yet attracted envy from agriculturalists. This now changed. At the goldfield sites, there was a great demand for food – which local squatters-turned-butchers and -gardeners did well providing.[15] As time passed and people arrived from further afield, pressure mounted to open up for sale cultivable land around the goldfields. This would mean putting onto the market land currently licensed for grazing, over which its Crown tenants had been given rights under the 1847 Order-in-Council. These rights were tacitly acknowledged even though the Order was not systematically implemented. This was because the interpretation of the terms on which the leases should be issued had not yet been resolved.

When the colony of Victoria came into being, instead of forcing through a settlement of the problem, Governor La Trobe played for time. Under various pretexts – incomplete surveys, instructions awaited – he postponed issuing the leases. He did not want to antagonise the squatters, but nor did he wish to allow them to gain such a degree of tenured possession as would block the development of townships, agriculture, industry and railways. During 1851 and 1852, many applications to purchase sections of their runs came in from squatters, the £1-per-acre upset price now seeming reasonable. The value of many stations, already raised by the 1847 Order-in-Council, increased further due to gold. Many changed hands at significant sums, on the assumption that leases and pre-emption were part of their value. Now came pressure on La Trobe to put desirable licensed land in the unsettled districts up for sale to smallholders to grow food for goldfield populations. But the hardline version of squatters' rights under the Order stood in the way, and they refused to compromise.[16] Dominating the new Victorian Legislative Council, they also blocked a motion there to solve the problem by extending the areas designated as 'settled' to make more purchases possible.

Using the only loophole open to him under the Order, in mid-1852 La Trobe protected the public domain by assigning several hundreds of thousands of acres as 'reserves'. This provoked an outcry from dispossessed squatters. Their stance had become decidedly antisocial, entirely dependent on the bare letter of the law rather than on the future good of the colony – of which they believed themselves better guardians than the Colonial Office or its creatures in Melbourne. Populist sentiment began to flow strongly against them. The *Argus* began a strident campaign to 'unlock the lands', but even in the *Herald*, a much less radical newspaper, the squatters were described as 'a class among whom absolute selfishness is the sole rule of conduct'.[17] La Trobe flip-flopped, and eventually referred the interpretation of the Order-in-Council back to London, encasing his request for a definitive ruling in a lengthy despatch of observations and recommendations. However, as a concession to the squatters, in August 1852 he gave permission for them to buy homestead blocks of 640 acres or one square mile. Although this was a help, at a station like Glenormiston, most 'improvements', including the house, farmstead, woolshed, sheep wash and dams, could not remotely be covered by such an area. They were all positioned at a considerable distance from one another.[18]

When Black left Port Phillip in 1850, the question of whether Niel Black & Company should purchase land at the earliest opportunity had been under consideration. This step would run directly counter to the original intention of the partnership, which had been established for the temporary exploitation of valueless 'wilderness' to graze sheep with a minimum of expense and investment in landscape improvement, just enough to ship a profitable wool clip home. From the outset, Black had gone beyond that remit. He had spent time and effort to find 'the best run in the colony'. Then he had wrought changes on it, on the grasses, the forest, the tracks, the watercourses, and he had significantly improved his stock. He had also mapped and surveyed his lands – in short, he had done whatever would be done by an 'improver' on an estate back home.

For years, Black had argued to his partners the case for consolidation and expansion, in the teeth of their expectation of maximum cash returns. The depression had been partially to blame for the early lack of income, but Black's constant ploughing of extra capital and company profits into stock and improvements was another reason cash income was lean. Gladstone, who had followed Black's actions closely, understood that he had been obliged to adapt to circumstances as he found them and as they evolved rather than as the partners at home had pictured them. And he respected Black's judgment and frequently expressed his confidence in him. Finlay had been more distantly involved. But he too was impressed by the abilities of their working partner – 'We have always thought, "come what may, if things can be got

right, Black will do it".' Black's flowing pen and self-conviction
had kept them on side, just. But pressure had been growing. In
1849, after the damaging effect on trade of the worldwide upheavals
of 1848, plus the outbreak of footrot in the Glenormiston flocks,
Finlay wrote: 'Given last year's circumstances, I understand that
you did what you did. But this year I do most sincerely hope you
will let us have £1000 or £1500 clear *each*. And that after this
you will give us annually a proportion, for example two-thirds
of your wool clip clear, as interest for our capital invested.' He
intended to withdraw from the partnership if he did not begin to
receive a steady return.[19]

Black might not be in the 'Big Clarke' league as far as land-
owning ambitions went, but he certainly believed that once a
Crown tenant had a lease with a pre-emptive right attached,
he must exercise it. The Clarke scare helped focus his partners'
minds. If someone scooped up Glenormiston, they would either
have to sell off their livestock at whatever price could be fetched
and seek compensation for their 'improvements', or else they
would end up paying Clarke rent for using their own amenities
and running their stock on what had been their licensed pasturage. Clarke had made Black's argument for him. Why would
the Leviathan of Van Diemen's Land covet their run and be prepared to spend £20000 buying 20000 acres of it if this was not
a desirable investment?

Finlay only half understood: he wrote to Black from Castle
Toward that 'we must be prepared to buy some stations', but he
was still not convinced about land.[20] Some squatters, including
Claud Farie, still thought bushland valueless. In late 1851, Archie
awaited advice on whether to go ahead when opportunity presented. 'I am afraid the Government will enlarge the Reserves
and have consequently resolved to apply for four or five sections

about Glenormiston. I must take this responsibility on myself as Farie is opposed to this plan.'

In the event, the only land Archie was able to buy before London delivered its verdict on the Order-in-Council was the homestead section. In August 1852, he bought for the company a block of 640 acres, with the house on its western boundary, for £1 an acre.[21] Some neighbours were similarly purchasing, but not all. By late 1852, the impact of gold on the colony and the pastoral industry was prompting many to quit. George Rodger wrote saying that he intended to sell up, 'and if I do so, I bid adieu to Australia for ever. And I thank God I have not ties to bind me to this infernal country.' Farie sold up in 1853, unable to solve his labour problems, and moved to Melbourne. Others, content to reap the profits from fat stock, held on. They remained hopeful that the authorities in London would come down on their side, recognising their contribution to the colony and their social position as its leading class of men. But, thanks to the swelling numbers of immigrants seeking their own promised land, both the popular and official tide had turned against them.

———

By mid-1852, even in Britain, anti-squatter sentiment was growing. Black, who read the Victorian newspapers regularly, wrote: 'A cry is got up against the squatters as a class as if they were an incubus on the progress of the colony, on the improvement of the country and of society. Mosquitoes and gadflies will startle, punish and annoy the strongest of us if their attack is made by numbers, collectively.'

Thus did Black decry claims by the mass of ordinary people to influence in public affairs. This view was entirely conventional in the world and circles he occupied. 'Democracy' would lead to government being dominated by agitators and the mob, eclipsing the role of wisdom and experience. His diatribe continued: 'They [the squatters] will be attacked and harassed by the influence of numbers … Squatting is doomed never to gain another point favourable to its existence. Inroads and aggression will from day to day be made upon its rights and privileges.'[22] This outburst was provoked by John Pascoe Fawkner, the 'tribune of the people', who used the pages of the *Argus* and his seat in the Legislative Council to lambast the squatters for stealing Victoria's patrimony from the common man.

With fellow squatters in Britain such as Alexander Mollison, Black tried to develop an association in London to plead their case at the Colonial Office. Mollison, a long-established grazier and active in public affairs, took passage from Melbourne on purpose to defend the cause of the pastoral industry. Black wrote to Archie from London in early 1853: 'I am here at present trying to urge on the government the impolicy of withholding from us the pre-emptive right.' He and Mollison lingered for weeks but their case was not well received. The Duke of Newcastle, Colonial Secretary of the day, kept them at a polite arm's length.[23]

Not until November 1853 did Newcastle reach a determination of the Order's disputed interpretations. When his verdict finally arrived, in March 1854, the squatters were horrified to discover that he had found against them. He agreed with La Trobe that, in view of the rapidly growing and more diverse population, the interests of some 700 pastoral licensees could not take precedence over the equitable development of the colony on behalf of all.[24] La Trobe's establishment of reserves and intended land sales in 'unsettled' areas were endorsed. If the squatters desisted from their extreme claims and sought compensation for genuine losses they would be accommodated. But the pre-emptive right was for homestead blocks only. Fawkner read out the despatch in the Legislative Council to raucous cheers. The *Argus* described it as the 'final downfall of a most odious monopoly'.[25] This triumphant tone proved premature.

The Crown tenants, as the squatters styled themselves, strongly protested against the breach of solemn promise made to them by the Imperial government.[26] They also resented attacks on their integrity – notably the suggestion that they were trying to gain monopolistic rights over the land for purposes of 'jobbing', or profiteering. They accepted the sale of some land near the goldfields with due compensation to the licensees, but claimed that 'it would be impolitic to disturb the pastoral interest generally'.[27] The changed character of the colony due to rapid immigration – which by now was vastly improving their fortunes with the growing demand for meat and produce – was a shock that they seemed unable to absorb. Many persisted in believing that they and only they were suitable custodians of the colony's future.

La Trobe responded by promising to lay before the Legislative Council a measure to issue the leases. But his tenure was due to expire in mid-1854, and he left the poisoned chalice to Sir Charles Hotham, his successor. Hotham chose not to offer the squatters leases whose terms they would oppose, and instead appointed a royal commission to examine the landholding situation from scratch. Its findings were generally unacceptable and the impasse continued. In the end, no leases were ever drawn up. Instead, grazing licences continued to be issued annually, and a 14-year limbo over rights of run prevailed from 1847. Strictly, the squatters had no rights, but actually a degree of tenured privilege was accepted.

Preparation for land sales in the unsettled areas began in 1853. La Trobe started by replacing Robert Hoddle, the Surveyor-General who 'never hurt any man's run', with the young and energetic Andrew Clarke. The first surveyed allotments on the Glenormiston run to be put up for sale were auctioned at Geelong on 7 June 1854. Archie Black had already been given the go-ahead to buy land when he could, and warned his uncle that the moment was at hand. Niel wrote blithely from Glasgow: 'If my idea of the present value of money is correct, I fully expect that it will sell at little more than the upset price', and instructed Archie to 'pursue a quiet, judicious course of action'.[28] He was seriously out of touch since the days when £1 was thought outlandishly high for an 'unsettled' acre.

He also underestimated the usefulness of Archie's 'bold, dashing rashness' – which he deplored. Land auctions in Geelong, and later at Warrnambool and Camperdown, were events at which the company's fortunes would be made or broken. Archie in his smartest outfit, mounted on Adonis, his favourite horse, 'clipping the King's English and thinking himself no sheep shank', was a familiar figure at the sales. He was also one to be respected. Quiet judiciousness would not have won for Niel Black & Company the estate his uncle desired. In their different ways, nephew and uncle were as one in the quest for acreage, and Archie's inclination to be 'expensive' was just what the company needed.

At the June 1854 auction, the sections for sale on Glenormiston were in its easternmost area, in Colongulac parish. This was Basin Banks, bordering the western shores of lakes Gnotuk and Bullen Merri. Most of Colongulac was occupied by the Manifold brothers of Purrumbete, and Camperdown – surveyed in 1851, and already boasting a post office – was its main township. The lake shores contained very rich soil and were much sought after. The 18 lots purchased by Archie went for high prices; on one section of 504 acres, the average price was £5 7s 5¼d an acre.[29] Niel Black must have been stunned; but he would have been more stunned to lose this jewel in the Glenormiston crown. The stratospheric prices showed how rapidly things were changing. Altogether, Archie spent over £6000 on 1460 acres.

Now that land purchasing had finally begun, Black's enthusiasm to get hold of everything they could was, predictably, not echoed by his partners. For the previous two years, significant sums – £10000 and £15000 – had been sent home, to everyone's approval. But now the old contest between investment on the ground versus cash sent home resumed, with the complication that Niel was at home and also needed cash. Gladstone feared that Archie might draw money on the partners in Scotland without their agreement. Niel wrote to Archie that 'drawing on home to a moderate extent will not be objected to. But it does not do to pounce even upon the richest with large drafts at a day's notice.'[30] He would have borrowed on his own security. Archie used the device of selling cattle, with the market now rapidly growing. Turning Warreanga into a cattle station in 1847–48 had paid off splendidly. Around 3000 cattle bought for 11s 6d each were sold fat for £13 a head two years later.[31] Such profits gave Archie confidence and calmed the partners down.

As sales of land became imminent over the bulk of Glenormiston, in its own parish and in Terang and Marida Yallock parishes, Archie needed more capital. Some sections contained large plots of 300 or more acres with stony rises or other unpromising soils, and there would be little competition; but even at £1 an acre, large sums were needed at one time. Land in areas of possible future township, with richer soils, close to roads or better watered, were divided into much smaller plots of 16, 20 or 40 acres. These ran up high prices. But they were often grouped with poorer land, and the squatter had to buy all the plots in a section or he would end up with a checkerboard. Unless he was careful, others might buy lots that cut him off from water, woolshed, even his homestead. Before long, 'land-jobbers' entered the scene, artificially forcing up prices of plots that were no use to anyone other than the existing squatter. Buying land was turning out to be no fool's game.

For Glenormiston, 1854 was a critical year. Archie, after much negotiation, was to be brought into the company as a one-eighth share partner for £2000, the sum paid equally by his uncle and his mother.[32] This gave him added authority, but he was still junior, and was now playing a role which Gladstone and Finlay would have much rather entrusted to Niel. But since Niel resisted going back to Victoria, Archie was landed with the responsibility and that was that. They all knew he was a spendthrift, they all knew he was erratic and rarely told them what he was about, and they all knew he was becoming increasingly impervious to his uncle's endless strictures.

Archie was determined to make the critical land purchases around the homestead and up to the neighbours' boundaries. For this he needed a great deal of money. At this key moment in the acquisition of the company's core assets, Archie received a visit. In August, Robert Gladstone, Gladstone's eldest son, arrived in Melbourne. He was making a tour of his family's overseas trading interests in the East. The two became instant friends.

Years later, Robert – married and settled in his father's old merchant house – still wrote with nostalgia of his time with Archie at Glenormiston. 'Often in my dreams I fancy myself back there, careering after the cattle and cracking my stock whip. Occasionally too a great longing comes over me to go back again, and I feel as if the air here was close and no room to move, and I long for the bright sky and limitless expanse of Australia. I keep my old stock whip, my cabbage tree hat, my cord breeches, and my spurs ready for use at a moment's notice, and a couple of Boomerangs and a Waddy in my Dressing Room remind me daily of the days that are past.'[33] The deep impressions of his visit, and his admiration for Archie's command of his wild western world, stayed in his imagination for years to come.

Back in Scotland, a great deal hung on Robert's report to his father. About Archie, Robert wrote: 'He and I get on beautifully, with a fierce argument now and then, just to keep us alive.'[34] Both his father and Niel were delighted, and the case Robert put to his father on behalf of Archie's intended land purchases transformed the situation. He rode out with Archie all over Glenormiston and saw the sections divided into allotments, and how the estate would come together. For the first time, Gladstone understood that it would be mad not to buy, to let the run be carved into pieces or pass to someone else. He even went to Scotland from France, where he was wintering with his family, to make available £12000 for Archie to draw on at forthcoming land sales.[35]

At the end of December 1854, long before this news arrived from Scotland, the first sales for land at the heart of Glenormiston were held at Warrnambool. Of land licensed to Niel Black & Company, nine of 31 sections in Glenormiston parish and two in Marida Yallock went up for auction. Most were on the northern and eastern perimeter of the homestead purchase. They were not all contiguous, and allotments on some were withheld for future sales, leaving glaring gaps which would have to be bought later to unify the patchwork. All were vital components of an estate based around the original block. Archie had to bid on 56 separate allotments, frequently against competition. He held his nerve and bought 3900 acres altogether, 3230 on Glenormiston and 670 on Marida Yallock. The cost was nearly £10 000. Many lots went for far above upset prices of £1 or 30 shillings per acre. For Archie, those two days spent at Warrnambool were adrenalin-charged. And this was only the beginning.

Three months later he was back in the Warrnambool sale-room, and again in August and October 1855, when further large parts of Glenormiston parish, including the home station, went under the hammer. News of the £12 000 that was on its way as a result of Robert's visit arrived in mid-1855 and boosted Archie's hand. In 1855, the second year of land sales, Archie bought 6210 acres at a cost of £7370. This process of land accumulation was enough to make any young man's head spin, and spin Archie's did. Altogether by now he had bought over 12 000 acres and spent around £24 000. Many pieces were still missing, but the nucleus of the Glenormiston estate was secure. Even his uncle was impressed, and for once full of congratulations. A new sense of proprietorship and social status encouraged Niel Black to give up 'the wandering life of a Bedouin' and become the tenant of a mansion on the seashore just north of Dunoon. Ericht Bank was owned by John Leadbetter, a Glasgow merchant, and the house enjoyed spectacular views across the Firth of Clyde.[36] Black had now become someone, even in hide-bound Argyll.

In December, Archie was back at Warrnambool to purchase land in Terang parish. This bordered John Thomson's Keilambete on the west, and Mount Emu Creek on the east and south. Terang had been laid out as a township around its lake, and prices were high. From this moment, there is a sense that buying land had become for Archie an addiction – the adrenalin of the saleroom going to his head, as the card table to a gambler. Two sections of land bordering Pejark Marsh were very expensive indeed, and the 2300 acres he bought on a steamy day in Warrnambool cost the company £4800. His uncle was pleased, but there was no way to argue that these lands were vital to the integrity of the estate, unless it was to be on a magnificent scale that Gladstone and Finlay would never approve. As 1856 dawned, these two began to realise that Archie intended to buy every acre currently under licence to Niel Black & Company. He had not been given any such permission and they determined to rein him in.

———————

Why did Niel Black fail to return to Victoria during all these years? He should have been there to conduct these transactions. Not only had Archie continually implored him to return, but Gladstone and Finlay also pressed him to go back.

He had intended to sail in 1852. Finlay was much relieved. 'There can be no doubt that a great revolution is going on in Australia, of which an experienced person with *freedom of action* such as you have, could take advantage … It gave me much pleasure to learn that you leave so soon to be on the spot.' Gladstone echoed these sentiments: 'I should not be dealing honestly with you if I did not tell you candidly that I think your presence out there will be advantageous to all parties.'[37] But from one month to the next, Black postponed his departure. The reason was that his intended, whoever she was, kept postponing her acceptance of his suit. In December he was still waiting 'for the lady to make up her mind'.[38] He wrote to Archie more than once that he expected 'to leave here very soon' but added that he should nonetheless act as if 'you never expected to see me again'.[39] For Archie, the prevarication was infuriating and unnerving. Gladstone wrote Archie that he could do nothing: Black glowered if he raised the subject of his return. By late 1854, Gladstone had given up. 'I know nothing of your uncle's plans for some time past, except that I do not think there is much chance of his going out to you, nor of his getting a wife tho' I wish he had one with all my *heart*. The fact is he is too particular and I fear now will never meet with such a partner as he thinks suitable.'[40]

Chafing in the Queen's Hotel in Glasgow, dangled on a string by a lady he would not give up on, had a depleting effect on Niel Black. He was now 50 years old. His best days were over, and he began to believe that no-one – except Archie – would be the inheritor of his Australian efforts. But Archie, while 'reaping a rich reward', was angry and ungrateful. Niel believed he had given his nephew a golden opportunity, better than anyone in his family before him, and that he complained unnecessarily. Niel's letters became more irascible and unkind as he transposed his black mood onto his nephew: '[Why should I] be forced to come out there to enter on a struggle for which I am now getting too old, devoting my declining years to the service of others from whom I may receive little thanks, *love* or attention?'[41] He talked of 'that unendurable purgatory which stands half way between [the position] of a Gentleman and a common Farmer', and feared he would never find a life companion, though the rumour mill continued unabated. Captain Eddington passed on to Archie the gossip from home: 'I had a letter from Elizabeth Turnbull last

GLASGOW, 14ᵗʰ March 1856

RECEIVED by me, Treasurer to the Glasgow Highland Society from Neil Black Esquire the Sum of Two Guineas being his Subscription Money, as a Member of said Society.

Wm Morrison Treasurer.

Niel Black's membership of the Glasgow Highland Society was
acquired in March 1856, at the height of his wife-hunting quest,
when he was living in a mansion on the Firth of Clyde.
Niel Black papers, Box 31, MS 8996, State Library of Victoria

week. All well in Scotland, your Uncle Niel *going* to be married,
as *usual.*'[42]

Black also hated the idea of the new Victoria – where things
were done 'to please the caprice of a stark stare mad moboc-
racy'.[43] He started to believe that his Australian life was over:
'Everyone returns but me and all my friends here say I will never
go back. I have not said this myself yet but doubtless my energies
are every day relaxing.'[44] The high prices cattle fetched as a result
of increasing population, plus the unappealing changes in the
colony, encouraged Niel to see himself as retired, with Archie
as the active working partner. It was quite clear to everyone
except himself that this was never going to work. Archie kept
the partners in ignorance of his plans, and was whimsical and
wilful. His uncle endlessly enumerated his faults as if this could
improve matters, but only succeeded in further antagonising

Archie and undermining Gladstone's efforts to bring him to a more cooperative spirit.

The crisis came in 1856. In March, Archie bought another five sections on Terang adjoining those already purchased. All the land went at the upset price, but the outlay was £3230. He was forced to cut back on the cash sent home. Gladstone was furious. He enlisted Robert to write to Archie and explain their predicament. 'The long and the short of it is that one must eat and drink and pay one's Bills, and this cannot be done without money, and as your Uncle has *all* his capital in the Concern, and my Father and Mr Finlay a large portion of theirs, they naturally look to NB&Co as their mainstay, and if all the Proceeds are put into land every year, the Partners might as well have put their money into the Sea so far as the present is concerned. What they want now is for you *not to buy a single acre more except what is absolutely necessary to consolidate our past purchases.*'[45] No further drafts on Gladstone & Serjeantson would be honoured.[46] Archie fired off a rejoinder that he was '*determined to make the cattle pay for it*'. His uncle ridiculed him: 'This is surely most absurd language. Can your determination fatten the cattle, or do you mean you will sell them whether fat or lean?'[47]

The final straw came when Archie wrote that John Thomson was selling Keilambete for £30000 and that he intended to buy it.[48] Such a purchase was way beyond any plan ever discussed. His uncle accused Archie of getting him into a scrape, although privately he would have loved to get his hands on Keilambete. His partners were appalled. Expenditure on such a scale was in direct opposition to their instructions. Niel wrote: 'You say "You can have little idea of the anxiety that *desire* to become possessed of this place gives me." Do you for one moment suppose that your partners will be content to sacrifice their own wishes to gratify your ambition or vanity. What have they to do with *your feelings?* … I fear, Archie, you forget that Pride goeth before a fall.'

Black spent autumn 1856 at Ericht Bank, unwell. There in November, the partners gathered for emergency discussions. Gladstone and Finlay intended to send orders to sell Keilambete immediately if purchased, thus bringing disgrace on Archie and ruining his credit in the colony. Niel did his best to argue them out of this. At their insistence, he finally agreed to return to Victoria and review the company's operations. A week after his guests had departed, he sat down and wrote to Archie at length. 'I have been very ill but am much better now. I am going to England this week to spend the winter there and on the continent. There is great anxiety for my going out next summer to re-establish confidence that has been too often shaken.' He then produced a bombshell: 'I have agreed to comply with this wish, and I may add that I don't come as a bachelor.'[49]

In so terse a way did Niel inform his nephew of his engagement. His fiancée was 22-year-old Grace Leadbetter, his landlord's daughter. On 16 December, the marriage took place in Leamington Spa in the softer air of England, where her family was then living for her father's health. Gladstone attended, but no-one from Black's family came south for the occasion. He informed Archie that his marriage had taken place, and who to, by sending him a cutting from the Leamington newspaper.[50] At the end of December, Mr and Mrs Niel Black set off for France for two months abroad. Soon afterwards, news came that Thomson had withdrawn Keilambete from the market. It transpired later that he would rather not sell at all than sell to Archie Black of Niel Black & Company.[51]

Finally, in late 1857, Black acceded to his partners' wishes and, accompanied by Mrs Black, took ship for Melbourne.

Chapter Eight

'TO STEM THE WILD TORRENT OF DEMOCRACY'

STEPPING OFF THE BOAT at Melbourne on her husband's arm, Grace Black, sprightly, intelligent and 30 years his junior, was everything Niel Black could have asked for in a wife. Although her grandfather had been a plain working man, her father, John Leadbetter, had been given a sound Scottish education and risen to wealth and civic prominence via the linen trade.[1] Grace's mother, Ann Hutton, had been born and raised in Newfoundland. So the 'improver' and colonial-adventurer qualities exemplified in Niel Black recommended him to the Leadbetters.

Niel expected to escort Grace on a 'short visit' to Melbourne, a year, maybe two – time enough to enable Archie to take a restorative trip home, and for Niel to conduct a thorough review of company affairs before returning to Scotland. There, the Blacks would live in comfort at Ericht Bank, the house above Dunoon that Grace had known from childhood. Having rented it for two years, Niel now proposed to buy it from his father-in-law. John Leadbetter happily agreed. His son Robert ran the family business in Glasgow, and they were both pleased to off-load the Dunoon property in so satisfactory a way.

In early 1857, when the partners in Scotland received the news that John Thomson of Keilambete had withdrawn his run from sale and that Archie would not therefore be spending £30000 against their orders, the pressure on Niel Black eased. But he had made a commitment to go out and he now had to fulfil his obligation. A delay occurred in mid-1857 when Grace was unwell, from that unmentionable cause, a miscarriage. Gladstone feared she was delicate. But finally the couple set sail via the Mediterranean and Suez, a route increasingly used as a less strenuous alternative to the Cape of Good Hope.

They disembarked at Melbourne on 8 January 1858, expecting Archie to meet them. Just before they left Scotland, they learned that he was engaged to an 18-year-old Highland girl, daughter of a carpenter. She was uneducated and so unused to society that Archie had taken it upon himself to send her to school. Archie dreaded his uncle's reaction, anticipating forceful opposition to the marriage. Even without this difficulty, the prospect of resuming close relations was alarming. So Archie was not on the quay to greet Mr and Mrs Black, nor had he engaged horses or a carriage as instructed. Despite this lack of proper courtesies, Archie's bearing – once he appeared at the hotel – made a favourable impression on his new aunt, his junior by six years. His engagement to Marion McLeod was not mentioned.

Niel was determined to think as well as possible of Archie's managerial performance. After all, he was responsible for leaving his nephew in charge and, later, for bringing him into the company as a one-eighth partner, and his insistence on Archie's ability to run things in Australia had provided the pretext for his own long absence. He wanted to believe that Archie had done his best for Niel Black & Company, even if he had inevitably made a few mistakes. He attributed Archie's sense of isolation to shyness and pride, which he also blamed for the misguided romance. He arranged to rent Claud Farie's house in Gardiner's Creek Road (now Toorak Road), on the south-east corner with William Street, and he paid his friend a generous £400 a year in rent: as ever, Farie was short of funds. Niel was sure that he and Grace would soon engineer Marion's replacement by a young lady of better class. Grace quickly developed a social circle as all Niel's old friends came to call, agog to inspect that phenomenon, an actual Mrs Black.

The promising start in the renewed relationship between uncle and nephew was paper thin, and cracks soon began to open. Archie refused to give up his 'inferior' friends, least of all Marion McLeod. Mrs Black did not call on Marion – her husband forbade it – causing Archie offence. With company affairs, things were no better. After almost eight years of epistolary ill-will, it was unlikely that Black and Black would see eye to eye. Niel had therefore obtained from Gladstone written agreement that he had final authority over company decisions. If changes had to be made, he was in a position to override

Archie. Nonetheless, he intended to move cautiously, not rush in and turn everything upside down in such a way as to provoke Archie's wrath. He saw himself as the older and wiser 'friend', keen only to advise the nephew whose well-being he wished to promote. But his long absence and his frequent strictures had fixed him in Archie's mind as a tyrant who found fault with whatever he did. Years before his engagement to Marion McLeod, long before Niel brought Grace back to Australia, Archie's animosity towards his uncle for the difficult circumstances in which he had placed him, and from which he had refused to relieve him despite repeated entreaty, had become bitter almost beyond reason.

Once Mrs Black was settled, Niel went down to Glenormiston. Very quickly, relations between uncle and nephew descended from uncomfortable to disputatious. Archie did not like Niel looking into station affairs and refused to assist his enquiries. Niel began to find that nothing Archie had done — with the exception of the land purchases — was to his satisfaction. The books were in such a muddle that he insisted the clerk, John Buys, redo them from the day he left, and promptly discovered an accounting error of £19 000 — fortunately in the company's favour. The store cattle were 'a disaster' and Archie sent them too young to market; the land was overgrazed so the cattle did not fatten; the purebred Shorthorn herd branded NB had been neglected and was no longer up to much.[2] The fencing, into which 'a fearful amount of toil and labour' had been poured, was falling apart because poor materials had been used. 'Stranger' horses were grazing on Glenormiston, and a rogue overseer had sold animals not belonging to Niel Black & Company and pocketed the proceeds. Archie had several outstanding lawsuits with aggrieved neighbours over matters that should never have gone to court. Once Niel began to find errors under every stone, the confidence he had reposed in Archie as ongoing company manager unravelled.

In this contest, Archie had no hope of outmanoeuvring his uncle. All the advantages – personal and corporate – were on Niel's side. He had come back hoping to wrap up his business and return to Scotland as soon as possible. But his standards were high, and even if Archie had not let certain things go, once Niel got back in the saddle he was never going to find that anyone else managed his company satisfactorily. One omission piled upon another until he declared to Gladstone: 'NB&Co would not be less than £80,000 to £100,000 richer than they are if I had been here for the last eight years. It was so good a business [when I left] it was scarcely possible to spoil it.'

He did not absolve himself of blame. 'Archie could not help it – it was a necessity of his nature in the circumstances in which he was placed, and probably if anyone can be justly blamed for bringing him into so bruising a set of troubles, it is myself for having left him so long and so young to himself', he admitted. 'If I had always remained here or even returned in 1851 or '52, Archie would have been a different man.' Occasionally in the voluminous letters he wrote to Gladstone at this time, he intimated that Archie had become unbalanced, a psychologically damaged person. But no sense of contrition accompanied this realisation. This was a hard age and Black a hard man. Archie not only refused to give up Marion McLeod, but also failed every management and personal test he was set. Even before the scandalous revelation of a time of licentiousness at the homestead, and of Archie's abandonment of his own illegitimate child, his uncle regarded him as 'used up' in the plan of Niel Black & Company. The whole sorry story of Archie's shortcomings was unflinchingly relayed to his partner as supporting evidence for the need to remove him from their joint affairs.[3]

In mid-1858, Archie's younger brother Walter arrived in Victoria to try his hand at squatting. With him was Archy Hamilton, son of a successful Glasgow banker who lived at Hafton House, an enormous pile along the coast from Ericht Bank, whom Niel had come to know. Archy Hamilton had been provided with £5000 to invest in a run under Niel's supervision. Like many well-born younger sons despatched to the colonies, Hamilton was entirely unsuited to pastoral life in brash, burgeoning and fickle Victoria. Walter, by contrast, flourished. Although Niel had previously thought little of him, his younger nephew grew in his estimation as he learned the grazier business. Even Grace, who had initially been swayed by Archie's dashing presence, now preferred the more modest and circumspect Walter. But no good prospect of an affordable pastoral station offered itself to the young hopefuls. Prices were high, and impending land legislation was playing havoc with the market for stations. The different status of Archie, a partner in the company, was a cause of friction between the brothers. But there was no question of Black asking the partners to let another nephew come in.

In March 1859, with his fiancée still in school, Archie finally decided to go home for a visit. This he had refused to do when his uncle had landed a year earlier, but as relations between them deteriorated and Niel reasserted iron-clad control, Archie's temper was perpetually fraying and giving way. By this time, Niel had determined that if Archie was 'used up', Walter could conveniently earn a salary on the company's books until an alternative prospect presented.

Archie was gone for 15 months, returning in mid-1860. It turned out that he had had two motives in going home. One was to consult medical specialists about his health: he was (wrongly) convinced that he was suffering from some sexually transmitted malady and might follow his father into madness. The other was to destroy his uncle's reputation with his Scottish partners and re-establish his own claim to eminence in the affairs of Niel Black & Company.

———•+•+•———

By the time Archie left for Scotland, his uncle had become the Honourable Niel Black MLC, an elected member of the Legislative Council of the Victorian Parliament. Given his intention of spending only a short time in Australia before going home to Scotland, and his earlier protestations of his unsuitability as a politician, this was an improbable turn of events.

Various things conspired to change his mind. One was his experience of Melbourne life with a delightful young wife at his side. He was pleased to find – although he brushed it aside – that a kind of weathered eminence attached to him. In his absence, a further crop of pioneers from more gentrified backgrounds who had come out when he did and slummed it in the bush long enough to make good had sold up and gone home. This left a smaller company of esteemed 'old settlers'. In Black's – or rather Farie's – elegant house in South Yarra, he and Mrs Black received calls from 'everyone of note', including the Chief Secretary, the Speaker and various others of gratifying distinction. In late 1858, Sir Henry Barkly, the Governor, was sufficiently gracious to take a small retinue down to Glenormiston for a kangaroo shoot.[4] Perhaps partly as a result of being put on the sporting itinerary of the colonial crème de la crème, Black started to think of building a new, much larger house.

177

Black was settling back into colonial life, and he was also moving in those exalted circles where the deplorable state of Victorian politics was a hot topic of conversation. Black knew all about the venomous, populist, demagogic, anti-squatter tirades that had punctuated the gold rush years. During 1857, when he was still abroad, the cause of egalitarianism in Victoria had advanced at full cry. The reformist Chief Secretary, William Haines, had put before Parliament a land bill meant to replace the 1847 Order-in-Council. The language of the bill avoided old controversies by sidestepping the 'pre-emptive right' and omitting any mention of leases. But it left in place the rest of the prevailing land occupation system: sales by auction, annual renewal of squatting licences, and compensation for improvements. Since plenty of land had already been sold to meet farming demand, its terms were thought uncontentious. The squatters would pay for being left undisturbed by large rises in their licence fees and livestock taxes.

When the bill was introduced to Parliament in June 1857 it caused an uproar in the Legislative Assembly. Charles Gavan Duffy, a well-known Irish nationalist who had generously decided to offer himself to Victorian politics as the poor man's saviour and the squatters' scourge, accused the government of deliberately contriving to deliver the colony's territory into the permanent possession of a handful of graziers. The obligation to pay heavy compensation payments would, he argued, exclude from the land sales any poorer contestant.[5] The political dynamics surrounding land had undergone another shift. Victoria was currently suffering once again from economic slump. Gold production, especially of the digger variety, was in decline, but gold-inspired immigration was at its peak. Unemployment was high, especially in the kind of occupations sought by shopkeepers, artisans and clerks – who had not travelled to the opposite end of the world to join the ranks of common labour. Distress led to agitation, and in mid-century Victoria, agitation invariably focused on land and its possession. Haines' nervousness about tackling the hegemony of the squatters and opening up land to ordinary homesteaders led to a major political crisis. As far as real demand for farming land was concerned, the crisis was synthetic, but the sense of grievance that incomers were being deprived of a foothold in the new society was very real.

Thus the campaign to 'unlock the lands' was re-energised, sending tremors through the political landscape. Since conservative interests in both chambers were still strong and opposition via elected parliamentary representatives had few prospects of success, an extra-parliamentary movement known as the Convention, after the name of its manifesto, was formed. The centrepiece of this manifesto was a set of revolutionary land acquisition proposals: free selection before government survey, deferred payments, the abolition of squatting, and open commonage (grazing) of anyone's stock on all remaining Crown lands, including those under licence. The squatters were naturally appalled by the rise of a Chartist movement dedicated to their destruction. Many men of a liberal stamp were nearly as dismayed, and even opposition figures such as Duffy disassociated themselves from the revolutionary Convention program. The casualty was the land bill, which – torn apart from left and right – had to be withdrawn. Offsetting this failure, Haines did succeed in passing a key measure of parliamentary reform – manhood suffrage. This inspired the land reform leaders to anticipate support in a differently constructed Assembly where their views would be better represented.

The bill for manhood suffrage that passed into law in November 1857 confirmed Victoria as the leading British colonial exponent of democracy. In 1856, the pristine Parliament had become the first in the world to adopt the secret ballot. Other reformist proposals now gathered pace. Not only manhood suffrage but abolition of property qualifications for membership of the Legislative Assembly, and a demographically fairer distribution of parliamentary seats. Just as the design of the new legislature mimicked the mother country's – the Assembly corresponded to the House of Commons, and the Council, the House of Lords – it had the same lopsided representational bias towards the establishment. The Assembly was dominated by merchants, bankers and propertied men, while the Council, where property qualifications were even more stringent, was a conservative and squatter redoubt. Urban and goldfields 'common man' populations were underrepresented, just as industrial towns were underrepresented in Britain.

The 1857 bill for manhood suffrage avoided serious opposition in either House by caveats and qualifications designed to disenfranchise diggers and itinerant workers and boost property owners' share of the vote. Haines claimed that the property vote was essential to prevent Victoria from becoming 'a naked democracy'.[6] But the advent of even qualified manhood suffrage caused huge anxiety. If there was one symptom of 'democracy' – a term which still rang in many ears with the sinister knell of the tocsin – that most appalled non-reformists, this was it. Men such as Niel Black were genuinely alarmed by the prospect that those whose background, education and experience equipped them to rule might find their place usurped at the next election by unqualified upstarts voted in by force of numbers. Parliamentary reform, with which land reform had become conflated, ground to a halt. In 1858, Haines' plan for fairer electoral representation became mired in dispute, and he resigned. A new administration was formed by the Irish-Catholic John O'Shanassy, along with his ally, Charles Duffy.

When Niel Black arrived back in Melbourne, the Haines administration was on the point of making way for this 'democratic' alternative. Black complained to Gladstone: 'Political power is in the hands of bold and brazen-faced adventurers, corruption is rampant, and high principle powerless, chained down by universal suffrage.'[7] His protests were couched in a hyperbole strange to modern ears, but this was the overblown language deployed on all sides. An Assembly made up of men whose horizons had been confined to the parish pump would not promote progress and prosperity for Victoria as a whole, but instead indulge in self-interest and class warfare: that was the assumption. Even those sympathetic to reform were alarmed by the prospect of 'tyranny of the majority' and 'government by the crowd'.[8] To Black, this miscegenation of unsuitable men with power was so opposed to the natural order of things that he did not believe it could succeed.

In 1858, when Black again took up his pen to write to his Scottish partners, an oft-repeated theme was political instability. Soon there would be new elections. In the 'reformed' Assembly – elected by manhood suffrage – there would be a new land bill. And the reformed attitude of the reformed Assembly towards such a bill could only be feared. Its purpose would be 'to restrict individuals and Companies from acquiring extensive freehold property'. Black sincerely believed that any law asserting such controls in transactions over the colony's key asset could not pass; or if passed, could not be implemented.[9] It would contravene 'free trade' principles and consequently prove unworkable. If not allowed by law, free trade in land would simply operate unlawfully via dubious practice and racketeering.

Already, the land auctions had produced a type of predator, known as 'land jobbers' or 'land sharks', who bought strategic sections of existing runs as a speculation, for the purpose of selling them at a profit to discomfited squatters.[10] Alternatively, such men demanded to be bought off in advance for being so obliging as to not bid up the purchase price. Black tried to set his own terms, refusing to deal with 'land sharks' at anything above the upset price.[11] But whatever misgivings he had about the evolving nature of transactions in land, he would not openly decry a system which helped maintain the squatter's supremacy at the land sales. The truth was, given the cards held by squatters and 'sharks', without some means of preferential purchase for people of modest means, it would not be possible to dislodge the new colonial 'inheritor' class from a monopoly of landed proprietorship similar to that the immigrants had left behind. Hence the significance of the movement for selection: it represented the demand for a new social and economic order in a new world. Resistance to selection was tantamount to refusal to create a more equal society. Men such as Black, who had earlier welcomed the chance to climb the social ladder and helped others do so too, now seemed to be pulling it up behind them.

In September 1858, Black was approached by some of his Melbourne connections to stand in 'the conservative interest' for election to the Legislative Council. The Upper House was already established as the legislative bulwark against the rising radical tide and the setting where a check could – and in the conservative view must – be exercised on democratic excess. This time, Black succumbed to pressure. If company reasons made it impossible for him to return to Scotland in the immediate future, why not use his presence in Melbourne for political purpose? The seat in which he was requested to stand was in the

Western Province. In October, he went down to Warrnambool, an O'Shanassy–Duffy heartland due to the large number of Irish farmers. The electoral rolls had been packed with 305 fictitious names for the Catholic interest, but he was persuaded to accept reassurances that these would be eliminated, and his candidacy went forward.[12]

There was self-interest in his decision, but in his own tortuous and subjective way, Black was quintessentially a man of principle. He felt the real sense of alarm pervasive in his circle about the Convention's influence, and believed that those of wisdom and experience must try to stop the reform agenda getting completely

Invoice dated 4 March 1859, detailing the election
expenses incurred by Mr Niel Black at Warrnambool.
Niel Black papers, Box 31, MS 8996, State Library of Victoria

out of hand. He told Gladstone: 'If I had not stood, the province would be represented without contest by a Roman Catholic nominee of the O'Shanassy Ministry. When no other would enter the lists, I felt it my duty to make an effort to stem the wild torrent of Democracy.'[13] Men such as himself should play their due role in government. 'It was on public grounds alone that I ever consented to become a candidate. I felt that, as the representative of an extensive property, I was playing the part of a craven in declining the duties while I clung to the privileges that attach to it. This, together with the knowledge that many of the evils squatters as a class complain of, we owe to our remissness, compelled me to seek a position that I as little courted as you would the privilege of standing in your own room while the vent is being swept.'[14] The next land bill would have to be opposed, and if responsible landowners shrank from the bear–pit of politics, then they would have no grounds for complaint if rabble-rousers tore down what they had built.

Black campaigned under the slogan of 'free trade in land', and the *Portland Guardian* approved him as 'a representative of the right stamp'.[15] He won by a solid majority: 484 votes to 230, which he reported to Gladstone with pride. 'Mrs Black is now the wife of an Honourable, a title I most unwillingly sought.'

He turned out to be right in his earlier belief that he would not be an effective politician. The first time he opened his mouth in the Council he was inaudible, and though he attended debates, he rarely spoke. Behind the scenes, and in committees, he did more. He described the work as 'tasteless', and declared he would happily quit if anyone suitable could be found to replace him. He also felt inadequate: 'I lack the advantages of a liberal education to strengthen my confidence in myself in the performance of the duties which devolve upon every man who takes a part in legislating for the benefit of his country and constituency.'[16] By the mid-1860s, his infrequent parliamentary attendance attracted formal complaint. However, he remained an MLC of the uncompromising conservative tendency for the rest of his life.

———— ◆ ◆ ————

By the end of the 1850s, the issues surrounding land had become a battleground for other political and social problems in a way that bore down heavily on the squatters. Their detractors – urban, labouring and digger – picked on the proprietorial class as the representation of the society they had left the mother country to escape. They neither knew nor cared about the hardships the pioneers had faced, nor about continuing challenges, or the efforts of many to transcend their own antecedents. And they knew nothing of the terrain they claimed to want.

The image they bought into was of smallholders nestling in English-style villages throughout Victoria's western plains.[17] This vision gained a political impetus that could not be stemmed, even though it was unrealistic. An extensive yeomanry living on small-scale agriculture was a non-starter in the Australian landscape, even in its kindlier patches. This was known by those who understood the environment because they lived in and from it, and by the government's surveyors. But that was the new settler dream, and all their gold-digging disappointments and unfulfilled aspirations became subsumed by the belief that all would come right if only they could wrestle a piece of land out of the squatters' tenacious grip.

The idea that vast quantities of good cultivable land were being hoarded as grazing for cattle was a delusion. Thousands of agricultural plots had been sold at the land sales, and many were languishing unused. Agriculture was developing at a steady but not a galloping pace. Land under cultivation rose from 55 000 acres in 1854 to 419 000 acres in 1860, and the number of smallholder farmers from 3000 to 13 000.[18] Around the towns, farmers growing potatoes, vegetables or cereals could do well. But elsewhere, until railways spread, markets were too far away for the independent cultivator of a few hundred acres. For the time being, grazing was the only viable use of 'unsettled' lands.[19] And despite the image of the wealthy squatter riding imperiously around his broad acres with a cash register ringing in his head, raising livestock was no picnic. All the 'improvements' he had made – including, in recent times, miles of fencing or stone-walling for enclosures, and prodigious clearing of trees – had still barely touched the face of the untamed bush. The costs of managing and developing this land could only be borne by large-scale investors. The risks they faced included droughts, fires, floods, fluctuating livestock prices, diseases in the cattle and thistles in the grass – not to mention continuing insecurity surrounding key sections of their runs.

From 1858, Black joined other squatters in asking Chief Secretary Haines and successive land ministers to put onto the market those parts of their runs they still needed to purchase in order to consolidate their patchworks of holdings. In Black's case, Glenormiston was reasonably complete, but very little of Niel Black & Company's adjoining run, The Sisters, had yet come up for sale. The government, needing revenue, and still respecting the terms of the Order-in-Council until its term lapsed (1861), usually obliged the squatters. Whatever the joys of gold, the pastoral industry was still economically vital to the colony. Its upper ranks comprised of leading members of Melbourne society, including many government ministers, and its transactions oiled the wheels of banking and commerce. The squatters could not simply be driven across the Murray River with their own stock whips, as Charles Don, a demagogic political advocate for the working man, absurdly threatened to do.[20]

Niel Black was personally keen to expand farming settlement where it would succeed. He frequently expressed the desire to see more farmers – owners and tenants – settled on the land, including on his own, but in a way ordained by practical wisdom and market rates, not by ideology. He saw all such people, where they were bona fide landsmen and especially if they were Scots, as natural allies, comprising a composite group. Their natural tendency was conservative, unless the 'infection' of democracy reached them surreptitiously, a development he wanted to avoid by easing their path. But it was hard to envisage, even if he wished it, the growth of a successful farming tenantry on the company's lands any time soon.

In November 1858, he told Gladstone that he wanted to have Glenormiston surveyed and measured out in farms of between 200 and 600 acres, so that the land could be managed to its maximum potential whether as one unit or many. But his intentions were limited. 'I have no immediate intention of attempting to let out farms on lease on a large scale at present. If a few *good tenants* offer, I might let one or two farms at the extremities of our land, but I would not breach the property by leasing in the middle of it … As an occupation, farming is far from profitable at present. My opinion is that it must ultimately prove the ruin of all who are engaged in it under the present system.' Under this 'system', the typical smallholder failed to nurture his land, instead planting and harvesting recklessly and exhausting its capacity. Such farmers were known as 'cockatoos': they scratched a piece of ground, took what they could from it, and moved on. Mixed farming was too much trouble and required too much capital, so farmers abandoned the land when its goodness was used. To an 'improver' such as Black, this was anathema. 'A field was pointed out to me a short time ago bearing its sixteenth crop in succession, without one spadeful of manure during all that time.'[21]

To Black, the key to farming success was size. 'The popular cry is for the poor man to get a bit of land. This is the very thing to keep a man poor and to make the country poor,' he declared.[22] 'Farming here ought to be on a very large scale and with a large capital to begin.' The farmer would need sufficient cattle for it to be worth dealers' while to travel around and pick up many small lots to take to market. 'By breaking up the sward and cropping for a couple of years, and then sowing with artificial grasses, such as clover and rye, the depasturing capability of the land will be enormously increased – I think nearly threefold.' In this way, Black believed, mixed farming on a moderately sized acreage might work. 'I would like to experiment on one or two fields of 640 acres where little or no outlay of capital is necessary in clearing. I think it would pay admirably.'

The company had experience with tenant farmers. A farm of 100 acres on Glenormiston was let to William Houston, a Gladstone recruit from home. Houston cleared around half his acreage for planting. In the drought of 1858–59 his wheat succumbed to hot winds, 'but his oats proved a splendid crop. He will make money for a few years as he is under no restrictions as to cropping, but when the soil gets exhausted he will pine, and sink again.' Unless Houston changed his system, the farm was too small to be profitably worked. 'Everything in this country where land has not attained a high value is done on an extensive scale.' Farming, in combination with crop rotation and depasturing, must also be done on a large scale to compete with stock-running. 'Without rotation of crops, farming can become ruinous to tenant and landlord.' Black knew this to his cost: the two small farms the company owned at Moonee Ponds near Melbourne were in a wretched condition because of the tenants' failure to nurture the land or undertake improvements.[23]

Whether or not his experiments would work, Black's grounds for finding fault with land reform proposals – which discarded all existing land-use experience, and installed a smallholder system whose margins were too thin and whose members could be ruined by one bad season – are understandable and even reasonable, once the adversarial rhetoric is discounted. As well as his desire to profit his company and himself, he had a strong commitment to developing the colony, its lands, soils, fruits, grasses, stock and agricultural abundance. A land bill that inhibited such development, by taking land out of the hands of those who could manage it and assigning it to those who would almost certainly fail, was in nobody's interests.

During 1859, as the dissolution of the first Assembly loomed, the provisions of the land bill to be submitted to the next Assembly were under discussion. The Honourable MLC for the Western Province wrote wearily to Gladstone in March: 'The Bill is already enunciated and is to be based on free selection of 250 acres, compulsory occupancy, commonage near townships, etc.' But he was sceptical: 'I think all this is simply a political dodge on the part of the [O'Shanassy] Ministry to gain strength at the election.' It proved later to be the case that O'Shanassy was not disinterested – he had secret squatter interests. 'If they are driven to revolutionary measures it will be for the sake of office of which their tenure is not likely to be very long. I think it possible that some fertile agricultural spots will be selected to experiment on for the express purpose of keeping the democrats in play. It is not improbable that more than one Ministry is destined to fall before the question is finally disposed of.'[24] This was indeed prophetic, but Black was wrong to think that selection could be staved off indefinitely: so strong had the movement become that any land bill had to contain it or risk provoking riots. However, he did accept that the old squatting system which privileged the owners of large herds by providing them with cheap grazing would soon have to end, so powerful was the clamour for commonage.

As election fever mounted in August 1859, and the vitriol in the press and on the hustings debased the political coinage, Black despaired. 'This colony is at present suffering under a severe attack of democracy. The patient though in a state of frantic delirium is under no restraint and there is little chance of dealing with him until a crisis has supervened.'[25] His solace was the Upper House – labelled 'the House of Obstruction' by O'Shanassy – which no ministry could sweep away. There, the line must hold. There, honourable members would oppose measures intended to ruin the colony, whatever damaging collisions they faced with the Assembly.

To his brother Archibald in Scotland, Black wrote even more dramatically: 'The elections are taking place at present and a pleasant set of scoundrels we are to have as Assembly members. Out-and-out radicals, men that have no principles and will promise everything and something more, are sure to carry the day. I am afraid they will ruin this splendid country.' Only the Upper House could prevent radicalism from sweeping every-thing respectable away before it 'like a destroying fire, bushfires sweeping over the face of the country and leaving dust and ashes behind'.[26] Black, along with many others, genuinely believed that the results of the 1859 election might descend on their world and destroy it like a biblical plague.

Much as he lamented the state of political affairs, Black's private life at this time was joyful. One reason he could not think of going home in 1859 was that Grace was pregnant again. This time she carried the child to term and their first son, Archibald John (who soon became known as Ian), was born in September.

Rejuvenated by parenthood and with Archie away, Black was firing on all cylinders. He had thrown away the plans worked out back at home for selling off livestock and scaling back in preparation for division of the company's assets. In March 1859 a good season was expected, and he decided to build at Glenormiston not only a new house, but new men's quarters and farm buildings – the old ones had become a disgrace. He professed himself unable to work out how to build a cheap house, and thought it would cost £3000. He told Gladstone: 'This sum will give you a very wrong impression of what this house is to be. It is only one storey with good-sized public rooms.'[27] The eventual cost was closer to £5000; building in the bush was extremely expensive because of cartage and high masons' and carpenters' wages. Since the company would clear more than £24000 in the year – thanks to good rains and an overstock of cattle – Gladstone did not remonstrate. To his brother Archibald, Black wrote somewhat differently: 'It was impossible to do without a respectable place on a fine property. A cry would be got up against us that all the money was going home.'[28] The house he wanted would be the pride of the neighbourhood, and a fitting homestead for Mrs Black to preside over.

Gladstone kept probing as to how the original plan – to consolidate as a prelude to a division – would be carried out. He was not at all sure that Black back in harness at Glenormiston and set upon expansion was what he and Finlay wanted. He also felt that Black had been very hard on Archie, and still hoped to reconcile their differences. Gladstone continued to assume that Black would want to come home before long and needed Archie as manager. But Niel Black had fully resumed his colonial persona and had 'not the most distant idea of leaving the country' for the time being. Archie had suggested he be bought out and Niel was ready to meet the full costs of purchasing his share: 'I am sure it would be an advantage to him to make a fresh start on his own account.' He had identified 2000 acres at Basin Banks on Lake Gnotuk as an ideal property to settle on Archie as part of a deal.[29]

Archie, as his uncle learned from many sources, had done his best to blacken everyone's opinion of Niel while in Scotland. Whomever else he convinced, he failed to dislodge Gladstone's trust. Gladstone wrote to Black: 'He has a most unfortunate temper and is not easily guided – but I hope I have made some impression on him and that he will go out and meet you in a proper spirit. I am sure with a little forbearance on both sides you may part good friends though I fear you could never again work well together.'[30] Gladstone sympathised with the young man and regretted what the company had done to him, considering the service he had rendered them over many years. But he had finally accepted that, given the antipathy between uncle and nephew, Archie had to be bought out.

Archie returned to Melbourne in June 1860 still carrying his burden of ill-feeling. After long and vexatious negotiations, he accepted a generous settlement. He built himself a stylish house of bluestone and wood on Lake Gnotuk at the company's expense, and became the owner of 6400 acres – many more than his uncle originally envisaged. In February 1862, with the house completed, Archie married Marion McLeod. Since August 1860, he had been living at Glenormiston with his uncle and aunt in their new house, and they repeatedly offered him to be married from there. When the wedding finally took place, he neither invited them nor told them in advance. Archie deliberately left Glenormiston without saying goodbye to his uncle, who had just stepped out to see to something in the yard. Niel's distress was genuine and heartfelt.[31]

Chapter Nine

'WE ARE FULL OF CORRUPTION FROM HEAD TO FOOT'

DURING 1860, A BILL to introduce a fairer land regime endured an agonising gestation in the Victorian Parliament. Since the failure of 1857, the battle of the lands had become increasingly bitter. Whoever won at the 1859 election – a conservative grouping, as it happened – the new ministry must bring in a bill offering free selection. The land agenda of the radicals had gained such popular sway that it had to be accommodated despite their modest parliamentary representation. Although free selection was contrary to free trade principles and might encourage capital flight and economic downturn, even die-hards such as Black had been forced to accept the political necessity.[1] But there was bound to be a fight.

The Land Act that reached the statute book in September 1860 turned out to be only the first of many. Others followed in 1862, 1865 and 1869. Each attempt to promote free selection and dislodge the squatters from their runs by means of the law seemed utterly to fail. Each failure led to a successor Act to resolve the defects of the last. Despite the political crises surrounding the passage of these Acts, the most serious problems facing selection turned out to be on the ground, not in the debating chamber. Black's prophecy that the interference of free selection in the market would prove unworkable turned out to be correct. This was thanks not only to the fact that smallholder agriculture on many plots offered for selection could not succeed; but also to the methods Black and others used to defeat it, and to the ploys of profiteers who used the squatter–selector contest to devise and develop 'a simple system of corruption' – in which MPs colluded[2] – in order to relieve the squatter of every penny they could squeeze out of him.

Although on the face of it the squatters' behaviour confirmed the popular view that they were overmighty barons prepared to go to any lengths to gain control of 'their' ill-gotten lands, what they did was perfectly rational. Either they could do their damnedest to retain the holdings they had spent years and been through fire – sometimes literally – to create, or they and their flocks and herds would be cast onto the scrapheap of history. In terms of contemporary agricultural possibilities, they were also correct in maintaining that free selection was economically flawed and would not provide most beneficiaries with a reliable livelihood. The squatters felt beleaguered, both by the democrats who adopted selection as their ideological and political cause, and by the 'agents' and 'sharks' who made themselves indispensable in managing – or deflecting – the devastating impact upon them. Although the battle for the lands turned out to be weighted in the squatters' favour, no-one could be sure of that at the time. Many players did their best to gain from the contest to the squatters' detriment, and smaller squatters without the means, energy or influence in the right places to save themselves from selector takeover simply went under. Others ended up crippled with debt for decades.

While the 1860 land bill was under discussion, the ministry continued to enable individual squatters to buy sections of their runs, on the understanding that this was a 'last chance'.[3] Ever since he returned to Victoria, Black had been trying to get land surveyed and put up for sale on The Sisters, the 36 000-acre run west of Glenormiston he had licensed since 1843. The 640-acre pre-emptive purchase was made in 1854, but since then no other land on The Sisters had been put up for sale. When Black enquired why, the Surveyor-General said that this and the adjoining Keilambete contained the only first-class agricultural land still unsold in this part of the country.[4] Most of The Sisters – named for its nest of volcanic outcrops – was stony, wooded or marshy, but some parts, especially those around its two freshwater lagoons, were cultivable. In August 1859, Black's efforts were rewarded when ten small and four larger lots, north of Kolora Lagoon and adjoining the Mortlake road, were auctioned at Warrnambool. Despite strong competition, Black bought them all. The remaining agricultural land was held back for the advent of free selection.[5] Black's plan for the division of the company's assets between himself, TS Gladstone and Alex Finlay – Archie having been bought out with the property at Lake Gnotuk – was to gain enough land to make three estates of 10000 acres each.[6] There was enough purchased land on Glenormiston for two of these, and The Sisters comprised the third. As ever, Gladstone remonstrated. Never had he dreamed of becoming a landed proprietor in remote Victoria – a prospect to him as distant as settling on the moon. But to move Black from his course was tantamount to dealing with a force of nature. 'To this plan I stick through thick and thin, without fear or favour',[7] he wrote, and so he did. If Finlay and Gladstone did not want an estate for one of their sons, then he could manage or lease it for them – even sell or buy it, once the market shook off the incubus of free selection.

When debate began on the 1860 land bill, Black had still bought less than 2000 of the 10000 acres he wanted on The Sisters. His hopes of gaining more before the bill went through were dwindling. In April, he sought an interview with the Chief Secretary, William Nicholson, a man with whom he was acquainted. He was 'the Grocer with whom I dealt for many a day', he told Gladstone, and 'in every respect a plain, decent, commonplace man', even if he was regarded as inadmissible to the Melbourne Club.[8] Black deplored this snobbery and wished it were otherwise – much might have been achieved if the gulf between men like Nicholson and the colony's social elite was not so acute and mutually reinforcing.

For his attempt to twist the ministerial arm, 'I had a litho-graphed map of The Sisters with me. I pointed out the way in which our purchases there stand detached, that our dairy and improvements are still unsold, that all the watering places were made by damming the water, all done at our private expense.' Nicholson promised to intercede with the Lands Minister, but nothing happened, so Black again pressed his suit. 'I better go hard with the Chief Secretary. His object is to gain my support for the Land Bill in the Upper House. This is tasteless work but out of it I will take all the good I can without compromising my honour but that is a line I never did and never will cross from mortal gain.'[9]

One of Black's problems was obstruction from the survey department – which he put down to a quarrel between Archie and Robert Scott, the District Surveyor. But this was not the only difficulty. The Lands Minister was James Service, a conviction democrat who also happened to be Black's local MP. Service was bound to oppose any monopoly over land by a squatting concern like Black's. He had smallholder constituents in Terang. These became increasingly vociferous in resentment against Black when they found that horses and bullocks they grazed on his lands had been impounded.[10] However, until the land bill deemed otherwise, he had exclusive rights to the grazing on land he licensed. The Terang farmers ignored these rights on the basis that *their* horses, cows and future mutton also needed to eat. But Black was enduringly tough about boundaries. 'Straying' animals risked introducing livestock disease: pleuropneumonia was currently making a devastating appearance in cattle. There was also outright theft: '[Some] villagers slaughter and feed on our cattle. We sometimes find an animal suffering a recovery from a bullet lodged in the head.'[11]

In May 1860 the land bill became mired and Nicholson resigned. News of this crisis was conveyed to Black by Sir Henry Barkly, the Governor, who flatteringly called him in for 'consultation'. Barkly's strategy was to summon obstructive Legislative Council members and persuade them to be more cooperative, or face the substitution of a more antagonistic – and democratic – ministry. Barkly's acceptance of this prospect amazed Black.

'Sooner or later he said, Duffy & Co must have a trial.'[12] Eventually, Nicholson resumed power, expecting the Governor's 'consultations' to bring the Legislative Council round. Black, who remained obdurate, knew his stance wrecked any chance that land on The Sisters would go up for sale before the bill entered into law.[13]

The Land Act's final passage was accompanied by high drama. After repeated standoffs between Assembly and Council, deadlock was finally broken by the democrats' inflammatory antics. On 29 August, 2000 angry rioters marched from the Eastern Market to Parliament Yard. Alarmed by the sound of stones on their windows, the members of the two Houses temporarily united against the mob, and made sufficient concessions for the botched-up Act to be put to the House. Only weeks before, the Honourable Mr and Mrs Niel Black had removed 130 miles away to their new house at Glenormiston, but Black rode back to vote. The 'most wretched piece of legislation ever to receive a Majority approval in this or any other colony' was finally made law.[14] Under it, a selector could apply for between 80 and 640 acres of surveyed 'country lands' at £1 an acre, or purchase part and hold a lease on the rest for one shilling a year. No-one could purchase more than 640 acres in a year. There were exclusions and caveats to appease the squatters, and 'improvements' had to be undertaken. But a law to help the small man become an independent farmer had come into being.

The price, however, was high. The bill's prolonged butchery in Parliament exhausted the government and launched a conflict between Assembly and Council that lasted 20 years. Nicholson lost his majority and again resigned. In November, the forces of democracy entered power, not under Duffy, but under modest Richard Heales, a coach builder, temperance campaigner, and working man's politician adopted as a compromise candidate. His ministry would oversee the Act's implementation, and no leniency towards the squatters could be expected.

The real prospects of selection had yet to be seen. Much would depend on how lots were brought onto the market by surveyors and land offices in the districts, and what happened when contestants – squatters, officials, selectors, speculators – came face to face on the ground. To his partner, Black was philosophical: 'If we cannot make the tree fall as we would like, we must watch the fall in its own direction, so as to avoid being caught by its trunk or branches as they reach the earth.'[15]

Immediately the Act came into force, notice of land sales followed. Black rode out to inspect lots on The Sisters, but in the volcanic terrain he came to grief. 'My horse came down, throwing a complete summersault [sic], in which process I appeared to rival him. The result to me has been two broken ribs and collar bone the same.'[16] At 56 he was lucky that the damage was no worse. Laid up at Glenormiston, his bones re-set by Dr Robert Farie, a nephew of Claud Farie's newly out from Scotland, Black could not attend the auction in person. Archie took his place.

Earlier in the year, Nicholson had suggested to Black that he employ others to apply for land on The Sisters as a device to get it onto the market. Black had replied that he had 'so far succeeded in life without having recourse to expedients that appeared to me dishonest'.[17] But once the Act came into force, he found it possible to trim his scruples. For this 1860 sale, with 1000 acres to buy on Glenormiston and 2000 on The Sisters, Black made thorough preparations. Prevented by the provisions of the Act from purchasing more than 640 acres himself, Black engaged surrogates to buy on the company's behalf. Apart from his nephews Archie and Walter, these were Archy Hamilton, Robert Farie, his long-time employee Donald McNicol, his tenant farmer William Houston, his gardener John Brown, and two others. Squatters had determined to evade the law and this was how it would be done. The land would be leased from the substitute purchasers until they could legally sell. Those who were his employees would receive 10 per cent as commission.[18] He guessed that nothing would be done to stop this 'not very immoral fraud': the government's need for revenue was pressing and small selectors could not afford the prices. He was right.

Archie returned from Warrnambool on 21 December to report unopposed success. Despite his relief, Black's conscience was tried. 'Yesterday I gave a sketch of the promising side of the picture', he wrote. 'This day I may give the reverse side, the feeling of having employed some of our own servants to buy for me is so far from being comfortable to my mind. My wish was to buy so far as we were able ourselves, stopping with Hamilton and Farie.'[19] He wanted legal advice as to whether, under a power of attorney he held on their behalf, Gladstone and Finlay would be eligible selectors, as well as his wife and baby son. But as he was not fit to ride to Melbourne and seek the Attorney-General's opinion, his employees were enlisted. After this experience, he buried his qualms but inwardly remained disturbed. His justification was in the universal descent into sharp practice that 'men of the most honourable and high principles are compelled to adopt to protect their interests'.[20]

'Dummying' soon became routine. 'I have this very moment returned from a land sale in Warrnambool', Black wrote in March 1861. 'About 1200 acres has been selected on Sisters. In

201

every case I employed an agent to buy for me.' This agent was Sam McGregor of Warrnambool, an ex-squatter he employed for many years, a friend whom he described on a later occasion as a 'thoroughly upright fellow'.[21] The law, it turned out, did not forbid squatters or their nominees selecting as agents for others. The greater problem was that large acreages were coming onto the market and squatters needed deep pockets. Those with insufficient funds had developed a new strategy for holding on to their lands. 'Capitalists arrange with the occupier to purchase as agent for AB&C certain lands in his occupation. This he agrees to in consideration of being allowed to lease the land at eight or 10% of the cost price for a period of years. These are good terms for the capitalist and save the squatter from untold sacrifice of his stock, which would be unavoidable in the case of his being bought out by small agriculturalists.'[22]

Over the next couple of years, Black implored his Scottish partners to keep the company supplied with funds so that, when chance arose, he could purchase land and 'complete' the estates. He wanted them to increase the capital, but they refused. He had offers of credit from his Melbourne bank, but did not want to be exposed to the institutions of the colony: he well remembered the years 1842–43 when banks had failed. In the next sales, some lots were beaten up very high – competition was increasing. One disappointed selector said that next time 'he would have a portion of Sisters if it cost him £10 an acre. So I must try to fall on a plan of supplying him otherwise.'[23]

Black might complain, but so much land was falling into the hands of the squatters that a popular outcry arose. In response, the new Minister of Lands, John Brooke, embarked on his own course of circumvention. One of the caveats put into the Land Act to mollify the squatters was to allow them to purchase at auction 'special lands', that is, lands within a mile of existing purchases, or half a mile in special cases. Brooke reduced this distance to half a mile generally.[24] He also encouraged encroachment by smallholders on pastoral runs for grazing, and began to cut off extensive blocks for commons and roads: '18,000 acres has been taken off Thomson's run for Farmers' Commons in one block, 2000 off us at Basin Banks and something more at Pejark Marsh'.[25] But Brooke's shrewdest anti-squatter device was to allow abuse of clause 68 of the Act, concerning 'occupation licences'. These licences were to be issued for inns, stores and developments of Crown lands for public purposes. In breach of this intention, Brooke began issuing occupation licences to agricultural tenants.

Black was in anguish: 'A cry has been got up that all the land is falling into the hands of squatters, and the present Ministry takes all its strength from the rabble so they must stop the sale of land. They have found out another plan of leasing under the 68th clause of the Act which is very popular, and where this may end it is impossible to see. Unless these men are speedily driven from office I would not be surprised to see Crown tenants authorised to settle down on the reserves in the midst of our property.'[26] And in fact, 40 such licences were granted on Marida Yallock, Glenormiston, Keilambete and The Sisters.[27] In mid-1861, as the administration began to collapse, occupation licences became its rallying cry. Parliament was dissolved and Heales fought the election on the cause of occupation licences for squatter dispossession. When he narrowly won, Brooke issued hundreds of such licences.[28]

Black's outrage at what was being done to fracture his land – including allocation of 'reserves and public roads passing through it in every direction' – had become so bilious that his wife advised him not to send his tirades to Gladstone. But habit died hard. 'I was out on horseback two days ago at six o'clock mustering cattle for the butcher', he wrote. 'The day was cold and rainy, the country wet and plashy but even at this early hour I met a party of Germans, five on horseback and eight on foot, hunting all over our ground in search of land for Occupation Licences and viewing with envious feelings our purchased land. But where were these men when we risked life and property to make this land of value?'[29] The occupation licences amounted to confiscation of land for political motives and they were opposed in both Assembly and Council, especially as many holders turned out to be absentee miners and tradesmen who made no effort to farm.[30] The Supreme Court declared them illegal, and in November 1861 Heales' administration fell. The new ministry, headed by O'Shanassy, was greeted with relief by the landed interest: O'Shanassy had shifted his allegiance towards the squatters. But Duffy was another matter, and he became Lands Minister, embarking at once on a new bill to right Nicholson's wrongs.

Whatever their protests about Brooke's tricks, the squatters had managed to circumvent Nicholson. Throughout Victoria, three-quarters of a million acres had been sold under his Act, mostly to squatters.[31] Between November 1860 and September 1862, Black purchased 5200 acres on Glenormiston, for £5400; and over 7500 acres on The Sisters, for £9000.[32] Although Duffy was a greater potential threat to the squatters than Nicholson, many in the Western District had already done much to consolidate their estates. And there was a good reason for not opposing a new Act: penalties demanded under Nicholson – against buyers of more than 640 acres in a year, for example – would be abandoned when his Act was replaced.[33] Black kept scrupulous records, but the tallies of purchasers on different runs, in different parishes, on different dates and at different salerooms were labyrinthine, and his lawyers believed that bounds had been breached.[34] If penalties were exacted, Niel Black & Company might suffer.

Duffy's Act reached the statute book within months, the Legislative Council offering only token resistance. Black actually spoke on behalf of the Act.[35] He explained to Gladstone – and more circumspectly in an address to the chamber – that it would be a pity to lose the new ministry after the disastrous Heales administration. Plus the squatters had been given the nod behind Duffy's back that evasion could continue. Black had spoken in private to two ministers, including the Attorney-General.[36] 'Both did not hesitate to tell me that it is vain to try to place restrictions on the free use of capital and that the land will be bought in other people's names. Better this, they say, than let the late Govt. remain in power – "Of two evils choose the least".' The ministers expressed regret concerning the prospect of duplicity. 'One, as honourable a man as any in the colony, frankly admits the demoralising influence and the injury to the principles of the rising generation if brought up fully cognisant of such a debased system of morality. God knows, human nature is bad enough under the most favourable circumstances.'[37]

Black would have liked to remove his family to an 'old country' where the old values applied and 'Men of Yesterday' were still respected. But he had to see things through.

———————•◆•———————

Charles Gavan Duffy was a principled politician with a mission on behalf of the decent and downtrodden, and he wanted his Land Act to work. He hired William Hearn, a distinguished professor, to draft the Act so that it would contain no loopholes for evasion. But Duffy and Hearn were innocents about the real prospects of agricultural settlement. They also underestimated the difficulties of implementing such an ambitious policy in a colony whose original settlers had long been the main source of authority and employment in the countryside.

The proto-villages full of cottage farmers that Duffy wanted to see spring into being, each around a 640-acre public block on which would emerge the emblems of civilisation – church, school, savings bank, mechanics' institute, public gardens, baths, magistrate's court, post office, market – were a dream. Detailed maps covering ten million acres altogether were prepared for 127 of these proposed 'agricultural areas'. Block upon block of tiny 'farmlets' were mapped out, layered and clustered around notional reserves, along notional tracks and roads, often in the midst of still-untouched bush. There was, actually, no queue of smallholders waiting to risk their modest all on semi-subsistence farming far from any source of supplies, market, railroad, public service or social amenity. No-one who understood the reality on the ground, compounded by the mores of pastoral society, the shadowy world of land speculation, and the determination of squatters not to have the best parts of their runs plucked out, believed Duffy's Act could work. Many doubted his sincerity. 'Is he a rogue, a fool, or a compound of both?' asked the *Geelong Advertiser*.[38]

The main absurdity lay in the process of selection laid out in the Act – intended to be 'as simple as getting a loaf of bread from a well-stocked baker's shop'.[39] A selector consulted the maps, viewed the blocks of smallholdings in his desired location, and had only to go along to the local land office with a downpayment of cash or a banker's draft to claim it. If he was eligible, and if no other person selected the lot he wanted within the day, he became the instant owner. It sounded too simple, and so it proved.

From the moment the first two million acres were declared open for selection on 10 September 1862, the whole process was hijacked. Within a week, 'the squatters have once more set the spirit of the act at defiance by employing agents to buy for them'.[40] Black explained the latest means of circumvention: 'The Selector of land makes a declaration that "it is for his own use and benefit". Now, if A lends money to B, and B buys land on A's run, who then rents it from B for one year at a handsome profit with the option of buying after, will this be construed to mean "for the use and benefit" of B?'[41] As B would do well from his bargain, the law must assent to the evasion. How much easier to earn money from commission and rent than to take up a plough and farm. By virtue of prior arrangements between A and B, the real selectors were almost all squatters, who thus obtained the land – which they formally bought after a year – relatively cheaply. The land offices were complicit, or in some cases, according to Black, were themselves 'the very centre of corruption'.[42]

By October, when the next areas were opened, the panto-mime had become evident to all and sundry. Black explained: 'The operation of the Bill was so different from what most of its framers expected that they stood aghast, not knowing what to think, say or do. The small fry of jobbers and land speculators have become so numerous that the squatters had to pay a con-siderable sum. In one case, I knew of as many as 86 opponents for one piece of land. Of this number probably 50 or 60 might be what is called "dummies", in other words dumb represen-tatives of the Squatters, for the use of whose name he paid a con-sideration and their expenses.' Where there was more than one selector, the process was to draw letters from a hat. The banks were willing to offer drafts for every selector with his name in the draw because there would be only one winner, so only one sum of money was needed. 'With 60 dummies drawing against 26 *bona fide* applicants, the chances were greatly in favour of the squatter. If this Act continues much longer in force, the game will be played with not tens but hundreds of dummies for each lot. What a disgraceful scene. The sale of Crown lands converted into a lottery of the very lowest description.'[43]

Black's purchases on The Sisters had by now brought his acreage there to 8500, but 18 000 licensed acres in Ellerslie and Framlingham parishes were still waiting to be sold, and he was never going to let them go without a struggle. After the surveyor's finishing touches, he had expected this land to be opened for selection in December. But such was the storm raised on account of irregularities under Duffy's Act that proclamation of other 'agricultural areas' was suspended. Duffy protested that the number of evasions reported was exaggerated and that by and large the land had been selected by bona fide farmers. Black ridiculed this, and saw its support in the press as politically partisan: 'The *Argus* goes in with him, shutting their eyes to facts that are as palpable as the sun at noonday.'[44]

Duffy's attempts to prosecute evasions of the Act failed.[45] Black sent off newspaper reports of the trials to Gladstone, commenting that the Act had 'brought out in bold relief the fallacy of the "Howl" that was raised by stump Orators to "unlock the lands" for the honest industrious labouring classes who came to this colony to seek a home they cannot find'.[46] Black would have been keen to see such people come into the countryside. 'If they could only change the cry of "put the people on the land" to "construct roads and railways", the true and sure agents for bringing the people to, and putting them on, the land, how different would be the character of a rural population springing up and thriving by habits of industry, from that of those placed upon it by political trickery and class legislation.'[47] Few of the 'honest and industrious classes' had presented themselves. An occupation vulnerable to pests, droughts, floods and frequent bad seasons did not appeal, especially when the expense of fencing, legally mandated 'improvements', and other sanctions had to be faced.[48] Some who did try it gave up and sold out to the local grazier. Almost all the serious demand was from the squatters, and the industry of gamblers and speculators feeding off this demand grew exponentially with every effort to back the mythical ranks of smallholders who failed to turn up.

In April 1863, sales of 'special lands' at auction resumed. But Black found it increasingly difficult to gain the freehold of any remaining sections of Crown land on either of his runs. An example was a block of 715 acres in the 'Big Bend' of Mount Emu Creek, in the south-east corner of Glenormiston. This land had been grazed by Niel Black & Company under licence since 1840, and came up for sale in April 1863. Where not on the creek, it was enclosed by grazing land the company had bought long since, so it was isolated, liable to flood and only of value to Black. If someone else purchased it, miles of road would have to be opened through his land to reach it, he would have to fence this road on both sides to contain his stock, and it would probably remain unused. Those who bid against him would be doing so purely to extract money from Black or cause him nuisance.

Before the sale took place, two people came to say they wished to buy a lot on the section. He managed to 'dissuade' them. But there was one whom he could not dissuade. 'A candidate appeared in the person of a successful Gold Digger who had just returned from New Zealand. He came up the country on pretext of looking for employment. He applied here and was taken on as a Bullock driver. One day was spent by him in seeing the bullocks put into proper places with the assistance of another man, loading his dray and showing him the work. The following morning the team was yoked up ready to start when my friend came to tell me the bullocks were wild and that he would not drive them. After a short exchange, he was told to leave – without the opportunity for making himself acquainted with the land for sale.' The man told Black that, at the auction, 'he would run me up as he wanted land, and revenge, both'. Walter tried to persuade his uncle to let the land go. That was not Black's way. He was forced up to 64 shillings and 3 pence an acre average, a total of £2300.[49]

These were not the only sections sold that month on Glenor-miston. Later in April, many suburban-sized allotments of 18–20 acres were up for sale, in areas originally reserved for possible townships along the creek, one at Mackinnon's Bridge and another along the Mortlake–Camperdown Road. Interest in these allotments was intense. Black expected to encounter a major effort to deny him 'his' land on these sought-after sections, and he needed someone to help him skewer the opposition. Since Sam McGregor was away, Black had to manage things himself: 'One man has told me that unless I allow him to buy a few hundred acres, no acre would be sold under 100 shillings. Another who wants a bribe of £200 said he would run every lot to £12 an acre.'[50] Black would never succumb to such tactics – they merely made him more obdurate. Not only the company's fortunes, but also his pride and standing were at stake.

On 23 April, in tones still infused with the excitement of the Camperdown saleroom, he wrote to Gladstone: 'Yesterday was the most harassing day in my past life. I bought all the land offered for sale, 2459 acres at £8252', including some he bought back on the spot from its purchasers. The price averaged 68 shillings per acre. On some lots he was beaten up to over 100 shillings, but in general he had done extremely well to keep the average down. 'I was most successful in bamboozling my opponent to get the land at Mackinnon's Bridge at 35 shillings.' He had an understanding with the bridge contractor, who duly bid for the land Black wanted, giving the impression that he was buying on behalf of his workforce. 'I ceased to bid at 30 shillings, which staggered and puzzled the enemy.' He also managed to buy most of Mount Noorat – he called it The Hill, as it did not qualify as a mountain to a Scot – at the upset price. The disjointed outpouring in this instantly penned account of saleroom antics indicates the extraordinary efforts by speculators to fix, deter, or cut Black out, and counter-attempts by Black to outwit all competitors to gain ownership of 'his' property. He ended: 'It is no small satisfaction to me to say that Glenormiston is now in such a state as to put it out of Mr Duffy's power to injure it. Glenormiston may almost be said to be complete.'[51]

Black believed that there were few bona fide farmers bidding for the sought-after lots. The whole operation was a scam to batten on his well-known desire to own all 'his' land, good and bad. John Buys, his clerk, had something of his own to say on this topic. 'Lately a practice has sprung up of persons offering their services as agents to buy on behalf of the Crown tenant which he can only decline to accept on the understanding that he will be opposed in every lot. To such an extent has this been carried [on] that these agents, professing to represent companies with a large capital at [their] command, have by a sort of tacit understanding divided the Colony ... The success with which these men carry on these nefarious practices has induced a daily increasing catch of smaller fry of bloodletting horseleeches to follow in their wake, attending all the land sales as their only means of employment.' Up till this point, McGregor had bought off the smaller fry by 'increasing his commission, usually a shilling an acre, and paying them a small proportion of it; but now the trade is becoming so numerous it is impossible to satisfy all. Everyone has to submit to these extortions – it is now the usual practice.'[52] Crown tenants, according to Buys, had become the victims of extortion.

Whatever the many immoralities and their degrees, by this stage selectors, squatters, agents, 'capitalists' and even local worthies all conspired to evade the law.[53] Officials in the survey department or land office themselves 'selected' or got their cut from others' purchases. Thus these transactions formed part of a skein of duplicitous land 'business' that was not supposed to exist.[54] Black commented: 'Experience proves that money, like water, has natural channels of its own. No Act of Parliament can make the water that flows down the side of Mount Macedon return to its source. Neither can capital be restricted from finding an outlet in the direction it seeks under the pressure of self-interest, which is as constant in the force it applies to men's transactions as the law of gravitation is [to] the flowing stream'.[55] In time-honoured fashion, the market had found its route.

During the rest of 1863 and 1864, land sales were few and only of 'special lands' not subject to selection. Black secured the valuable Pejark Marsh at the lower edge of Glenormiston near Terang – to the annoyance of Terang smallholders who wanted it for commonage. He also tidied his western edge by purchasing the west flank of Mount Noorat from Thomson, making the Terang–Mortlake Road their boundary.

Black still hoped to purchase on The Sisters when the Duffy disaster was legislated away. New elections came in October 1864, but to his dismay, the democrats swept all before them. 'If Nations are visited with punishment in the present day for their sins I think Democrats must be the character in which the Devil bestrides the earth', he complained to Gladstone. 'We have been dragged ten times lower by our last election.'[56] The next land bill was put together by JM Grant. This tough ex-gold-digger Scot had an unpleasant habit of referring to guillotines and other implements of revolutionary destruction as suitable for disposing of squatters.[57] Grant's land bill would be Duffy all over again – only worse. It aimed to make things easier financially for the selector, and tightened up the controls against resale to the squatter. 'This Bill is so stringent as to make it impossible to evade its conditions, at least so say the lawyers.'[58]

Black spent six weeks in Melbourne taking part in discussions on the bill – an exceptional length of time for him, and a penance as the amendments put forward in the Upper House were almost universally removed. Twenty thousand acres on The Sisters would be thrown open immediately the Act came into force. 'The whole world will be entitled to partake of this land at 2 shillings per acre of rent', and if selectors did not turn up, the land would still be left open for three years for selection before anyone could offer to buy it. The Upper House tried fruitlessly to reduce this to one year.

They also proposed an amendment to enable reserved roads not yet made or in use to be closed by written authority of the shire council. Roads intended for 'agricultural areas' that never happened were a sore point with every squatter. Not only did they carve up his paddocks and cost him dear in fencing, but regulations required roads to have wide grass verges – taking away his pasturage. There were many miles of redundant roads on Glenormiston and neighbouring runs.[59] This Upper House amendment was also thrown out. 'Every surveyed road in the colony must be kept open unless the Board of Land and Works sitting in Melbourne grants authority for closing them. This prevents us from converting our land into commonage; or forces us into open war with all the surrounding small fry.'[60] Black's local MP, champion of the common man, would back his constituents to keep open all redundant local roads to enable them to graze their livestock on the grass verges; to Black, this meant on land usurped from him and fellow proprietors.

Various methods of evading Grant's 1865 Land Act were discussed. One was for the squatter to pay someone a fee to select, meet his annual rent, and then fail to carry out the necessary improvements, making the land forfeit after two years. This would hardly work if it was again put up for selection – as Grant intended. To Black, the best prospect of beating the Act was with 'land certificates'. These had been issued under Duffy as compensation to those who had selected under Nicholson and suffered from more onerous payments. A certificate allowed anyone with a grant of freehold under Nicholson to rent additional land, up to a maximum of 320 acres. Because land next to the initial purchase might not be available, the certificates were made transferable. As a result they were traded as currency, selling at various rates. The claimants were meant to be small-time, poor selectors; but anyone who purchased under Nicholson was eligible. That included Black and his dummies.

Now he sought to improve his chances. 'About a week ago I bought 12 certificates at 15 shillings an acre which, together with what is held before, will entitle us to select 6400 acres. If we can get this off the best land on Sisters it will not leave much land to be selected.' Here was the new scam. As under Duffy, lots would be drawn between selectors for the same allotment, so the trick would be to put in multiple certificates. Among squatters and their agents, certificates would be borrowed and lent. Some land sharks were by now a very sophisticated breed, with MPs as well as officials in their expansive pockets, and Black clearly believed that his notoriously anti-squatter MP would accept such a bribe, even one that favoured Black – whatever his constituents might think. The shark would arrange for the squatter's land to be put up for selection at a place and time to suit him. 'Suppose I have an area of 3000 acres on our land proclaimed for Selection on a certain day, I can put two certificates on each lot and I borrow 6000 certificates for 6000 acres more. In this way I have four chances on each lot. In every instance in which one of the borrowed certificates has been the successful number, I return to the owner one of equal value. The plan will work well if the sales in different places take place on different days.'[61]

When sales under Grant began, chaos ensued. Black sent Gladstone the newspapers 'for information as to the National Raffle of land to which Victoria invites the World'.[62] The first was in late May at Hamilton, where a stockade was built to contain thousands of people. 'The colony is swarming with Selectors wandering about in every direction like locusts. Ninety out of every 100 are mere speculators, trading on the chance of getting money out of the squatter in some form or other.' Black had received a letter from a 'gentleman who proposed to attend with 500 Selectors for us for a trifling consideration, as he calls it; I had another such offer yesterday'. Both were refused. The most eminent land jobbers were purchasing 'extensive numbers of certificates. They hire the services of an equal number of men to whom they assign each a certificate, and with these they go about from place to place to be employed by the squatters at so much per acre selected.' A shark might offer someone as much as £500 to select. If the person was successful, the land would be transferred to the existing occupant – but without title or security, and with the obligations of improvement.[63]

Despite Black's sense of degradation in using such methods, he succumbed. But it did him no good. Nor did his certificates. At Warrnambool on 17 June, Black deployed 'over a hundred backers, Walter says nearer 200, and yet not one of these had a call from the ballot box to select. We have therefore incurred heavy expenses without getting one acre to cover it.' Black believed that 90 per cent of selections were made 'in the hope of being able to sell to the squatter. Where a block of land is very valuable to the squatter being situated close to his woolshed or homestead, he will in a state of frenzy and desperation take any risk to save his position.'

Among the selectors trying to make money from the 'raffle' were many decent citizens. 'The Treasurer at Warrnambool told me he had hoped to select on our land as he is in want of funds to buy seven acres of freehold which adjoins his suburban cottage. He had hoped to obtain the money from us for doing so, as we could be under no fear of apprehension in effecting an illegal purchase from a man of honour like him. The manager of the Bank of Victoria told me he tried his luck for a similar purpose. Every day the township was crowded with multitudes seeking employment to select land, just as you may have seen reapers at home offering their services to cut down the crops of yellow

'Recd from the Honble Niel Black the sum of one thousand and nine hundred
and twenty pounds on account of purchase money of Land Certificates,
the balance to be paid on selection.' Signed Geo H Davenport, countersigned with
Niel Black's initials, dated 23 February 1865. No-one could say these
land-purchasing dodges were performed in secret.

Niel Black papers, Box 32, MS 8996, State Library of Victoria

corn.' There was worse. '[We see] the Commissioner of Crown
Lands hobnobbing and rollicking drunk with the lowest scamps
every evening; crowds of young girls not over 15 attending the
Selection Stockade day after day to select land, make declarations
that they are 21.'[64]

Most of the lands put up at Warrnambool on 17 June 1865
were on The Sisters, in the parishes of Ellerslie and East Framlingham, and according to John Buys, consisted of 13 300 acres.
There were more than 1500 applicants. Of these, 237, including

one certificate holder, were successful. Around 12 000 acres were taken up and the rest withdrawn. 'The chance here was one in every 42, and although NB&Co put in more than one hundred applications, not one was successful. But afterwards several of the successful applicants made their leases over to NB&Co.'[65] Black went off to Melbourne to consult his lawyer on whether this was legal. It seemed that selectors were entitled to let the grazing on their land for three years as long as they did not enter into an agreement of future sale.[66] In this way, 7550 acres were leased on The Sisters, with the hope, but no guarantee, that one day ownership might follow. Altogether, Black's purchased freehold was short of the full acreage to which he aspired, but with 26 700 acres on Glenormiston and 11 400 on The Sisters, it was very substantial. Whatever he might protest to his partners about the ragged nature of the company's domain, it was a major achievement. And, circuitously, it was done within the law.

Black's disillusionment with life in the colony deepened during this process – which lasted most of a decade. Government was so inadequate, the motives of its leaders so suspect, and policy towards rural settlement was unrealistic and antagonistic to men of capital whose efforts were vital to the colony's success: 'We are full of corruption from head to foot', he wrote to Gladstone in 1867. 'It is the Almighty Sovereign that rules all.'[67] It grieved him that nothing could be done by any normally upright man to secure the future of everything he held dear without resorting to immoral practice. 'Can my son, born and brought up in the midst of such corrupting influences, enter on the active duties of life with the same purity of mind which was instilled into the Father by more favourable circumstances?'[68] Gladstone repeatedly asked him why, feeling as he did, he did not come home. But Black believed himself by now unable at his advanced age to build a prosperous career in 'an old country'. 'I often ask myself whether it would not be sound judgment to sell out and clear away altogether before it is too late. But then comes the question: What could *I* do elsewhere, and can I forsake Victoria, my bride of five and twenty years?'[69]

Under pressure from his wife's family, he had long ago given up Ericht Bank, the house in Scotland. He needed all his resources for Victoria. He had promised to take Grace home to see her adored father once more before he died. In May 1865, as the land saga rose to yet another crescendo, news came that John Leadbetter had passed away. Black chastised himself bitterly for failing to fulfil his word.

Chapter Ten

'ALL EFFORTS TO REACH AGREEMENT HAVE QUITE FAILED'

SINCE MOVING INTO the new house at Glenormiston in 1860, whatever other tempests were ruffling a squatter's calm, the life of domestic contentment on a country estate that Niel Black had long aspired to was wonderfully fulfilled. On 14 April 1862, Grace bore him a second son, named Steuart Gladstone after his partner. She delivered at home rather than in Melbourne, despite the doctor's recommendation. A third son, Niel Walter, followed in June 1864. Like his own father, Niel Black was 60 when his youngest child was born. He loved fatherhood, but the need to leave an unencumbered inheritance for his three boys became a constant preoccupation.

The creation of a gracious homestead and a reputation for hospitality brought both Mr and Mrs Black great pleasure. His garden was laid out by a faithful employee, John Brown, working under his and Grace's guidance. The fruit orchard was his pride and joy. 'The garden is fenced with corrugated iron, and apples grow to 5¾ inches in circumference, also peaches. The iron fence has very much increased the temperature of the garden, making our produce mature earlier; but we are still a month later than Melbourne.'[1]

Despite its cooler climate, Glenormiston did experience extreme heat. One late January day when the temperature rose precipitously, Black went to the garden 'in the evening after the bustle and anxiety of the day was over. Where the trees were loaded with a rich and luxuriant crop of nearly full-grown fruit, but before any tendency to ripen had begun to show itself, guess my surprise on seeing every apple, pear and peach exposed to the northern aspect cooked, ready baked in their skin while hanging on the tree. The baking was as perfect as the most careful cook could wish.' The bustle and anxiety of the day had been fire-fighting. The night before, he had seen the threat to come. 'Our horses were nearly knocked up with the heat, and consequently I did not get home till after 12 o'clock. Riding home at night I could see the glare of the bush fires to the north-west, the point from which hot winds always come. From this I knew what was to take place next day.' The lookout posted on Mount Noorat was falsely reassured at dawn when 'the dews of night had damped the fires so that no smoke could rear, and he returned home in comfortable security'. Anticipating otherwise, Black got the men up at 7 am – in time to save the run.[2]

Fighting fires became so routine every January and February that elaborate precautions were put in place, with a lookout always on The Hill and horses saddled ready to gallop wherever needed. Most fires were accidental, caused by men boiling up their tea, or 'some half-drunk mortal staggering homeward, lighting his pipe and throwing away the match'; but some were deliberately set. 'Finding bush-fires so frequent and hearing of men threatening them as a means of punishment or revenge, I originated a Mutual Bushfire Protection Association which has taken very well. We have notices posted all over the district offering £100 reward to anyone who will give information that will lead to the conviction of one raising a bush-fire wilfully, or £20 for raising a bushfire through carelessness or neglect.'[3]

One of the worst fires was in 1863. Fire in the north 'was seen from the top of our Hill, but before men on horseback could ride six miles to meet it, it had entered on our run and no earthly power could check it. The flames jumped before the hot wind 10 to 15 feet, and the tinder-like grass caught it up when dropping to expire.' The hot winds drove the fire into 'the Big Pond' at the bend of Mount Emu Creek, where it burned out, but not before cattle had stampeded across the plains, and large areas of pasture were reduced to cinder. Forced to send cattle to market, he was short-handed when another fire arrived from the south.

'A system has been adopted of cutting a ring round the trees where the forest is too heavily timbered. These withered trees caught fire which ran up the bark, from which sparks were carried a considerable distance. During the heat of the day we were so enveloped in smoke that we could not see from what point the fires were approaching. The few hands we had were so dead beat that they were barely able to face a fire. I am certain Walter did not sleep twelve hours during that week. At last we had to kindle back-fires along the road to Terang, beginning at Mackinnon's Bridge, where the fire was at last stopped by keeping watch night and day on the road, watering the edges in case of sparks crossing. It seemed as if destruction fierce and uncontrollable was approaching us from every side. In some places the earth itself was burning, I could not ride over it without burning my horses' feet. On one day, and that not the hottest, my wife took a note of the thermometer. It registered 106 [41°C] in the shade of our Verandah.'[4]

Rains brought other problems for Grace. In her early days at Glenormiston, 'the verandah and fowl-yard are her chief walks as we have as yet no made [surfaced] roads or walks dry enough for winter. Walking for three months is almost impracticable. We do not even go to church during that time.'[5] Travel in the district gradually improved. The Hampden Shire Council, set up in 1863 with Daniel Curdie as president, vigorously pushed road-making. The council consisted of prominent local squatters, including Niel Black, Peter McArthur and Daniel Mackinnon, and all contributed generously for roads.[6] Still, rainy weather carried risks. Grace became very ill in the spring of 1864 after driving in a buggy to Terang on a cold wet day. 'As she was charioteer she could not protect herself from getting soaked through on the chest and arms, and sat in a little cold shop while the horse was being shod at the blacksmiths.'[7] His wife's illness kept Black at home for weeks, prompting protests about his non-attendance in the Upper House.

Black regretted the lack of neighbours for his wife to befriend. Society around Glenormiston was at a premium. Archie and

Marion Black at Gnotuk were not visited or received after Archie crossed a line in his relations with his uncle by threatening to bid against Niel Black & Company at a land auction; this was to extract from him a paddock Archie wanted.[8] Mrs Claud Farie, who took Grace on holiday to Tasmania and often brought her children to stay, died of cancer in August 1863. The Blacks' closest friends were the Mackinnons at Marida Yallock. Daniel Mackinnon was 14 years younger than Niel, and also close to Archie, their friendship formed in the 1850s when Niel was away. Mackinnon remained on good terms with both uncle and nephew through every twist and turn of their own complex relationship.

If her life was isolated, Mrs Black did not complain. Her house was always full, mostly of young men – called Farie, Hamilton, Gladstone or Steuart – who had come out from Scotland to join what Black wryly termed his 'College for Squatters'.[9] Then there was Claud Farie and his children for the holidays; Walter Black en route from Warreanga, droving fat cattle to market; a Scottish cousin Walter Buchanan and his wife, stopping by indefinitely on the chance of employment; and the new Police Magistrate, waiting for a house. 'We are often favoured with visitors who do not think it too much to stay with us for six or 12 months', wrote Black. Grace did protest occasionally; so did the servants.

Some attendees at the 'College for Squatters' required forbearance. Peter Serjeantson, prodigal son of Gladstone's Liverpool partner, put Black on best fulminating form. 'I do not quite approve of having a young man forced into my house for the short space of five years. Perhaps it was desirable to get him out of the Office, and this was the readiest way of accomplishing it. Now to be plain I don't intend to ask my wife to set up as a reformatory for the benefit of young men who cannot be controlled by their own parents at home.'[10] Young Serjeantson complained about his reception, and to assuage Gladstone, Black afterwards controlled his pen. No matter what case he made against sending out young men who were failures at home as if succeeding in the colonies were the merest bagatelle, he and Grace were not to be spared. His friend William Campbell wrote from Scotland to say that an entrant for Black's 'College' would not be coming after all. 'You will be relieved, for the numerous "waifs and strays" that have been entrusted to your care must weigh on your mind. In my day, a youngster was always well worth his grub and lodging. But times are changed.'[11]

One of the 'waifs' was Archy Hamilton, Walter's companion from Dunoon. 'Kind-hearted and correct' though young Archy was, Black found him unsuited to the exigencies of managing anything, including his own life. Hamilton and Walter soon parted company. Niel continued to act as Hamilton's guide, mentor, banker and travel agent – helping him to go off to New Zealand in 1861 with another intended partner, and always keeping his father abreast of his activities. But times had indeed changed. 'Today', Black wrote, 'the habits of a real squatter are as little seen here as on the Banks of Loch Lomond or the Braes of Skye.' The cost of stations and other expenditures were too high – and, thanks to selection on any land worth owning, too insecure. Eventually, young Hamilton went off to South America.[12]

Another 'stray' was Adam Steuart, arriving in October 1862. There was little attempt to disguise the fact that the youngest son of William Steuart, Gladstone's uncle and an original partner in Niel Black & Company, was a reprobate sent into exile. By some mysterious process, Adam was to be put on the path of redemption in Victoria under Black's supervision. Black could not refuse. The pill was sweetened by Adam's remittance, which included a promise of £10 000 to be invested in a squatting partnership.[13] He was to be occupied, but his resources were to be tied up so that he could not access them without Black's endorsement. 'Break-outs' began at an early stage. He was a guest at Glenormiston at the same time as Serjeantson, and the young dissolutes made a pretty pair. One morning they borrowed horses and rode off to Terang to get drunk. Steuart just managed to get home, but Serjeantson – after three days of excess in the township taverns – fell off his horse, walked into a bog and nearly drowned. He had to be rescued by Mr and Mrs Black in their gig.[14]

Black despised Serjeantson. Even put to riding the boundaries to check cattle, he wrecked his horse, he remonstrated to Gladstone. 'No doubt his accounts will be sent me one day and I would like to know if his father wants them paid.'[15] Adam Steuart, he genuinely liked. But the only way to keep him straight was to have him under his and Grace's supervision. 'Like "Lady Audley", he has his own secret which he can as little put aside as the shadow inseparable from his body whenever the sun shines.'[16] Things sometimes improved, but never lastingly. Black saw Steuart's alcohol addiction as a sickness of the mind. 'He can resist every temptation for a time but the disease keeps steadily increasing until its generating power at last breaks through every obstruction.'

In 1864, Adam Steuart became a partner with Walter Black and Robert Farie at a station they took up at Boort on the Loddon River north-west of Bendigo. His family contributed £6000 of the £13 000 capital, and later added £10 000. For a time all went well, but gradually 'break-outs' restarted. Ejected from Boort, he returned to Glenormiston. Niel did not want to send him home while his father lived – he feared it would break the old man's heart.[17] Adam remained with them, a 'supernumerary', until 1869. His sister Elizabeth wrote Black a touching letter of thanks. 'You write so kindly that we are sure you feel for us and that we may count on you as a friend. As regards *this world*, all hope of a career seems at an end but if we may only by God's help save his precious soul, this is what we look to.'[18]

Glenormiston absorbed Adam Steuart and other 'stayers' and was a contented place. William Campbell captured Mr and Mrs Black's sentiments: 'You will doubtless find the attractions of Glenormiston militate against Melbourne life: for who that could roam over its green aspect and revel in its sunshine and enjoy simple pleasures with little alloy, would look back to the fleshpots of Melbourne?' A glimpse of life at the homestead is provided in a letter of 1863 written by a visitor, Charles Maplestone. He became lost heading east towards Camperdown and, in the dark, found a track which led him to the 'handsome and beautifully furnished mansion of Hon. Niel Black. Here, I was hospitably received. Mr Black was not at home, but there were several guests, one of whom, a Police Magistrate, I know. Mrs Black is a very elegant lady-like woman. After a little preparation in a bedroom assigned to me I was ushered into the dining room and at 8 o'clock, the dinner bell rang. The whole conduct of this establishment – the dinner table, plate, furniture etc. are very much in the style of an English Gentleman. Next day, Mrs Black (with whose manner of conducting family worship in the morning and with whose whole demeanour I was much pleased) kindly pressed me to remain until Mr Black's return.'[19]

In 1857 in Scotland, a five-year deed of partnership for Niel Black & Company had been drawn up. At the end of 1861, a division of the assets was to take place and the company be dissolved. Black's decision to take charge again at Glenormiston, followed by the negotiations over Archie's exit, complicated this timetable. So the deed was renewed until 1867. Claud Farie, a trusted arbiter in company matters, wrote to Gladstone in Scotland: 'I think the landed property should be divided in three, or kept as a joint partnership property. It would greatly facilitate the business if you would take a run out here yourself – your interest is now a very valuable one.'[20]

But Gladstone could not be persuaded to travel so far. Black would have dearly loved to entertain his mentor at Glenormiston, ride out with him and demonstrate why buying and fencing land was essential, show him the dams and culverts, and talk into the night about politics, trade, finance, what to do about Adam Steuart, and the future of his own small boys, now 'growing like mushrooms'. He also yearned for the stamp of approval he was certain would be his if only he could bend the ear of a discerning confidant from home. He had to be content instead with a visit from Gladstone's second son, Steuart, who arrived in early 1864.

Steuart Gladstone, aged 27, had already made a fortune in the India trade. He and Black corresponded regularly, especially over horses Black sent to him at Calcutta for pig-sticking.[21] The prospect of Steuart's visit had been building in Black's mind for a long time. He believed that his report would finally 'wipe off the last faint blotch of all the imputations' that Archie had made against him, and confirm that he never deviated from the course that would best serve Gladstone's and the company's interests.[22] In fact, so important was the visit to him and so keen was he that it succeed that he feared disappointment. He was right.

The young man from Calcutta hoped for adventure and sport, riding down cattle wild as buffaloes on the American plains; but they were too docile. As for shooting, kangaroos were few. Day after day, it rained, and the dwindling embers of frontier life in western Victoria seemed disappointingly tame. Steuart found Black's tirades against democracy irritating, and he had no desire to examine exhaustively the studbooks, maps and accounts laid out for his inspection. Mrs Black invited over some young ladies, 'a new thing in this house'. By local standards, life at Glenormiston was gentrified, but to Steuart Gladstone, it was paltry compared to Calcutta races and balls, and the attentions of his father's partner, with his Scottish brogue and old-school prejudices, were too assiduous. So he went off to Melbourne with his cousin Adam Steuart and soon afterwards left prematurely for Calcutta. Black was devastated: 'It is like withdrawing from the thirsty lip the half-finished cup.'[23] The Honourable Member had received politeness, but not the seal of confidence he sought.

It was with much less enthusiasm that Black learned in late 1865 that his other partner, Alexander Finlay, and his son Campbell, were soon to arrive. Finlay, whose wife had recently died, was a difficult character, embittered by disappointment in Indian ventures.[24] Outwardly, he was courteous and gentlemanly, but his inner self was hooded and he gave nothing away. He had a powerful sense of his 'inheritor' status as compared to Black, whose farming family he knew. He treated Black not as an equal partner but as his agent or employee – which in a sense he was, since the company paid him a salary. Finlay had rarely been actively involved in Niel Black & Company, and he did not understand Victorian affairs. He had refused Black's requests for extra capital and repeatedly complained that his remittances were too low. A windfall year in 1865 gave Black a respite. But he suspected Finlay's motives for coming out and worried that Gladstone, Finlay's friend since boyhood, might allow his view of operations to take precedence over Black's own.[25]

The question of the company's division was looming. Black had been trying to buy sufficient land for three estates: Glenormiston divided into two, North and South, plus The Sisters. But he had failed to achieve the intended purchases on The Sisters. He had held back improvements there, to avoid driving up prices on its licensed lands – which he still hoped to buy eventually. So The Sisters was still 'in a state of nature'. Since early 1864, he had also been going back into sheep, pleuropneumonia in cattle having caused such a scare. Black thought the infection could be kept down and was unsure about sheep, especially given the investments required in woolsheds, sheep washes, and drainage to counter footrot.[26] But Gladstone liked wool – the clip came home, so it gave him more control. So Black put 30 000 sheep on his drier lands. Almost immediately, the flocks he put on The Sisters became scabbed from sheep on adjacent selector smallholdings. If the Crown lands were put up for sale, scabby flocks would be a liability. Sheep versus cattle was one of many imponderables related to the value of his stock and lands: freehold, rented or licensed; improved, semi-improved or 'in a state of nature'. Black could never have brought everything to a state of 'unity' prior to the division entirely satisfactory to himself. But he did expect to do things by means of his own devising.

There were many questions about arrangements post-division. Would Black remain manager of lands owned by the other partners? Might all of them lease to his nephew Walter? And there were questions about the division itself. Since all values were speculative in the absence of a regular, established market, how would an equal division of such varied lands be effected? The land could not be divided 'equally' by area, since The Sisters was not united or improved.

Meanwhile, Glenormiston had been conceived as a whole, based on the 1853 pre-emptive purchase, with the house and farm buildings in the centre. Drawing a line dividing the northern part from the southern as 'equally' as possible left all the buildings on the northern side. Given discrepancies in soils, water access, improvements and prospects, there would have to be a process of adjustment and compensation. When divisions of land were contested, as Archie had done from 1860 to 1862, they involved a large cast of valuers, lawyers and arbiters. During negotiations, prices might seesaw, sheep get scabbed, a railway open or new Land Act pass, further complicating every calculation.

The deed of 1857 stipulated that the division would be made by drawing lots. Then, Black had no thought of remaining in Victoria for more than a year or so. The new house had not been built nor his family established. Now he wanted to retain the house at Glenormiston; the gardens, orchards and trees he had planted; the elm-lined drive; his paddocks; the stables supervised by James, his coachman from Dunoon; and the home in which Grace managed their happy domestic life. He hoped – even assumed – that the allotment to him of the homestead section would be approved so long as the partners received an estate of equal value; after all, neither was intending to live there. Farie backed this assumption. 'The manner in which Black has managed the affairs of NB&Co from beginning to end, I think entitles him to be not only fairly but liberally considered by them in the division', he wrote to Gladstone.[27] There was no doubt in Gladstone's mind either. He told Black that he could have the place of his choice; and also that if Black wanted to purchase whatever fell to Gladstone himself, he would try to accommodate him. Neither of them expected Finlay to be much interested. How wrong they were.

———————

Not long after Alex Finlay arrived in January 1866, Black wrote to Gladstone in consternation: 'My energies are not a little paralysed and a shock communicated to the whole system as I do not find that Finlay and I can come to any arrangement for the future.'[28]

Black spent days riding around and showing Finlay everything, to be greeted with a wall of obstruction. To every proposal of Black's he raised objections. He did not see any reason why Black should wish for a choice of estate, even though the three sections would be independently valued and inequalities made good by arbitrated compensation. He rejected the idea that, if Black did not draw North Glenormiston, there could be any exchange or sale so that he could retain his home; or that in such a predicament he was entitled to sell up and leave, thereby withdrawing from his managerial-employee role. Black had hoped after the division to lease or buy their future properties from his ex-partners. This was also unacceptable – and Finlay told Black that Gladstone felt the same way, which was not what Black understood, and nor was it true.

Finlay queried all the values Black had assigned, and said The Sisters was worth more than he claimed. Black told him that if he was allotted The Sisters, he would not go there: it would mean starting all over again. 'I would like to sell out at once while the price of stock and land are both high, either with a view to retire altogether, or buy a larger and more civilized place.' As for

South Glenormiston, although Black rode with Finlay over the land several times and pointed out its good qualities in terms of soils, water and other features, Finlay thought this a blind. His attitude and behaviour were mystifying. 'I never met a man so close', Black wrote to Gladstone. 'I have opened to him every chamber of my thoughts, just as I would to you. It appears to me that every truth and openness tends to excite suspicions in his mind ... Not one yard could be passed without inspection, though as a stranger he could not know the land he had inspected the day before.' Black showed Finlay a draft plan for the division, 'making the acreage nearly equal, with a rough valuation classifying the various qualities', but he waved it aside.[29] In the end, Finlay decreed that they should have the freehold valued and draw lots for it within a year. He would not agree to anything else until this was done.

Black was profoundly disturbed. Finlay's behaviour towards him was humiliating – as if he was inspecting the operations of an untrustworthy factor on his Scottish estates. Although the environment was alien to Finlay, he appeared to discount Black's professional knowledge. Thinking to strengthen his partner's confidence, Black encouraged Finlay to consult others in the district. This included Archie, who – as Black knew – had accused his uncle of being prompted by self-interest in making improvements on 'the best end of Gleno'.[30] Black could not believe Finlay would place more value on Archie's opinions than his own; after all, Finlay had described Archie to Black himself as 'vain, headstrong, vindictive, dangerous' and a blister on the company they had done well to get rid of.[31] But when Finlay returned from Gnotuk he said nothing about his discussion with Archie. And when his neighbours told Black later that Finlay had canvassed them repeatedly on the relative values of the estates he felt mortified, as it advertised that Finlay distrusted him. Finlay clearly thought Black wanted to fix the division to get North Glenormiston cheap.[32] In fact, if anything, Black wanted his homestead so badly that he attached less value to the underdeveloped South than it deserved.

What made Alex Finlay think that Niel Black would perpetrate such deceit? After so many years running their enterprise with no hint of financial impropriety, what would make him act unscrupulously in so vital a matter? As Black pointed out, if he was capable of such deviousness, his partners would have long since found him out cheating them in many small ways.[33] Black blamed Finlay's suspicious nature. 'He has the manner and refinement of a cultivated intellectual, coupled with the instinct and secretiveness of a detective on duty',[34] he wrote to Gladstone. But there were mitigating factors. The immorality and corruption of Victorian public life, the low reputation of colonial wheeler-dealers, and the paucity of a reliable gentleman's code in this brash society disoriented Finlay. He would have learned all about land-purchasing shenanigans, and he knew Black was a deft practitioner and master of deals that, at home, would be disreputable. The 'almighty sovereign' of corruption had had its effect on every successful squatter. The exploits of country members would have been the subject of tongue-wagging at the Melbourne Club, in whose panelled embrace Finlay, an ex-Westminster MP and shooting companion of the Duke of Argyll, was more at home than Black.

At the bottom of everything there was snobbery. Even if Finlay could imagine a managing partner acting impeccably, this would have to be someone of his own class. It could not be someone who began life as a tenant farmer doffing his hat to Finlays and Campbells in their native Argyll, whose family quarrelled and whose brother was mad, even if he had rented a mansion on the Firth of Clyde and married the daughter of John Leadbetter Esquire. Finlay chose to believe embittered Archie's version of his uncle's affairs. It played to his resentment and social pique. How could an astute old fox such as Niel Black, Honourable Member of the Victorian Upper House notwith-standing, have done so well – honestly? How could he have built up a hugely successful stock enterprise in an outlandish part of the world without being a little crooked, while he, Alexander Struthers Finlay of Castle Toward, had looked business failure in the face and was burdened and mortgaged to the hilt?

In March, when Black was in Melbourne on parliamentary matters, he went to see Charles Klingender, his lawyer. Together they devised a plan for valuing, apportioning and conveying the company's freehold in three parts, adjusting the differences in value, dividing the profits, stock, and so on. Since this was what Finlay wanted, Black signed the necessary letter to set in motion the dissolution of the partnership.

Then a new element appeared. When his father went home, young Campbell stayed on in Victoria. Finlay prepared a power of attorney for his son to act on his behalf – a power of attorney that clashed with an existing one held by Black on the company's behalf. Finlay appeared to be reducing Black's authority in Niel Black & Company in favour of his son, a youth with no colonial experience, not even a spell at the 'College for Squatters'. Campbell – who spent all told very little time at Glenormiston – behaved when there as if he had equal managerial rights to Black and was entitled to ride any horse he liked or issue an order to the men in his presence.[35] Finlay also opened a special bank account with company money for Campbell's use. Black protested: how could such actions be consistent with his own authority over company affairs?[36] Campbell later confessed to him that his father had told him to report back every detail of Black's actions relating to the division. He also discovered that Finlay wanted Archie, not himself, to be Campbell's squatting mentor.[37]

After this, nothing would have induced Niel Black to go on in business with Alex Finlay.

———•◦•———

Throughout 1866 and 1867, the political situation in Victoria was in a state of continual crisis. The ministry of James McCulloch, elected in 1864, had set out on a course of radical change. This took antagonism between the two parliamentary chambers to such an extreme that all legislation ground to a halt and government revenues were in crisis. The Governor, Sir Charles Darling, abandoned the required stance of neutrality to side with McCulloch and the radicals, and was recalled in disgrace to London. Darling's recall led to petitions and public meetings championing 'the people's governor' as a martyr, and the feeling against the Upper House became quasi-revolutionary. Black went to Melbourne to take part in deliberations when his presence was keenly sought,[38] but he was much preoccupied by company affairs and his health was bad. He wrote to Gladstone: 'I know my wife would rejoice were I to sell out tomorrow and return home. She believes I am shortening my days here ... But I am chained to Glenormiston by a natural attachment, and I cannot find it in my heart to turn my attention to other things until I know its fate.'[39]

Black was determined to make the three estates as 'united' as possible in the time remaining before the division. He reversed his policy of no improvements on The Sisters. Many selector-lessees were keen to sell to him as soon as legally possible as they made nothing from their holdings. So he decided to risk improving them even with no guarantee about the future. He also used the services of Thomas Asche, the supreme 'land shark' of the day, to get key land on The Sisters – the Kolora Lagoon and swamp – put up for sale. 'A "land shark" fees and retains so many MPs, who back up his application to have certain land sold by auction', he explained to Gladstone. 'The [Minister of Lands] yields to the pressure; the land is sold. The Squatter buys it at auction, and pays his agent 40 or 60 shillings per acre; this sum [is] apportion[ed] among the MPs he retains.' Asche visited Black to agree on terms for performing this alchemy. 'He said he should know what sum he would be allowed, to guide him in his dealings and promises to his retainers ... I could have believed at one time that I would sooner be hanged to a tree than submit to such degradation but what can I do? ... I tell you most distinctly as a matter of fact that this is the system under which every acre of land has been sold for many days and I am obliged to receive and treat the agent as a Gentleman when he comes to my house.'[40] The nefarious Mr Asche, his tame MPs and the stranglehold he exerted over the squatters, became a refrain in Black's letters to Gladstone. 'Not an acre of land has been sold in this district for two years but what has been put up by Mr Asche's influence. There is not a man in this neighbourhood that has not employed him. When the matter comes to a push no-one will decline his services. Everyone is striving to complete their properties and by no other means can it be accomplished.'[41]

In late September, the final preparations were put in place for the division of the freehold lands held by 'our firm'. Black wrote: 'Every acre worth having from Geelong to the Glenelg is now freehold and with a very few exceptions, such as Manifold, Big Clarke and a few others, the owners are staggering under a load of Mortgage that must ultimately crush not a few of them. In times past, the profit derived from the occupancy of Crown Lands was applied to payment of the debt upon freehold, but the last two years have swept away this collateral security.' Among those with holdings in a relatively secure state was Niel Black & Company. But they would never be secure enough to satisfy Black. Many questions bothered him about the valuation of company property. What was the value of land on The Sisters that they leased and might never own? What was the financial effect of scab? What was the life of fences and stone walls, of which there were over 100 miles? How did you value anything in the absence of a regular market? Never mind, it must be done. 'I put this place [Glenormiston] in its Sunday dress to receive the valuers. It never was before in such order.'[42] As it happened, a critical vote on budgetary appropriations was due in the Legislative Council on 26 September. This was the day the valuers were due, and Black's absence would be deplored. It could not be helped.

For some days the valuers – Paul de Costella (Gladstone's designate), William Swan (Black's) and Walter Clark (Finlay's) – rode around the two runs to view the three proposed estates, and made their own assessments against Black's estimates of land, buildings, dams and other improvements. The draw by lot took place on 1 October 1867. Black never described the trauma of the actual draw. His lawyer, Klingender, was present and devised the method: two hats, one for order of draw, one for the draw itself. The valuers were present, as were Black's superintendent John McIntyre, Walter Black, Adam Steuart, Campbell Finlay acting for his father, and Claud Farie acting for Gladstone. The first name drawn was Finlay; Campbell drew North Glenormiston. Next was Gladstone, and Farie drew the South. Black was left with The Sisters lot, in which was included the two small farms at Moonee Ponds near Melbourne to bring its value closer to that of the other two. By prior agreement, Gladstone and Black would swap. But Campbell had no permission from his father to make any such offer.

Within half an hour, Black rode off to Melbourne to take part in yet another vote on the appropriation bill. He did not even have time to discuss the catastrophe with his wife. He was struck dumb. For three whole weeks, there are no letters in his copybook.

Black arrived back at Glenormiston on 21 October, feeling very shaken and sick. He then wrote formally to Farie, asking to effect the pre-agreed swap. In an accompanying note, he wrote: 'I believe this is the saddest day of my life. I am resigning any right to the offspring and fruit of my skill and labour for the last 27 years, with all its associations during that time, and that when I am too much worn out to have any hope of creating another like it. It is a cruel hardship and ought to be an eternal disgrace to anyone that would inflict so great an injustice on one who unselfishly devoted his time and his money to benefit the Coy. Gladstone has fully justified the high confidence and trust I reposed in him since the first day we met, but the other in soft and sugared phrase has adopted an opposite course.' Black knew Farie felt deeply for his old friend, as did many others. 'The sympathy and indignation so universally expressed by word and letter, though kindly meant, is to me and especially to my wife very painful. I cannot drive the feeling out of her mind that this is no longer our house. What my future plans may be I cannot yet determine but the public seems to have made up their mind that I will go home.'[43]

He had also to write to Gladstone, a letter that could be shared with Finlay. 'I agreed to submit to the game of chance and inexorable fate has written the divorce that separates me from the scene and sympathies of all my past life. It now only remains for me to try to start again. My name will not be altogether dis-associated with Glenormiston since you have so kindly agreed to let me have your lot in exchange.'[44] In an accompanying private letter he was less guarded. 'Just fancy yourself leaving Capenoch House, handing it over to my son in its present state and begin-ning a new home for yourself somewhere on the moor or hill-side. What grieves me most is my wife's silent uncomplaining look of depression and stifled disappointment. Had matters been left to you and me as they were heretofore, no third party would have been called in to value or settle matters between us, and what a gratifying testimonial that would have been to me, in place of a Board of Enquiry such as sat there to betray to the world evidence of distrust and limited confidence.'

Despite everything, Black was not beyond all hope that Finlay would reconsider. In this he was encouraged by Campbell, who was pained to see the old pioneer so brought down by the pros-pect of ejection from his home – a home his father did not want or need. Campbell wrote asking his father to do nothing until he returned: he was sailing in November. The evening before he left Glenormiston, Campbell talked everything through with Black, telling him there was no need as yet to fix the North–South dividing line. 'He thought it probable his father might be disposed to selling out, and expressing his most earnest desire that we should come to some arrangement to keep Gleno as it is.' Campbell told Black that his father was in desperate need of money, fostering his belief that there was a real chance he would sell.[45] And so Black began to consider taking his family home, to treat with Finlay and enable Grace to enjoy a long-postponed visit to her family.

———————

In August 1866, Black had received the son of the new Governor, Sir Henry Manners-Sutton, for some days of country sports. Black's original reputation was for kangaroo shoots, but since they had been decimated, snipe was now the thing.

The visit must have been a success, because when Prince Alfred the Duke of Edinburgh, Queen Victoria's 23-year-old second son, visited Australia in late 1867, Glenormiston was one of the Western District homesteads placed on the royal itinerary.[46] So even as his personal crisis unfolded, Black had to equip Glenormiston to receive a royal entourage and prepare to play his part in the prince's tour. The visit is barely mentioned in Black's correspondence, other than that he covered in the verandah to make space for a 'Corrobory'.[47] Either his mind was too full of other things, or the royal visit provoked reflection in a manner best left unsaid.

From the tactfully penned account in the *Warrnambool Examiner* of 10 December, the tour was characterised by royal rudeness and imperviousness towards the desire of Her Majesty's colonial citizens to pay their respects. The prince wanted as little as possible to do with the rustic colonial throngs who turned out to welcome him. He wore shooting attire throughout and wished that sport could be the tour's exclusive purpose. The party included Governor Manners-Sutton and Chief Secretary McCulloch. First stop was Thomas Austin's Barwon Park on

3 December, where rabbits were plentifully despatched. On to William Robertson's homestead near Colac on 4 December, and from there via Camperdown to Glenormiston for the night of Thursday 5 December.

Decorative greenery, flags, platforms, escorts of mounted horsemen, reception committees and loyal addresses were prepared by all the towns along the prince's route. At Camperdown, Daniel Mackinnon, Chairman of the shire council, was on the platform, along with Daniel Curdie, Black and other leading squatters. The prince, who had ordered his carriage to drive straight through Colac without pulling up, stopped only long enough to hear Mackinnon's address, smirk at its fulsomeness, and nod an acknowledgement. The carriages whisked onwards, while McCulloch, who had alighted to shake a hand or two as a courtesy, was nearly left behind.

A few miles further, a delegation from Terang waited at Mackinnon's Bridge. Black had dressed his older boys, Ian, aged eight, and Steuart, aged five, in full Scottish regalia, and they too were waiting on their ponies, to form a mounted escort on the last leg to Glenormiston. But the royal equipage turned off the highway along the Castle Carey Road so as to avoid Mackinnon's Bridge and reach Glenormiston by the back route. Black himself had to gallop off in order to greet his royal guest, who promptly went out shooting. In the evening, at Black's special request, the disappointed Terang citizens were permitted to come in and make their address privately, on the closed-in verandah. Bonfires lit the sky, from the summits of Mount Leura, Mount Meningoort, West Cloven Hills and Mount Noorat.

In the morning, HRH again went out snipe-shooting. The royal carriage and luggage were sent on ahead, and when the prince's desire for sport was sated, Black drove him to Mortlake in his buggy. A crowd of 1000 waited for four hours in the heat; no beer was served, all riders were told to dismount, and horses were removed from their carriage shafts so that no annoyance could occur of dust, unruly hooves or people enthusiastically crowding around. On the way from Glenormiston, Black persuaded Prince Alfred to accept an address from the people of Mortlake, and accordingly halted outside the hotel. But because they had been forewarned not to deliver one, Thomas Cumming, their shire president, informed the prince that they understood he did not like such addresses and so they would desist. With a few orderly hurrahs, and some raising of hats, the visit was completed with sufficient speed and sobriety to elicit the royal pleasure. The prince rejoined his waiting carriage up the road, and travelled on to Chatsworth, homestead of John Moffat.

The royal progress over, Black drew breath. A few days later he decided to do what Campbell Finlay had suggested. His nephew Walter agreed to take over at Glenormiston temporarily, and the Honourable Mr and Mrs Black and family took ship from Melbourne towards Castle Toward and home.

Chapter Eleven

'I DREAD SOME FATAL CATASTROPHE'

AFTER A TERRIBLE VOYAGE in which two members of the family were dangerously ill, Niel Black, his wife and three young sons disembarked at Southampton on 20 February 1868. He then proceeded to London, where he met Gladstone and learned that Alex Finlay had rejected all overtures for reordering the division. Gladstone strongly disapproved of Finlay's insistence on denying Black the homestead section, and had even offered £6000 as an incentive to sell or exchange. But, in spite of Campbell's earlier expectation, Finlay was unmoveable.

Shortly before Black left Victoria, an anomaly had been identified in the division of land, and on this he began to stake a great deal. Before the lots had been drawn, the arbiters had walked over the land and Black had pointed out the intended boundary between North and South Glenormiston using certain landmarks. But Adam Steuart had instead drawn on the map of division the government surveyors' line for the original allotments. The difference was around 1000 acres in favour of the North – the lot drawn by Finlay. It was weeks before this confusion emerged, and when it did Black clung to it as to a lifeline. Clearly, the boundary would need to be settled before the process of division could continue.

In late March, Black visited Castle Toward. Finlay behaved courteously as they went over company affairs. Black, forewarned to expect rejection, could not bring himself to request a sale or exchange on Glenormiston – even though this was the whole purpose of his trip.[1] But he did raise the issue of the mistakenly mapped boundary line, asking that it be resubmitted to the arbiters. This Finlay flatly refused. He said that Black would not be talking about any 'mistake' if he had not lost the draw, and implied that he had concocted the confusion to gain for the South an extra slice of the more valuable property.

If the trip home was proving pointless to Black as far as its main purpose was concerned, to the family it was a joy. They spent time at Robert Leadbetter's place at Rhu on the Clyde estuary, with Grace's mother and their Leadbetter cousins. Niel went to see his poor mad brother, Walter, in his asylum, and took Ian and Steuart to visit their uncle Archie in Glasgow. Now that hopes of retaining Glenormiston were at an end, he suggested to Grace that he take a house for her and the boys in England. But Grace would not hear of his going back to Victoria alone

– which he would have to do to complete the division. So he booked the family's return passage on the SS *Great Britain*, departing in July 1868. Once underway, the voyage aboard Brunel's famous iron ship turned out to be a pleasure. Grace had space and comfort enough to give the boys their lessons every day in their cabin, and the family spent two hours every afternoon walking on deck. The respite was welcome. But on landing at Williamstown, Black was greeted with news that Finlay had hired no fewer than four of the best counsel in the colony to secure at law all the land to the north of the disputed boundary line. Black responded by serving a writ.

Thus began a bitter and protracted battle which, to Black, represented far more than a contest over the balance of land on Glenormiston. He saw it as a defence of his reputation against imputations of conduct and motives 'dishonourable in the highest degree, such as should disqualify me, if true, for the society of gentlemen or Men of Honour'.[2] Hence the volume of sworn affidavits, acreage calculations and comparative estate evaluations in *Black v Finlay* filled endless files and many lawyers' pockets. Black was obsessive to the point of neurosis about the dispute, writing screeds of self-vindication to Gladstone and employing clerks and assessors to produce a confetti of information. Even Walter, Black's nephew and a witness in his favour, was bemused: the amount of land involved – especially as it shrank when resurveyed – did not seem worth all this expense and ill-feeling. Claud Farie tried to get Black to rein himself in and come to terms with Finlay. But to Black any compromise would be tantamount to admitting the truth of Finlay's accusations. Given that they supported him, he could not comprehend Farie's and Gladstone's entreaties to reconcile, while Black's inflexibility and excess of wounded pride seemed to them quixotic and bad form.

In November 1868, Alex Finlay arrived back in the colony. Black's legal counsel persuaded him, after all, to submit the boundary line to arbitration. There were still many hitches: Black found it impossible to drop the question of the 'mistake', since to him the whole problem was that Finlay had impugned his honour by saying he had concocted the 'mistake'. On his side, Finlay refused to accept that any local landowner or member of the Legislative Council could act as an arbiter in neutral fashion. But finally a cast of characters, dates, times and procedures were set.

The two alternative boundary lines, marked red and blue respectively on a map, were staked out on the ground, and on 22 December, everyone, including the government surveyor, arbiters, witnesses and Finlays father and son, tramped up and down and viewed the latest calculations and the position of roads, woolshed, water points and possible sites for a new house. The witnesses and the surveyor believed the blue line – the boundary Black had identified at the earlier valuation, not the one drawn on the map by Adam Steuart allocating more land to the North – to be fairer. But Finlay dissented, and Walter Clark, his arbiter, complained angrily that none of the witnesses could be believed as they were all Black's men. This was absurd: who could know the terrain better than those connected to Niel Black & Company, or even know it at all? At the lawyers' offices in Melbourne on 31 December, final evidence for the adjudication was heard. The damp squib of a resolution, given in January, was to split the difference, adding half the contested land to the South. Black was content, for the decision showed that the dispute was real, not a mistake he had invented.

By this time, the Black family was getting ready to leave Glenormiston. In November, they had held a farewell ball for 60 guests. 'Dancing was kept up till half four in the morning, many of those present had come 40, some 80, miles distant. Our health was proposed after supper, coupled with regret at our loss.'[3] In the New Year, Black leased a property, Moorabbin House at Brighton, which was by now accessible by train from Melbourne. It was a handsome mansion, close to the sea with a fine view over Port Phillip Bay. There were 22 acres of grounds, its rooms were spacious and well furnished, and Grace liked it.[4] The family did not move in until late March 1869 because Black could not leave Glenormiston until the divisions of company stock and assets were complete. Walter Black and other ex-company, now his own, employees moved into an empty farmstead on South Glenormiston.

The estate was renamed Mount Noorat. For a while, Niel Black tried to see the positive side of the hand he had been dealt. The boys gained from Melbourne schooling and socialising. The summer of 1868–69 was very dry, 'ruin to a great number' but a bonanza for those in more drought-proof land. The superior quality of grazing on Mount Noorat began to show itself. Black had always thought the South good, but because the homestead purchase was on the North, that had been more developed. He now instructed John Smith, his manager, to start on improvements, and went down to supervise from time to time. He stayed at the Mount Noorat farmstead and tried to accommodate himself to the Finlays' usurpation of his house and social position. Since he wanted his boys to grow up knowing about land and stock, he took the family down for the holidays, and they all enjoyed country life.

Alex Finlay's continued presence in the colony was, however, like salt in a wound. Everything about the final division – the distribution of the purebred stock, what to do about the furniture, the date of Black's last salary cheque – was made the subject of suspicion or dispute, with Farie trying to arbitrate.[5] Finlay wrote to Gladstone suggesting that Black's management of The Sisters on his behalf was neglectful. And Black, whose displacement to Melbourne made him vulnerable, had to defend himself against Gladstone's queries. 'You will hear of no end of bad management of your property. You will tell me this will have no effect on you and that you will treat it with the contempt it merits and I believe this to be true, but yet it is tolerated. This is exactly what the public does. No doubt the feeling is widespread that Finlay's conduct and accusations against me has been bad and unjustifiable. This is openly said behind his back. Nevertheless his acquaintance as a man of good position at home is sought and even coveted by many.'[6]

That the Finlays imputed 'malversation' to Black – behaving corruptly in a position of trust – was recorded by a journalist, Henry Hyndman, a college friend of the young Finlays visiting Victoria, who went to stay at Glenormiston.[7] Farie wrote to Gladstone that Finlay did 'all in his power to blacken Black's character not only in your eyes, but with the people here, and so far as I can understand matters, without a shadow of reason'.[8] So Black had grounds for being put out, even if he overreacted. Stories against the Finlays' 'Scotch agent', described as 'a wily old highland shepherd', were repeated to guests around the dining table over which he and Grace had presided. When Black heard of such things he was enraged. Easily able to cope with the acrimony of the land sale, the bear pit of politics, even the meanest land shark or anti-squatter demagogue, he could not let Finlay's slights slide off him. On the contrary, he allowed them to prey on him to a damaging extent. He was like a bull with a wound that never healed, easily angered and occasionally vicious.

Then something truly disastrous happened. Black's nephew Walter was killed. On 16 September 1869, on his way to a cattle sale at Skipton, 38-year-old Walter jumped out of a runaway buggy and mortally fractured his skull. The news came to his uncle by telegram, 'passing through my head like a bullet from a gun'.

This was the first in a series of tragedies which descended on Black over the next two years, causing him deep distress and landing him with major responsibilities. In their different ways, these involved trying to keep the victims' assets out of the hands of lawyers, banks, the Master in Lunacy, the Curator of Intestate Estates and other hovering vampires. In the case of Walter, not only was there profound grief, but his nephew's demise also sent Black's own plans for the future crashing. Walter would have been the guardian of his boys and Grace's right hand in the case of Niel's own death. Alternatively, Walter would have managed Mount Noorat for him, and The Sisters for Gladstone, should Niel decide to take the family home. Now he had to sort out Walter's affairs, dispose of his Boort interests, and secure his own sons' future without Walter's aid. And he had to shoulder alone the problem of Archie.

On Niel's return to Victoria in 1868, Walter told him that he feared his brother was following their father into madness. Archie's behaviour was increasingly erratic. He spent fantastic sums of money he did not have on land he did not need. But Archie's doctor talked only of maladies of 'the nervous system', as if the patient was subject to anxiety but not insanity. Niel held on to the idea that his nephew would recover if he could get away to New Zealand or Scotland for a change of scene. This was a diagnosis of wishful thinking, encouraged by Archie's spells of kindness, concern, and 'perfect reason'. But there were other times, of hallucinations, manias, delusions, disjointed speech, and bouts of 'extreme irritability' verging on violence. Archie believed that a league of Freemasons in Camperdown were poisoning his cattle's drinking water, laming his horses, and generally conspiring in his downfall.[9] Unexpectedly, Niel found himself removed from the rank of villain and cast as Archie's friend and helper. In the glow of Archie's altered behaviour towards him, Niel shed his own grudges against his nephew and tried to sort out his affairs.

By the time of Walter's fatal accident, Archie's condition had deteriorated to the point where it seemed likely that his Gnotuk property would go under.[10] All his uncle's efforts to convince Archie to put his estate into a trust failed: he refused to sign the deed. He had done well with his fat stock in the drought of 1868, but in 1869 he had a disastrous season. Bushfires ravaged his grazing, many bullocks burned to death and £500 worth of fencing was destroyed, all of which inflamed his anxieties and added to his debts.[11] When the telegram arrived informing him of Walter's death, 'initially his grief was irrepressible and agonising to behold, but suddenly he started up, saying it is untrue'. He was taken to Melbourne for the funeral by Daniel and Jane Mackinnon, but the doctor advised that he not attend as 'the incessant repetition of sympathy might end in confirmed lunacy'.[12] Niel felt bound to tell the whole unadorned story to Archie's mother, Jessie, because – not having been previously fully informed of Archie's state of mind – she did not understand why Niel was handling Walter's affairs, nor why he was trying to get Archie's property into trust. Her complaints about Black's management of her sons' affairs would have tested anyone's goodwill. But he made allowances, recognising her agony at losing one son to death and another to madness, thousands of miles away.

At the end of December 1869, Black received an offer from Gladstone. Gladstone knew that Black had originally hoped to own both ends of Glenormiston by buying the other after the division. So to realise his own profits and compensate Black for his disappointment, he offered to sell him The Sisters. The price was high, £60 000. But Black leapt at it, accepting enthusiastically by the return mail. But when Gladstone's two eldest sons found out about their father's offer, they objected strongly. Their opposition implies that they did not share their father's confidence in his partner. Neither wished to go to Australia as a proprietor, so owning a run there required a manager. Black's management was being criticised by the Finlays, and the young Gladstones were friends of the young Finlays. So Finlay influence could be detected in their demand that their father withdraw his offer.[13] They probably anticipated giving The Sisters to the Finlays to manage, even selling it to them. After all, the Finlays had already tried several times to oust Black from TS Gladstone's favour and service.[14] Steuart Gladstone had found Black irksome on his 1864 visit, and maybe he and his older brother Robert, Archie's good friend, believed the story – planted by Archie in the Finlay consciousness – that Black feathered his nest at his partners' expense. This at least was what Steuart told Henry Hyndman, the journalist friend he shared with Campbell Finlay.[15] Whatever reasons the sons gave for wanting to keep The Sisters, their father now appealed to Black to withdraw from the deal, if he could do so 'willingly and cheerfully'.[16]

If there was one thing Black did not want, it was for The Sisters to end up with the Finlays. That area of the Western District had been opened up, settled and improved by Black on behalf of Niel Black & Company. If he now lost The Sisters to the Finlays, they would outclass him in the district, and he, Niel Black, the pioneer, would become a nobody there. These were fears he kept to himself at the time but expressed later on.[17] His place on the shire council, his presidency of the Terang Mechanics Institute, his chieftaincy of the Western Caledonian Society – all would be at risk. Stuck in Melbourne, it was already hard for him to attend shire council meetings and keep a finger in district pies. If the young Gladstones wanted to own land in Victoria as an investment, why did they have to own that particular run? It had no special meaning to any of them. Surely they could buy – he would willingly help them buy – another property than the one they all knew he wanted so badly.

So Black put pressure on Gladstone. No, he would not let him go back on his word. He had banked on the deal to secure his own sons' future. It was not a question of money, but of the insecurity into which he and his family had been plunged by Walter's death. Despite his and Gladstone's long relationship, he would not withdraw in order to oblige his sons. This was regarded at home, even by Robert Leadbetter, as somewhat shocking, and not reflecting well on his brother-in-law.[18] There was a qualm that this was not gentlemanly behaviour.

While The Sisters' fate hung in the balance, more deaths intervened. In March 1870, it was Black's sad duty to send bad news to Gladstone. 'The soil on Walter's grave was not yet green when I sent you the news of John Buys' death.' (Buys had been Black's accountant and map-maker for many years and had contributed much to the company.) 'Now it is my painful task to make known to you the death of Robert C Gladstone, your nephew, who died at the village of Terang on Saturday 15th March at 3.30 a.m. from the effects of a fall from his horse.' This Robert was another – very promising – 'College of Squatters' entrant, who had been working at The Sisters. The fall itself was minor: Robert had toppled sideways when the horse shied. He had then stood in front of the animal, holding the reins, but lost his balance when the horse shot forward, trampling him.[19] Robert Gladstone's funeral in Terang, at which Alex Finlay and Niel Black were the pallbearers, 'he at the feet, I at the head', was attended by a large crowd: Robert had been popular on the station.

This sad occasion was nearly the last time Black and Finlay spoke. A few weeks later, after a year buying and selling various properties, Finlay tired of the Antipodes and left the colony for good. His son Campbell was installed at Glenormiston and would henceforth be in charge. Finlay had by now accepted that the southern end of Glenormiston was as valuable as the north, if not more so. Consequently, Farie suggested that it would be gracious of him to apologise to Black for accusing him of trying to fix the division in his favour and for tarnishing his name. Finlay refused. He would not admit to traducing Black, although he would have liked to reconcile. But this Black had no stomach for. On the contrary, he went down to the ship on which Finlay was embarking to tell him to his face, on deck, in the presence of Campbell and anyone else listening, that in the light of Finlay's repeated and unrepented imputations of dishonourable conduct on Black's part, he would henceforth cease to know him. News of this insult to the laird of Toward spread to Scotland, and was reported in detail to Gladstone by Black himself.[20] The gesture was ignored by Gladstone, but his son Steuart disdained it and wrote to Black accordingly.[21] Black was impervious. His antagonism towards the Finlays had become hard-wired.

As time went on, everyone – except the unflinchingly loyal Grace – wanted him to end the feud. Daniel Mackinnon thought that his indulgence in it risked unsettling his senses, and told him to forgive and forget, as a good Christian should – but to no avail.[22] Finlay's second son, Alec, who had played no role in the dispute, joined Campbell at Glenormiston in the mid-1870s, and wanted to be on good terms with Black. Relations in the neighbourhood generally would have been eased by a rapprochement. But Black's demand for an unqualified apology was rejected.[23] Only after Niel's death did his son AJ Black (Ian) negotiate an end to the Western District's most notorious social cold war.

───────

As 1870 drew on, Niel Black awaited Gladstone's decision over whether his mentor would defy his older sons and renew his offer to Black of The Sisters, which in turn awaited the visit to the colony of Gladstone's youngest son, John. The young man was entertained at Moorabbin House and stayed with Black at the Mount Noorat farmstead. But when the Honourable Member was summoned to Melbourne on parliamentary business, John went to Glenormiston to stay with the Finlays and there remained. Black offered to assist him in the purchase of an alternative run to The Sisters on behalf of the Gladstone family. Many squatters had recently gone bankrupt, ruined by drought, debt and the low price of wool, and the market was flush with properties. But John was not interested in inspecting any, which reinforced Black's suspicion that he was a stooge for Finlay takeover plans.

After John went home in 1871, his father finally decided to sell The Sisters to Black. Black paid £30000 up front and the other half on mortgage at 5 per cent; the price was well above what Gladstone would have received from any other buyer at the time.[24] Occasionally later on, Gladstone demurred about this deal. Black was slow to repay him the capital, and Gladstone's income from the interest on the £30000 loan and the Moonee

Ponds farms, his residual assets from the company division, fell short of the stories of high returns and growing wealth – including of Black's – he kept hearing from Australia. But Black justified himself calmly, replying that easily made fortunes were rare and usually exaggerated and that even the greatest could fail – which was not uncommon. The monthly letters went back and forth between them as regular as clockwork, and whatever awkwardness there had been over the deal did not spoil their relationship. Black often expressed appreciation that despite the severe pressure exerted on Gladstone's trust in him, his partner had held faith and refused to believe Black's detractors.

In August 1870 came another blow: the death of Claud Farie. Farie had been a president of the Melbourne Club, active in the Turf Club, a leading light of colonial society. At the time of his death, he was both Sheriff and Inspector-General of Penal Establishments, but his stipend barely covered his expenses. 'He lived and died a popular man, but could not make money', wrote Black.[25] The Bishop of Melbourne conducted the funeral, but the orphaned family were almost destitute. The will was dated 1847, and of six trustees, the only one still living was Black. When Farie lay dying, Black sent a message to his oldest friend in the colony to reassure him that he would provide a home for his four about-to-be-orphaned children.

Black genuinely grieved for Farie. Claud was 12 years his junior, a different mettle of person from a different background, but they had arrived within weeks of each other and set out together on the colonial adventure. Squatting was not Farie's métier, but the two had always stood by each other. 'He was the finest, purest feather in my wings, and his death will make my flight dull and heavy for my short remainder of time', wrote Black. Now he found himself responsible for sorting out Farie's affairs as well as taking in the children. The presence at Moorabbin House of the two Farie girls, Jane and Kate, aged 21 and 19, quickly became permanent; the boys went off to boarding school and later to Scotland.

In November, while Black was still coping with the problems thrown up by Farie's death, his brother Archie wrote from Glasgow saying that his remaining days were few. Archie left everything he had to Niel – although of all his relatives, Niel least needed the £8000 in his estate. This doughty old Scot, whose education was far sketchier than Niel's and who would never have graced a Gladstone drawing room, continued to value their fraternal closeness despite the physical and social gulf that had opened between them down the years.

Over the 1870 Christmas holidays, the Black family stayed as usual at the Mount Noorat farmstead. But their celebrations were marred: Niel became so ill with bronchitis that his own life was in danger when news came in early January of Archie's death. However, whatever sadness he felt about the loss of his brother was overwhelmed by the crisis now engulfing the other Archie, his 41-year-old nephew.

———•◆•———

During 1870, Archie's manic behaviour had so disquieted Daniel Mackinnon that he had been pushing Black to take action to protect Archie's wife and five children – all aged under seven with one a babe-in-arms. Niel was loath to do anything drastic: he did not think Archie a dangerous lunatic. Besides, what action could he take? There was no way without Archie's agreement of taking away the management of his property unless he was declared insane. And Niel did not want Gnotuk to fall into the hands of officials. When he was a small boy, that had happened to his father's estate. He had grown up listening to his mother fight to prevent every penny of her sons' inheritance being lost to lawyers and unscrupulous trustees. Throughout 1870, he was criticised by his friends for failing to intervene in Archie's affairs, and by Jessie writing from Scotland accusing him of too much intervention in Archie's affairs. She thought Niel was trying to get his hands on Gnotuk for himself.

A turning point in Archie's deteriorating condition came in October 1870. Daniel Curdie wrote to Niel about 'the melancholy affair' he had heard on the Camperdown grapevine.[26] Archie had got into a raging temper and expelled two maids from his home at Gnotuk. He then seized Marion and 'shook her most violently', making her fear for her life. When a friend was visiting Archie, Marion slipped out in the dark with her baby and crawled to a nearby cottage. She was taken in by the postmaster's wife, Mrs Duigan, from where Mrs Mackinnon fetched her and the baby to stay at Marida Yallock. The Mackinnons were to bear the brunt of the Archie crisis over the coming months.

The question of how to proceed became critical. Black saw his own and Archie's lawyers in Melbourne and was in daily contact with Mackinnon. He agonised, as he wrote to Jessie: 'Bundles of letters came to me urging me to take immediate steps to place the persons and property under the protection of the Court. I stated the case to lawyers and barristers who are ready enough to take action on the petition of his wife, but to my dismay I find that once in Court, the law takes possession, and his person and property is handed over to the Master in Lunacy.' Before this official could take action, a trial would take place. 'Archie can get any number of lawyers ready to defend his case, and his poor wife must prove that he is unfit to manage his own affairs.'[27] Violent behaviour towards one's wife was not a symptom of lunacy in the eyes of the law, so if Archie refused to cooperate they might lose. The only alternative course of action was to have Archie declared a lunatic, which would require two doctors' certificates. Marion held back from the fatal step, persuaded by Archie to return home to her children once more. 'I dread lest some fatal catastrophe takes place', Black wrote.[28]

In late December, Marion again fled from Gnotuk to the Mackinnons with the baby, leaving the four other children with Archie. Niel was already unwell, and although he went over to Gnotuk, he and Mackinnon did not go up to the house, because Archie had threatened to shoot any intruders who came to remove his children. When Niel returned to Mount Noorat, he took to his bed and became dangerously ill. Finally, when news came that the children ran wild at Gnotuk with nothing to eat, Mackinnon persuaded Marion to sign the petition. 'Archie was committed before Mr Mackinnon and Mr Pickles, on two doctors' certificates', Grace wrote to Archie's family in Scotland. 'Mr Mackinnon felt exceedingly at having anything to do with depriving him of his liberty. He saw it could not be avoided but that did not make it any less painful. Poor Archie took it very quietly, he was sent down in a private coach to the Asylum. He has been very quiet and in good spirits since, always saying that he will be at liberty again in a few days.' By this time, Grace was also at Marida Yallock. At the rough and ready farmstead, Niel had been exposed to draughts and extremes of temperature, so the Mackinnons had insisted that the whole Black family decamp to their homestead. 'We got your uncle over here in a close carriage and he is now, I am thankful to say, very much better', she reported.[29]

When Niel returned to Melbourne in February 1871, he succeeded in persuading the Master in Lunacy to let him manage Archie's property on behalf of his wife, family and the court for the time being. All Black's applications and presentations around government offices to gain permission to remain in charge paid off. He personally met the expenses of putting cattle on the Gnotuk property, employing stockmen and paying interest on Archie's debts, thereby keeping the property productive and solvent until things were resolved. For these efforts, no-one gave him much credit – certainly not his sister-in-law Jessie, who wrote with unstinting reproach. The whole saga, and the accompanying distrust – which he blamed on the cloud in which Archie and Finlay had jointly enveloped his reputation in Scotland as much as in Victoria – debilitated him physically and mentally. But at least Archie seemed calmer.

Black's main worry was that, at a time when the market was depressed, he might be forced to put Gnotuk up for auction to clear Archie's £30000 debt. He could not bear to see Archie's superb 7770 acres fetch only £3 each, well below their value. Black would have bought Gnotuk himself at £4 an acre, but he could not do so without mortgaging his own property, and this would force the sale of that too, should he die himself in the near future. Since his health seemed so fragile, he did not want to expose his family to such a risk. But in the end he decided to go ahead. He persuaded his bank to advance him the money to purchase the property on his own security, with the idea of paying off Archie's debts and holding on for long enough to get it in better shape and let the market recover. It would then be resold and the reversion go to Archie's wife, children and mother. No sooner had he put this strategy in place, however, than events overtook him.

Archie had been moved to the Cremorne Private Asylum in Richmond. There he stayed, refusing to sign a deed of trust or anything at all. By now Niel accepted that his nephew would not recover, but he felt Archie would get better treatment back in Scotland. He and Grace were frequent visitors, as was Jane Mackinnon. Marion could not visit – she was again pregnant. In early July she had another baby, a fifth son and sixth child. But Archie's physical condition now began to deteriorate. In August 1871 he had a heart attack. 'I was called down hurriedly to see him but after the first attack, he gradually began to recover from day to day, and we lost all apprehension of immediate danger. His delusions became less frequent and he took his food without any expression of poison being mixed with it as he used to do', Black wrote to his brother-in-law.

On Monday 28 August, at 9 am, Archie had another heart attack. 'His doctor informed me that he had two eggs, toast and tea to breakfast which he took with relish. He then took up his Newspaper, reading and making comments on the Tichborne case, when all of a sudden he made a loud moan and never spoke again.'[30] Jane Mackinnon came up with Marion to Melbourne, and on Thursday 31 August, at a small private funeral, Archie was buried in the same grave as Walter. Daniel Mackinnon wrote to Mrs Black in Scotland: 'No young man had a brighter prospect before him but there was a cloud overshadowing his mind for many years back which marred these hopes and rendered his life gradually more unhappy.'[31] But, his dear friend believed, since God had chosen to end Archie's troubles, he now enjoyed relief.

Since Archie had made no will, his property should have been taken up by the Curator of Intestate Estates and the Master in Equity. Niel Black fought off this scenario by having Marion petition to be put in charge, with the freehold to be sold under the authority of the Supreme Court. By the time the legal and administrative arrangements had been struggled through, the price of wool had risen dramatically, and with it the value of the Gnotuk property. In December 1872, it went up for auction. There was strong competition, and the 7770 acres that Black had feared would go for £3 an acre 18 months before fetched an extraordinary £9 5s per acre. With the cattle and other assets, the estate raised £75 300, enough to pay off the debts and provide a very substantial sum of £45 300 for Marion and her children.[32] Niel, in part fortuitously, had managed the business superbly.

Black himself was now feeling more robust. The long spell of catastrophe was at an end. Walter's, Archie's and Farie's estates were sorted. Marion and her brood were going home to Scotland. And he had reached a decision of his own. He would build a homestead at Mount Noorat and cast his lot permanently for the colony.

Chapter Twelve

'THE CROWNING FOLLY OF MY LIFE'

WHEN ARCHIE DIED in August 1871, Niel Black was 67 years old. The strains of the previous few years had damaged both his health and his peace of mind. His temper was more inflammatory, worsened by his strangulated stomach, for which he daily consumed quantities of patent medicines, and his unreliable humour and obsession with the Finlays were hard on his family and friends. 'We get queer and crotchety when we get old', he had once reflected to his brother Archie. Twelve years in the Upper House of the Victorian Parliament had expanded his self-importance, and he defended its bristling ramparts more readily. His bark was worse than his bite, at least within the family circle where Grace coped admirably. She and the Farie girls enjoyed their respites at Moorabbin House when the old bear was uncaged and went to Mount Noorat to play the pastoralist – which he often did for weeks at a time. He never took to town life, his heart ever with his stock, his men and his 'place', some part of which was always under improvement.

The bronchial illness which had felled him at the draughty Mount Noorat farmstead in early 1871 convinced him to build a weather-proof house as a replacement, and he commissioned the architect Charles Webb to design him a small but solid and elegant manager's 'cottage'. In March 1872, he supervised the laying of its foundation at the base of The Hill. At the same time he selected a site for a future residence on a grander scale, to which he would move his family and reassume the role of country proprietor; 'but whether it is to be built upon in my day is a problem I cannot solve at present'. He was still ambivalent about competing with his earlier creation. 'Glenormiston has never yet been surpassed in the colony. The English trees and shrubs are now full grown for greater effect, but my new house will command a far more extensive view, of a country abounding with hills and lakes with a mountain range in the distance'.[1] This mountain range featured more strongly in his mind than in the visible landscape: only on a good day could distant peaks towards the north be glimpsed. However, such adornments to the future house's prospect would impress his Scottish in-laws.

The cottage was completed in early 1873. He then began to address more seriously the question of whether to go ahead with a homestead to its north, with stables, cellars, outbuildings, avenues, gardens and grounds. He had the area flattened and planted with trees in preparation. To avoid incurring further debt, he would use his brother Archie's bequest of £8000 to pay for the house. Grace was unsure about the project, fearing that he would not live to occupy it. But he was convinced that he must leave his sons a proper country home, equivalent in style and ambiance to those of other leading district families. On maturity, Ian, Steuart and young Niel must assume the responsibilities of managing the estate, and thereby contribute to the colony's development. Many times he wrote that he did not want them leading a pampered city-bound existence off income derived from his assets. Grace was determined to educate the boys in England – if not at school, certainly at university – as many well-off squatters now did. Black did not want them to return to Victoria as idlers.

'I went last week to the Caledonian Games and Warrnambool Races where I saw the young Australians coming out very strong, the first born of my comperes whose Fathers in many instances have left fine estates to their families', he wrote to his brother-in-law. 'It grieved me to see the fast, flash doings of many who completed their Oxford and Cambridge education, came out here and having nothing to do, go in for horse racing and fast doings. There were no fewer than a dozen four-in-hands driving about and a brace of six-in-hands showing off, driven chiefly by young men from the universities at home. I can't help thinking, will my boys take to such work?'[2]

In March 1873, the lease on Moorabbin House expired, and the family, with their Farie guests and Claud Hamilton – yet another young Gladstone connection sent out into Black's tutelage – moved to D'Estaville in Kew.[3] This imposing house belonged to Chief Justice Stawell who had gone home on leave. Black waxed lyrical about the 'beautiful place, garden and grounds surpassing everything I have seen in the colony ... Water laid on to every room, even to hoses in the garden ... 40 acres, clean, pure and healthy. But I am heartily sick of being kicked about in this way.'[4] The high prices being fetched for sheep and cattle rekindled his interest in his prospective new homestead. 'Money is as plentiful as mosquitoes among the "shepherd kings"', he wrote. But he did not get carried away. The high prices of wool and meat 'create a feeling of prosperity amongst our monied class closely bordering on madness. I even dread that the prevailing mania may infect myself and induce me to erect a more expensive building than will be suitable for the estate under more adverse circumstances, which I fancy I see looming.'[5] When prices rose very high, Black anticipated bubbles and crashes.

By early 1874, he was having second thoughts about building the house. He had had a good year in terms of prices, but he found himself with little cash surplus. His estate increased in value but did not bring in a high annual yield. Gladstone kept repeating stories circulating at home about Australian wealth, with more than a hint that, since the returns on his residuals from the company division were unimpressive, he was being left out. Black derided such stories as 'bounce'. He would never submit to the lure of unsound speculation, and if this was what the Gladstones wanted, it would not be pursued through him. As a general rule, he took a dim view of people who invested in the expectation of excessively high profits, as such windfalls were normally based on the ruin of someone else – something he believed was illegitimate as a business aim.[6] He was irritated when Gladstone was fed, and repeated, such stories, because they came from people whose business acumen was less than his own and who enjoyed capering about on self-erected pedestals, lauding their financial success. No doubt land would go on increasing in value, 'as it has done in the mother country, but here we are subject to fluctuations of a sudden and almost revolutionary kind. A tide of destruction sweeps over the land and sudden fortunes are made on the remains of those who have fallen victim to overwhelming ambition'.[7] Tales of easy profits, he insisted, were exaggerated. Yes, every now and again someone might make a fortune, but many crashed. 'But for the debt I owe you without reducing it one farthing for the last few years, it would be hard for you to believe that I am unable to save any money', he told Gladstone – a refrain of cash shortage his partner had been hearing for 25 years. 'The profits are barely equal to the expenditures.'[8] And to prove it, Black sent off his accounts. By now so many doubts had been sown about his integrity that he was not fully believed.

The new threat he feared was of heavy taxation on big land-owners, against whom popular attacks in the press and Legislative Assembly were as strong as ever. With this new tax looming, he did not think it made sense to lay out large sums on building a new house. The situation was too volatile, labour too scarce and expensive. In some contexts – to improve the land or its stock – his purse was wide open, but in others it was well sealed. 'I am anxious to build for the benefit of my wife and family but I fear to encumber the estate for such a purpose. It is more prudent to go on as I am and diminish my debt, rather than increase it.'[9]

Black thought that when the next goal had been reached, that would be the time to stop – to build, go home, take his ease, his debts paid up. But whenever he reached one goal, another presented itself. The new goal he now set himself was to build up his NB herd so that its natural increase would keep his land stocked without the need to purchase further store cattle. In this, his final decade, his energies were no longer consumed by 'the battle for the lands' but by 'the battle for the bulls'.

Niel Black had intended from the first to develop a fine Short-horn herd, even though at the outset of pastoral life in the Port Phillip District there was no market for meat. Only wool, and later tallow, could survive the long voyage home.

His first request to Gladstone to send him 'two or three Pure-Bred Durham Bulls of first rate quality' came in May 1840. Two were sent in 1841, the first of many imports. Black kept immaculate stud records, culled his stock from the start and was the first Australian herdsman to spay his cows routinely.[10] But while he was in Scotland during the 1850s, the purebred stock deteriorated under Archie's management. Although Niel soon put things back in order, a further setback occurred when, after drawing North Glenormiston as his share in the division of Niel Black & Company, Alex Finlay insisted that for a year in advance of the final separation of the company's assets, 'no animal should be removed from one part of the station to another'. As the heifer paddock with all the best young cattle was on North Glenormiston, Finlay 'took away about 400 of the cream of the herd' and refused to sell any of them to Black or Gladstone.[11] Black was forced to accept in numbers of stock what he lost in quality. But within no time, he was again importing bulls and improving his herd.

In the late 1860s, John Mickle, a squatter and stockbreeder, went home to Britain. Mickle replaced Gladstone as Black's agent in the purchase and despatch of bulls with gloriously grandiose names to Melbourne. 'I know you will be anxious to hear how Prince Christian is getting on', Black wrote Mickle in August 1871. 'The little Bull has not grown much, though head and ears in rye grass and clover ever since he came here. He is hardly big enough to reach up ... [unreadable]. Some of the heifers in the same paddock are beginning to show in calf, thus proving that he did duty somehow.'[12] Within a few months, Black was less enthusiastic. 'I never was so much disappointed in any animal. He has not grown, he yet looks an old, odd fossil, a sort of curiosity. I have made up my mind that he is not fit to be head of the harem of my pure cows, so I ask you the great favour of sending one or two bulls to take his place. My only instruction is that there is nothing in England too good for my herd.' He was worried about the competition: 'Robertson Colac and Finlay Glenormiston is striving hard to come up to the NB brand.'[13]

Black was naturally goaded by the thought of the Finlays on his heels, but William Robertson and his sons, at their fine estate at The Hill, north of Colac, were the real competition. They had taken over Foster Fyans' herd – hence their FF brand – and replenished it with imported bulls and local bovine dignitaries of exceptional provenance. Black and William Robertson, a man who 'began life as a Hawker carrying a pack on his back, and before his death, entertained the Duke of Edinburgh',[14] had a cagey respect for one another. Robertson referred to Black as 'that old serpent',[15] and both he and Black would have happily used any legitimate means to steal a march on the other over land, stock or reputation. Robertson, with his 40 000-acre estate, a herd to die for, and four married sons each with his own homestead, had the edge in spectacle and repute. The sons were excellent organisers and born salesmen.

However, Black did not approve of 'over-fed animals got up for exhibition in the show yards' – which was decidedly the Robertson approach. At market, Black's fat cattle regularly attained the highest average prices, and on these grounds, he boasted that his was the premier herd in the southern hemisphere – and some observers agreed.[16] Even without the hyperbole, his herd of red Shorthorns was widely celebrated for purity of blood, size, symmetry and strength of constitution.[17] These animals, and those of other well-known Victorian breeders, were sought by graziers establishing herds in Queensland and the Northern Territory. In the early 1870s, this led to an unprecedented boom in Western District Shorthorns, in which competition became steely.[18]

For his herd's prowess Black owed a great deal to Mickle's choice of 'sires of high lineage'. In 1872, Mickle obliged Black by despatching two of the best bulls he could find: Bedesman and King of the Day. They arrived in November, and Black had insufficient superlatives to describe King of the Day, who became for a while his favourite creature on earth. 'What a free, light step he has, just like a Blood horse, and Countenance as bland as that of a high born Lady.'[19] This prancing life was unexpectedly threatened. In June 1872, an outbreak of foot-and-mouth disease, then raging in Britain, showed up in the neighbourhood of an imported bull. Charles Gavan Duffy was Chief Secretary at the time. Black wrote to Gladstone: 'A Commission was appointed by Duffy, who at once destroyed the infected animals and placed a cordon of Police round the infected district. Every animal imported was to be destroyed on entering the Bay.' Fortunately for King of the Day, 'Duffy went out of office, and the present Chief Secretary [JG Francis] asked me to suggest a new committee that he would appoint. This has been done and I think we will hear no more of their wild raving.'[20] One of Black's bulls had already fallen under the Duffy axe, and he was determined to avoid such a fate for Bedesman and King of the Day, now landed at Sandridge. But only with great difficulty did he extract them from the clutches of the Chief Inspector of Stock.

The Honourable Member would have been happy to see his bulls quarantined at Sandridge, he told the Legislative Council on 15 October 1872, if the accommodation provided was 'suitable'. But it was entirely unfit. He offered to convey the bulls in a covered railway truck to his own place – Moorabbin House – where he could sequester them. But this was objected to, because 'to carry the animals such a distance along the railway would create too great a danger of contagion'. He then offered to have the bulls placed on board a small steamer, landed at Brighton, and escorted up the beach to his grounds. This too was refused. Instead, they were taken in charge by the Chief Inspector of Stock, and with far less security walked through the open streets to a yard near the Yarra. Here 'the wooden partitions between the animals were so weak that the man in charge was frightened lest they tear down the boards and gore each other to death'. After 40 days, the Chief Inspector – who must have had his fill of Black's protests – released the animals to his care. At Moorabbin, under his own eye, they had the suburban luxury they deserved, before going off to the wilds of Mount Noorat. Black's experiences were regaled to the Legislative Council with a view to having these evils repaired. Some Honourable Members ungraciously suggested that Black was wasting their time. Black retorted that as he now had on hand 'a six years' supply of imported stock, ... it was not to be supposed he was personally interested in the question he had raised'.[21] In fact, he still hoped to avoid a ban on stock importation. But in April 1873, such a law was passed.

Other more positive developments were having an effect on the livestock industry. A solution had finally been found to the longstanding problem of preserving meat so that it could reach home in a palatable condition – although not yet by a method that preserved the meat intact, only by making 'extract of beef' and sealing it in cans. There had been many experiments in the search to develop a 'dead meat trade' beyond pemmican, a substance fit only for armed forces' rations. Early efforts were bankrupted when the gold rush pushed cattle prices through the roof.[22] In the 1860s, the quest restarted. 'Efforts are being made to cure beef and mutton to bear the voyage home without tainting. Some has already been sent home in good condition, made into hams with melted tallow poured all over to exclude the air', Black wrote home in 1868.[23] 'I have sent a barrel of preserved meat to R Leadbetter for distribution among friends', he wrote to Gladstone.[24] But when the cask arrived and was opened, the stench put everyone to flight. 'It nearly put us out of the warehouse', Robert Leadbetter informed his brother-in-law. 'Nevertheless the clerks and partners took some home and I did also and had it boiled but as soon as the cover was off I had to send it away.'[25] Coating in tallow was clearly not the answer, and freezing with ammonia had led to 'the check of an explosion'.[26] Black backed many such experiments and bought shares in some of the companies.[27]

When success eventually came, he regarded his investments as well repaid by the increase in the price of stock. 'The Agents at Ballarat say that the preserving establishment has added 2 shillings a head to the price in that market throughout the season.'[28] The first cargo of frozen meat made it to London in February 1880. Black must have heartily celebrated the news.

———•◆•———

The fashion for Shorthorns reached its Victorian peak in the mid-1870s. The day Robertson Bros advertised their second large sale of purebred cattle, on 25 February 1875, the *Argus* commented: 'Given a form demonstrating excellence of blood, and an undoubted pedigree to back it and, these united in a shorthorn of the fashionable strain, we know of no combination that will so surely succeed in extracting golden acknowledgements of merit from the pockets of occupiers of land. Of late years shorthorns ... have gradually, like rare old wine and excessively large diamonds, been held for what are deemed by outsiders fancy prices.'

The animals were huge, and at the peak of their parade, their fashionable enormity was matched by fantastically extravagant prices. The annual Shorthorn sales initiated by the Robertsons, which included a champagne lunch for all comers, were a new kind of grand social occasion. The Robertsons held their sales at The Hill, and every breeder worth the name attended. At the March 1875 sale, Black had his manager John Smith keep an 'abstract' of the animals and prices: 265 Shorthorns and Herefords, some with pedigrees, some without, fetched £20 714.

Within no time, Black was planning his own sale. In May 1875, his stock agents, Eaglestone & Ettishank, expressed delight: 'The [NB] brand is so well-known that no doubt can exist as to the result.' The first small ad was inserted in the *Australasian* of 19 June. Pressure had to be exerted on Black to spend money on advertising 'throughout the colonies ... as done by Mr Robertson'.[29] Interest was widespread, pleasing the 'old serpent' enormously and confirming his boasts about his herd. A fulsome article appeared in the *Australasian* a month before the sale: 'The recently obtained average in the Ballarat market-yards of nearly £30 a head for 14 prime NB's [sic] has confirmed its claim to be regarded as the premier brand of the Australian colonies', the writer purred. There followed an account of Black's imported stock, purchases and herd improvements over 35 years. Star billing was given to the Earl of Waterloo, 'a dark red bull, very evenly and heavily fleshed', the last to be imported before the recent ban.[30]

A sale of this kind necessitated changes in the animals' management. Black's bulls, who had never previously seen a shed or been fed in any way other than by grazing, had to be put in stalls to make it possible to handle them. They instantly lost condition. Special yards had to be erected, as well as places where the visitors could view the stock. Black was far from happy about these preparations, but he had to follow the style of things laid down by the Robertsons. That was what people expected.

When the time came for the sale to take place, disaster struck. In 1875, the rains poured down even in the dry season, and as the day of the show – 18 November – drew nearer, the specially built yards at Mount Noorat resembled a mud bath. Worse, far worse, was a thunderbolt delivered to Black two days before the sale in the form of a letter from Robert McDougall, another Shorthorn breeder. McDougall had an old quarrel with Black, having in the past accused him of being a less than impartial judge of cattle where McDougall's beasts were concerned.[31] He now wrote that he had looked into the catalogue for Black's forthcoming sale and seen '*things*' there which, without a satisfactory explanation, would prevent him attending. He then painstakingly showed, citing herd books and his own recollection of studs he had visited in England, that the pedigree assigned to a roan bull called Montebello was in fact the pedigree of quite a different Montebello – a creature now residing in Prussia.[32]

Black was aghast. The bull had been bought for Niel Black & Company in May 1860 by Alex Finlay from a Mr Fawkes of Farnley Hall in Yorkshire as his best animal. In the correspondence, accounts and the bill of lading, it was named Montebello, but it had arrived without a written pedigree. *Coates's Herd Book*

– the cattle-breeders' bible – contained only two Montebellos for that year, so an assumption had been made by Eaglestone & Ettishank, with Black's tacit acceptance, as to which one it was. And the breeder of those two Montebellos was not Mr Fawkes of Farnley Hall. Since McDougall had waited till the last moment to deliver his blow, there was too little time before the sale for Black to find out what the truth was about the pedigree. Quite a number of the 400 animals up for auction were descended from the Montebello now labelled an 'imposter' by McDougall, an undesirable situation from everyone's point of view.

What to do? If the sale went ahead, Black might be accused of selling animals under a false prospectus. McDougall's qualms were bound to become public, and anyway the last thing that Niel Black would do was to risk his reputation as a breeder by allowing any suspicion to hover over his herd book. At ten thirty on the morning of the sale, he prepared to make an announcement. He would read out McDougall's letter voicing legitimate concerns, and he would also read out Gladstone's letter from 1860 describing the purchase of the bull from Mr Fawkes, and the bull's bill of lading. This would 'relieve ourselves of the responsibility of selling under a false pedigree'. Black had every confidence in his bull's bloodlines, and he knew that most breeders – including McDougall – would know that there was no attempt to deceive. There had to be an explanation, which in time would be revealed.

Then, at the last moment, he changed his mind. 'The weather was dreadful – it had rained all night the previous night. On our reaching the yards it was found necessary to let one of the pens escape to prevent suffocation or smothering in the sticky mess. After an anxious consultation it was decided that it would be impossible to carry out the sale to the end without destruction to numbers of the cattle. This being the case it was deemed unnecessary to raise the uncertain point as to the identity of the Bull.'[33] Black cancelled the sale, served the lunch, and offered to repay the expenses of those who had come from Melbourne. Since there had been no effort to keep McDougall's letter secret, it was widely whispered that something other than the weather was the real reason for the postponement. Buyers declared themselves incredulous that the sale could have been stopped for so 'trivial' a reason as the mud, but undoubtedly animals were at risk, especially as they were unused to being penned. The postponed sale became as notorious as McDougall could have wished, with news flashing by 'electric telegraph' from Camperdown that one of the largest, best attended and most widely anticipated cattle sales in Victorian history had been stopped in its tracks by its eccentric progenitor. There followed an outpouring of stories in the press and wildly embroidered rumours.

Black rushed to Melbourne to telegraph London to solve the mystery of his Montebello's exclusion from *Coates's Herd Book*, but breaks on the line meant it took over a month to get a reply. All this he explained in a letter to the *Australasian* published on 11 December. Although he insisted that the weather and the state of the yards were his sole reason for the postponement, it is hard to picture Black putting his purebred beasts under the hammer with a question mark hanging over their ancestry. In such a fix, stress to his purse or inconvenience to buyers from afar were his least consideration. In due course, the mystery was resolved. And when Montebello's proper pedigree was sent, it turned out to be as good as or better than the one wrongly attributed.

One major loss from all of this was the Earl of Waterloo. On 29 November he slipped and fell in the infamous mud. At home in Melbourne, Black received a telegram from Mount Noorat

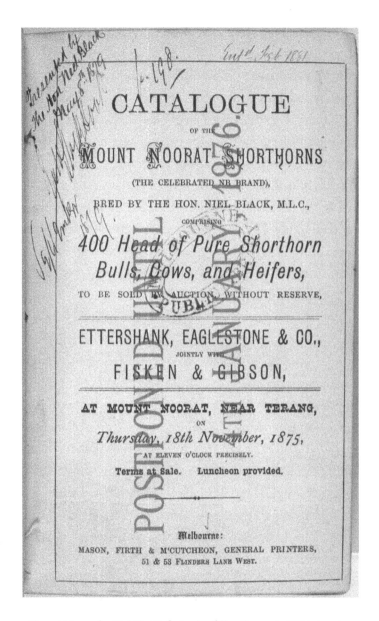

The catalogue for Niel Black's first sale of Shorthorns, in 1875, showing the last-minute postponement. The pedigree of a parent bull, Montebello, was challenged by another breeder, Robert McDougall.

YA 636.2 B56, State Library of Victoria

asking urgently for a veterinary surgeon to be despatched. This 'last surviving imported Bull is very ill and not likely to recover', he wrote to Gladstone. 'This Bull I bought three years ago for £500. So wonderful is the change in prices seen here I am sure I could have got £2000 for him a few days ago.'[34] The Earl of Waterloo did indeed die, and his passing was much lamented and reported in the press as a great loss to Black.

The postponed sale was readvertised for 4 January 1876, three days before the Robertson Bros' next sale at Colac, which annoyed them considerably. When the day came, all the expectations of the earlier sale were dashed: visitors were fewer, buyers sparse, and some animals went for no more than fat stock prices.[35] To an extent this was Black's choice: he did not put reserves on any lot or animal, and accepted whatever price they were knocked down for. At the end of January, Black wrote his usual monthly letter to Gladstone. He confessed himself deeply disappointed with the results of his sale, while the Robertsons had had a sensational success. A few months earlier, they had purchased the entire Mount Derrimut Shorthorn stud from Robert Morton, paying £27 000 for 37 animals,[36] and some of these champions had fetched an incredible 1000 guineas each.

Black felt understandably sore. The 'worst bustle I had in my life' had made a large hole in his pocket. He complained of his agents, who had conducted his sale poorly, and of the buyers from Queensland who would not come to Mount Noorat a second time. 'Everything was against me', he railed. 'I have only the overseer's place [to put people up in]. I could not ask persons from a distance to come to stay here – the accommodation in the neighbourhood is scant. The four Robertsons have each a large house and all are married to neighbours' daughters. I hear they had 150 Gentlemen staying with them for a week.'[37] And then of course there was the 'blunder committed at home in the neglect of having the Bull Montebello entered in the Herd Book'. He did not need to say whose fault that was: Finlay's. He admired the Robertsons for 'their very dashing enterprise. The fortune that was adverse to my interest was the flood tide that carried them on to a higher success.' Whatever his views about over-feeding, 'it is useless to attempt to compete with such animals. At the sale, people will get a long price for them.' The Robertsons' marketing, their showmanship, the fame of their pedigrees and the size of their bulls had triumphed. But despite all the pomp and circumstance, Black's cattle were still the best. 'I regard the butcher with his beam as the best judge, and there no-one has yet been my equal.'[38]

The following January, 1877, he held another Mount Noorat Shorthorn sale: they were annual until 1879, by which time the boom had peaked. He sent the 1877 catalogue to Mickle to illustrate the impact of the Earl of Waterloo on the quality of his herd, but was pessimistic: 'The reduced price obtained for wool has placed a damper on the courage and energy of breeders which will deter them from buying.' In fact the sale did well, realising £15 252 6s[39] – his best ever result. Still, he protested to Gladstone about laying out large sums on lunch, pavilions and 'huts' for visitors' accommodation. 'Such sales in my opinion is a most disgraceful affair but singly and alone I cannot put the system down … Just fancy 600 persons sitting to a sumptuous lunch with no end of champagne and ice, my former drunken cook taking his seat alongside my own boys and drinking champagne from out of tumblers. Robertson set the example in all this and woe to the man that would set his face against it.'[40]

The truth of the matter was that the Robertsons had won the battle of the bulls, if the butcher was left out of the picture. Most of the buyers at Black's sales were local: Jeremiah Ware, Alec Finlay (Campbell had gone home to Scotland), John Thomson and others. Black himself put his finger on what was happening: 'There are two sorts of buyers. Buyers for stud purposes cannot pay too high in price. The higher the price, the greater the name, and it answers their purposes to pay enormous prices to get up their name. There is another class of buyers that try to improve their general herd. They do not deal in oat cake.' By this he meant that they did not stall their animals and feed them up solely to boost their prodigious size and price. 'They work for quality at the lowest prices at which it can be procured.' These were the buyers that came to Black's sales. The next year's sale, in 1878, brought in £10 490. 'You will probably say this is not too bad, but compared to the Robertsons' sale it is a wretched failure', Black wrote to Mickle. 'Their best Bull fetched £2500, my best sold for £300.'[41]

In January 1879, the last of his sales gave him much pleasure. On this occasion there were a few buyers present from Queensland and New South Wales. But by this stage, Black had long given up the idea of doing anything other than sell for relatively modest prices purebred cattle that would improve the quality of beef locally and generally. He never put reserve prices on his stock: if they went for well below their value, that was fine. The 1879 sale fetched £5733, and was described by the *Camperdown Chronicle* as 'the best of the season' in the light of a plunging cattle market. What pleased Black was the good-spiritedness of the occasion, the fine encomiums on his cattle, Daniel Mackinnon's address on the splendour of the NB herd, and the three hearty cheers with which he was personally applauded.[42]

In December 1875, at the height of the Montebello crisis, Black asked Charles Webb to put the plans for Mount Noorat House out to tender. Maybe the Robertsons' fine houses and the '150 Gentlemen' who stayed for a week pushed him to a decision. Whatever the impulse that made him go ahead, over this final grand project of his life, Black's usual sagacity deserted him.

Mount Noorat House turned out to be an extravagance on an elaborate scale – just the kind of thing he professed to deplore. His declining powers, and a vision of himself as the proprietor, observing his livestock lying in the shade of his English trees, allowed him to be led by the nose by architect, carters, masons, plumbers, decorators and designers of every fancy and novel contraption. Ambition to put the 'far-famed Glenormiston' in the shade, and enthusiasm for the town houses he and Grace had recently lived in rather than the gracious, one-storey homesteads with wide verandahs – such as Glenormiston, Marida Yallock, Meningoort and others built in the 1860s – turned his head. He wanted a two-storey house similar to one he had admired near Melbourne, but Webb told him it was impossible to cut bluestone into 'peaks, towers and turrets' of the Scottish baronial style, 'such as to my mind would harmonize with the surrounding scenery'. And since there was 'neither firestone nor dressed bricks within a reasonable distance', he was obliged to settle for bluestone and something less ornamental.[43]

Mount Noorat House was two-storey, with a colonnaded verandah looking out over Mount Emu Creek and into the far distance towards Camperdown. Stuccoed and Italianate, it had a long drive coming in from the direction of Terang, a grand gateway, and an imposing portico on the southern side where coaches drew up before departing to the stables. This was essentially a town house – or more accurately a mansion – and to build

281

a town house in the far-off bush, and fit it with all the latest in water connections and gas illuminations, was a hugely expensive and complex operation. It led to delays, frequent changes of mind, altercations with Webb, a court case with the building contractor, ruptures with the boilermaker, problems with novel contraptions that could not be made reliably functional, and a price that spiralled beyond control.

When Webb originally drew up the plans, the house was supposed to cost £8000. When it went to tender in December 1875, most estimates were far higher, so Black decided to abandon the project temporarily. 'The season was so unfavourable that I regarded it as quite impossible to carry out the work, the land being so saturated with rain and besides, labour was a fabulous price.'[44] Black then asked Webb to reduce the size of the building to bring costs down, but was talked out of this on the basis that wages were expected to drop. They did not. Again at the end of 1876, 'tenders were called for and the lowest was £12,000. To withdraw the building again would render it ridiculous and none but inferior contractors would tender for it. So with unbounded reluctance, I closed. I think the architect pressed me into unnecessary expense in the shape of decoration but it is a most substantial building and will, I believe, be an elegant house.' The successful contractor was Thos Walker & Co, and the agreement was signed in December 1876.[45] The foundations finally began to be laid in January 1877.

The dry season of early 1877 was perfectly suited to carting and construction, and the house rose quickly to its second storey. When Black and Webb went to inspect in April, they found 100 men at work. The pleasure of this spectacle to Black was offset by the sight of all their horses eating up his grazing for free.[46] The intention was to take possession in March 1878, but inevitably things overran. Black became ever more perverse and difficult, changing his instructions, trying to rein in Webb's poorly calculated expenditures, and failing to sign the paperwork when requested. Webb briefly threatened to resign from the project, and because he was not satisfied with some of the interior decoration, Black refused to make the final settlement with the contractor. Even Black's own lawyer became exasperated with him, and Black did what he had sworn never to do, which was to land himself unnecessarily in court.

The issue ended up in the letters page of the *Argus* in April 1879, where Black and Thos Walker engaged in a series of ripostes about 'blotches on the walls' and 'falls of plaster from the ceiling'. The installation of a gas machine for lighting also led to volumes of correspondence. Since half a ton of brackets, globes, fitments, and a generator for which a special vault was constructed – 'same as for Mr WJ Clarke' – had to be carted from the railhead at Colac, naturally there were glitches. The house was at the limits of the practicable. The minute the plumbing or lighting failed to function properly, the head of the firm would be summoned from Geelong or Melbourne for an 'inspection'. No plumber or decorator wanted to desert his business for days at Black's drop-of-a-hat command. Nor did Black wish to pay their travelling fees.

Such matters had a tendency to vex the Honourable Pro-prietor, who frequently wondered why he had embarked on such a project. To Gladstone he wrote: 'I look upon it as the crowning folly of my life. I was swept into building it as the drowning man is drawn into the stream he cannot resist. I regard it as a burden that may encumber my son's life. It will be a fine house proving a burden on one third part of my estate.'[47] In town, such a house could be sold, but not one buried in the countryside. Despite being assured by his clerk of works that his extra costs were less than normal, he knew he had been 'humbugged'. 'When an architect gets hold of a man who has the name of having command of money, I believe they make it a point to pick his pocket by every possible means.'[48] With all the extras, including £3000 for furniture and its transportation from Melbourne, the bill came in at over £20000 − more than twice what he had planned to spend.[49]

On 6 July 1878, Black took delivery of the house and prepared to move in. The two younger boys, Steuart and Niel, were enrolled at Geelong Grammar, to which they would ride over at the start of each term; and James, in charge of Black's horses since 1858, would bring their ponies to collect them when it ended. Niel's eldest son, Ian, was about to leave Melbourne for Trinity College, Cambridge. This was his mother's choice. Black had lately begun to feel that it would be best for the young man to stay at his father's side and study in a 'squatter college' in Melbourne, given that the duties of head of the family would soon devolve onto him. But he allowed Grace the final say. On 9 July, the 18-year-old left for Britain by the mail ship. Black said goodbye with a heavy heart. He could not expect to see his firstborn again.

The resumption of the life of a countryman, which he loved, was not destined to last long. Black was now 74. His various health scares included an alarming 'apoplexy' in 1876 which nearly swept him to oblivion, and his digestive organs frequently faltered. His ill-humours had a lot to do with pain, but he made light of it, taking up the reins at Mount Noorat with renewed zest.

His last battle was with the rabbits that had infested the entire district, moving westwards from Barwon Park where they had first been introduced and run riot in the early 1860s. With typical bombast, Black set up to be the pioneer of their local extinction. 'It is impossible for anyone who has not experienced the ravages of rabbits to form the most distant conception of their destructive powers or of their ferocity where pasture is abundant', he wrote to Gladstone. 'I have now close to 60 men employed in putting them down. I have taken a lead in the work of destruction hereabouts, hoping that others will follow my example.' He was on the trail of a gas-emitting machine that would destroy them in their burrows. 'I have put a rabbit-proof fence all around the Hill [Mount Noorat], which is a favourite nursery in which thousands are bred month after month. By this means I hope to destroy all of those outside the enclosure and afterwards attack them in their stronghold. I have been informed on good authority that Robertsons of Colac spent close upon £40,000 to destroy the rabbits on their land.'[50]

By early 1879 he had 'six patent rabbit exterminators at work on the Hill, and 12 men and two boys employed in working them. The machine generates gasses most destructive to animals' life by burning charcoal coke which is blown by bellows into the burrows, when death instantly ensues.'[51] Apart from his rabbit skirmishes, in that dry season he rode out with the firefighters on several occasions to combat bushfires on the border with Glenormiston.

As the shadows began to close in on him – and also on TS Gladstone, whose own health and eyesight began to fail in 1879 – his preoccupation was with what would happen to his lands and his family on his demise. Although he remained a 'no surrender' member of the Upper House, helping man the redoubt against the reform of the Legislative Council, the payment of salaries to MPs, and the introduction of higher taxes on large estates, and still occasionally fulminated that a bloody revolution must be on its way, he had effectively given up political life. In the Council chamber, he spoke only in debates on fencing, pests, thistles, diseases in cattle and other matters of squatterly importance, and on education. If it were not for the earnest entreaties of fellow MLCs with similar views such as Sir Charles Sladen and William Campbell, he would have opted out. He had long since become, in his own phrase, 'a Man of Yesterday', on retreat from the public stage of life, and in particular from the democrats of the day, who – confound them – enjoyed 'a majority in all things'.[52] Even at the local level, he was no longer active. The nearest railhead to Mount Noorat was at Colac, and travelling long distances in a jolting carriage made him ill. He preferred to stay at home and engage himself in the management of the estate, especially as he found that 'it becomes very extravagant' when left entirely to others.

Black cogitated long on the decision to send Ian home to study. He planned to leave the property jointly to his three boys, under John Smith's management until they came of age; Mount Noorat House would pass to Ian, or 'AJ' as he was later known. He deeply regretted the loss of control over his eldest son's life, and over the shaping of Ian's ideas and skills for the future management of the inheritance. Steuart, the second boy, was often unwell, and both he and young Niel were still at school. Black became anxious about Ian: he was spending too much money at Cambridge, studying too little, and wasting good opportunities for travel and self-improvement. As with his nephew Archie in the past, he became a lecturing and hectoring correspondent. Other squatters heard all about their sons' activities, he complained, but

Ian barely kept his parents abreast of what he was doing. 'I advise you to cultivate society, more especially Ladies' society, you take no notice of any advice I offer. All I can say on this or any other subject is treated with such indifference.'[53] The neglected father, unable to prompt his son to open up and confide his views in the way that he did so easily himself, was agonised at the thought that – despite Ian's obvious promise – his son was headed for an idle, insignificant life. But at thousands of miles' distance, all he could do was hope that his uncle Robert Leadbetter, and Gladstone too, would bring to bear the fatherly influence that he himself proffered in vain.

Early in 1880, Black suffered a stroke. 'I had for days over-worked myself out on horseback all day under the rays of a burning sun, travelled all night in a crowded coach, was out the following day on foot from 7 to 7 o'clock measuring fences and boundary lines. Next day I was insensible.'[54] Although his spirits remained indomitable, his health was giving out.

In early May, he again became ill. As the days proceeded, 'those about him noticed a circumstance that has invariably been found a harbinger of approaching death. He began to talk in the language of his childhood – Gaelic – the language in which his earliest thoughts had found expression and which is entwined around the heart-strings of every true Highlander'.[55] On Thursday 13 May, the doctor told Grace that his liver was on the point of collapse. Black then dictated 'My Dear Gladstone' for the last time. Sir Charles Sladen arrived unexpectedly from Melbourne, and after a conversation between the two old friends, a codicil to his will was drawn up. Having signed his name, Niel asked to be alone with Grace, 'and told me that he was in perfect peace, that God had put it into Sir Charles' mind to come and relieve his mind of all earthly care'. After passing into a morphine-assisted delirium, he died just before midnight on Saturday 15 May. Steuart and young Niel were present.[56]

On 18 May the *Warrnambool Standard* reported: 'The funeral of the Hon. Niel Black took place today, and was the largest I ever saw in the district. People from all parts of the Western District and some even from Melbourne testified to the respect in which the deceased was held in the district where he had so long acted a prominent part. The cortege was of unusual length, covering nearly a mile of ground, and consisted of over sixty vehicles, exclusive of equestrians and those who followed the procession on foot. A start was made from Noorat at noon, and the Terang Cemetery was reached in less than two hours.' After a description of the elaborate coffin, the report concluded: 'The funeral services were conducted in accordance with the simple ceremonies of the Presbyterian Church.'

Thus was the redoubtable pioneer and Honourable Member, 'a loving and wise husband and father', laid to rest. On his tomb was written, from the Song of Solomon: 'Until the dawn breaks and the shadows flee away.' His love for the poetry of the well-chosen word, and the Old Testament cadences which had infused his spirit, never deserted him.

EPILOGUE

IN 1881, FOLLOWING a longstanding plan, Mrs Grace Black set off for Scotland with her two younger sons. Steuart and Niel were destined, like their older brother Ian, for Cambridge University, and Grace wished to consult doctors in Edinburgh about her arthritis. Advised not to take the steamship route via the Suez Canal as the pounding of the engines would 'vibrate' her, she booked their passage in a sailing ship around Cape Horn. Her sons, alarmingly, spent most of the voyage in the rigging. In the family's absence, Mount Noorat Estate was managed by John Smith.

Mrs Black and her sons all returned when the young men's education was complete. The estate had been divided into three, in keeping with old Niel's will, and the boys formed a partnership, Messrs Black, and proceeded to manage the runs of Mount Noorat and The Sisters. They purchased an estate at Grassdale for John Smith, in gratitude for his long and faithful service. In

1915, in a letter he wrote to the daughter-in-law of his former employer, Smith described having kept every single letter he had ever received from the Honourable Niel Black. Here again was evidence that this was someone who inspired great loyalty in his workforce.

In 1890, Black's detested neighbours, the younger Finlays – their father Alex Finlay had died in 1886, Campbell had already gone home and only his brother Alec remained in Australia – decided to sell their property in the Western District. Glenormiston was put on the market, and when it was announced that Niel's second son, Steuart Gladstone Black, had bought the house and 1700 acres of the run, a cheer was raised in the saleroom. Thus did 'the far-famed Glenormiston' find its way back into the Black family's possession.

Niel's oldest son, Archibald John (AJ or Ian) Black, married Agnes, daughter of Daniel Curdie of Tandarook. They lived at Mount Noorat House, as did his mother. The couple had three sons: Ian, Donald, and Niel (who died in infancy), and a daughter, Grace. Steuart Gladstone (SG) Black married Mary Mackinnon, daughter of Daniel Mackinnon of Marida Yallock, but she died in childbirth and her daughter, also Mary, died in infancy. In 1903, SG Black married Isabella Moat, whom he met while she was visiting from England with her friend May Leadbetter, Grace Black's niece. SG and Isabella had two daughters, Cara and Margaret, and a son, Archibald Niel (Archie), father of the author.

Isabella's friend May Leadbetter and Niel Walter Black, the third of old Niel's sons, also fell in love. As they were first cousins, they were refused permission to marry. But after his mother Grace died in 1907, the family relented. In 1909, at the age of 44, Niel set off for Scotland to marry May and bring her to live at Dalvui, the house he built for her on a part of the Mount Noorat estate. Sadly, the *Warratah*, on which he sailed, disappeared in a storm off South Africa, leading to months of fruitless waiting. The ship's fate has never been discovered.

In the 1890s, Messrs Black switched from grazing to dairy cattle, becoming pioneers in the Australian dairy industry. The Glenormiston Butter and Cheese Factory opened its doors in 1895, and the NB Shorthorn beef herd was sold up in 1899. In 1904, AJ Black set up Trufood, one of the earliest companies to manufacture dried milk. The Glenormiston dairy enterprise and Trufood successfully absorbed other small dairy operations for many decades. In 1986, together with other companies, the Glenormiston brand was amalgamated into Bonlac Foods, with AJ's grandson John Niel serving on the board.

AJ Black died in a motor accident in 1912. Agnes, his widow, took her family to England, and both sons joined the forces to fight in the First World War. Donald, a flyer, was killed. Ian Gladstone Black returned to Victoria after the war and took up his role, with his uncle SG Black, in the family business, while Agnes lived on at Mount Noorat House with her daughter. By this time, much of the land had been sold, some of it under requisition as 'homes for heroes' after the First World War. Lightly fictionalised under the name of Carruthers, the family features in many of Alan Marshall's stories about his childhood, based on Noorat, where the nationally acclaimed writer was born in 1902.

Glenormiston House was enlarged in 1909 by SG and Isabella Black, who added a storey to the original 1860 house, making it much more imposing but less elegant. Their children grew up there to begin with, but Archie, born in 1912, was sent to school in England in 1923, and it was impossible then to travel back and forth regularly. When the Second World War came in 1939, overseas travel effectively ceased, and he married and made his life permanently in the UK. SG Black died at Glenormiston in 1940. In 1949, Archie brought his young family to Australia for an extended visit in order to settle the estate, and Glenormiston was sold to the government.

Ian Black, the successor to Mount Noorat, married Hope Austin and they had a daughter and a son. In 1939, Ian, still in his forties, died of septicaemia contracted after fighting bushfires. His mother, Agnes, had herself just died. Alone with two small children, with farming depressed and the Second World War about to start, Hope Black decided that Mount Noorat House had become an expensive liability and demolished it, raising her family in Mount Noorat Cottage instead. Thus did old Niel's fear that he was unnecessarily encumbering his estate by building such a folly of a mansion eventually become realised.

John Niel Black, Ian and Hope's son, died in 2012 in an accident on Mount Noorat. Gina Hope Black continues to live at the Cottage and to farm on part of the original run. Neither brother nor sister had children. Thus the Western District dynasty established by old Niel Black of Glenormiston and Mount Noorat is slowly coming to a close.

BIBLIOGRAPHY

ARCHIVES

The principal source for this book is the manuscript archive containing *Records and personal papers of Niel Black & Co.*, 1838–1938, MS 8996, held in the State Library of Victoria. The total archive contains 154 boxes. The correspondence from 1839 to 1880, on which the book chiefly relies, includes Colonial Correspondence (incoming letters from within Port Phillip/Victoria); Incoming Correspondence from Abroad; and Outgoing Correspondence, i.e. copies of letters written by Niel Black and occasionally by others acting for him. Some of the many outgoing letterbooks, whose principal content is letters Black wrote to his partner TS Gladstone in Liverpool and Scotland, individually contain up to 150 000 words. Altogether therefore the archive contains millions of words. The author has made her own transcriptions of many of these letters, backed up with transcriptions of excerpts from the incoming correspondence of TS Gladstone (also in the Black archive) made by Margaret Kiddle in the 1950s; these typescripts are held in Margaret Kiddle's archive at the Baillieu Library, University of Melbourne. Given the deterioration of the original Niel Black copybooks, and the difficulty of reading and interpreting nineteenth-century handwriting, there may be minor errors. The archive also contains a photocopy, and a typescript, of 'Journal of the first months spent in Australia, by Niel Black, commencing September 30th 1839, the day after his first landing in Sydney', which has also been published (see McKellar, under Books). The original of this journal, in two notebooks, is held by Gina Black.

Other archives

Addis, CP, *Abstracts*, a compilation of material associated with Archie Black (nephew of Niel Black), mainly from the letters of Niel Black and Daniel Mackinnon, 1976, MS 10042, State Library of Victoria.

Ewen, Stephen, Correspondence, 1839–1875, MS 8758, State Library of Victoria.

Kiddle, Margaret, Papers and correspondence associated with research for *Men of Yesterday*, University of Melbourne Archives, Baillieu Library, Online Listing: Kiddle, ML (1964.0002 and 1977.0106).

McArthur family, Papers, 1849–1970, MS 9144–MS 9148, State Library of Victoria.

Mackinnon, Daniel, Records and personal papers, Mackinnon family, 1854–1944, MS 9470, State Library of Victoria.

OFFICIAL RECORDS

Historical Records of Australia, Series I, vol. XXIII, July 1843–September 1844.

Victorian Hansard, Debates and proceedings of the Legislative Council and Assembly of the Colony of Victoria, vol. V (1859–60) to vol. XI (1864–65); Victorian Parliamentary Debates, Legislative Council and Legislative Assembly, vol. XI (1870) to vol. XX (1874).

BOOKS

Arkley, Lindsey, *The Hated Protector: The story of Charles Wightman Sievwright, Protector of Aborigines 1839–42*, Orbit Press, Melbourne, 2000.

Baillieu, Darren (ed.), *Australia Felix: A miscellany from* The Geelong Advertiser, *1840–1850*, The Craftsman Press, Melbourne, 1982.

Billis, RV and AS Kenyon, *Pastures New: An account of the pastoral occupation of Port Phillip*, Macmillan, Melbourne, 1930.

Blainey, Geoffrey, *Our Side of the Country: The story of Victoria*, Methuen Haynes, Melbourne, 1984.

——*A History of Victoria*, 2nd edition, Cambridge University Press, Cambridge, 2013.

Boldrewood, Rolf (Thomas Browne), *Old Melbourne Memories*, Macmillan, London, 1896.

Boyce, James, *1835: The founding of Melbourne and the conquest of Australia*, Black Inc., Melbourne, 2011.

Bride, Thomas Francis (ed.), *Letters from Victorian Pioneers*, Public Library of Victoria, Melbourne, 1898.

Brown, PL (ed.), *The Narrative of George Russell of Golfhill*, Oxford University Press, London, 1935.

Clark, Ian D, *The Port Phillip Journals of George Augustus Robinson, 8 March– 7 April 1842*, Monash Publications in Geography, no. 34, Melbourne, 1988.

Clarke, Michael, *Big Clarke*, Queensberry Hill Press, Melbourne, 1980.

Critchell, James T and Joseph Raymond, *A History of the Frozen Meat Trade: An account of the development and present day methods of preparation, transportation, and marketing of frozen and chilled meats*, Constable, London, 1912.

Critchett, Jan, *A Distant Field of Murder: Western District frontiers 1834–1848*, Melbourne University Press, Melbourne, 1990.

Curr, EM, *Recollections of Squatting in Victoria*, George Robertson, Melbourne, 1883.

Dawson, James, *Australian Aborigines: The language and customs of several tribes of Aborigines in the Western District of Victoria*, George Robertson, Melbourne, 1881.

De Serville, Paul, *Port Phillip Gentlemen: And good society in Melbourne before the gold rushes*, Oxford University Press, Melbourne, 1980.

Henderson, Alexander, *Early Pioneer Families of Victoria and Riverina: A genealogical and biographical record*, McCarron, Bird & Co, Melbourne, 1936.

Hyndman, Henry Mayers, *The Record of an Adventurous Life*, Macmillan, London, 1911.

Joyce, Alfred, *A Homestead History: Reminiscences and letters of Alfred Joyce of Plaistow and Norwood, Port Phillip, 1843–1864*, edited by GF James, 3rd edition, Oxford University Press, Melbourne, 1969.

Kiddle, Margaret, *Men of Yesterday: A social history of the Western District of Victoria, 1834–1890*, Melbourne University Press, Melbourne, 1961.

McAlpine, RA, *The Shire of Hampden 1863–1963*, Terang Express, 1963.

McKellar, Maggie (ed.), *Strangers in a Foreign Land: The journal of Niel Black and other voices from the Western District*, Miegunyah Press in association with the State Library of Victoria, Melbourne, 2008.

MacLehose, James, *Memoirs and portraits of one hundred Glasgow men who have died during the last thirty years, and in their lives did much to make the city what it now is*, no. 49, John Leadbetter 1788–1865, John MacLehose and Sons, Glasgow, 1886.

Peck, Harry H, *Memoirs of a Stockman*, Stockland Press, Melbourne, 1942.

Powell, JM, *The Public Lands of Australia Felix: Settlement and land appraisal in Victoria, 1834–91*, Melbourne University Press, Melbourne, 1970.

Roberts, Stephen H, *History of Australian Land Settlement 1788–1920*, Macmillan, Melbourne, 1924.

—— *The Squatting Age in Australia 1835–1847*, Melbourne University Press, Melbourne, 1935.

Serle, Geoffrey, *The Golden Age: A history of the colony of Victoria, 1851–1861*, Melbourne University Press, Melbourne, 1963.

Shaw, AGL (ed.), *Gipps–La Trobe Correspondence 1839–46*, Miegunyah Press, Melbourne, 1989.

Shaw, AGL, *The History of the Port Phillip District: Victoria before separation*, Melbourne University Press, Melbourne, 2003.

Sinclair, James (ed.), *The History of Shorthorn Cattle*, Vinton & Co, London, 1907.

Sinclair, Sir John (ed.), *The First Statistical Account of Scotland*, vol. 5, no. XXXV, 1793.

Sutherland, Alexander, *Victoria and its Metropolis: Past and present*, McCarron, Bird & Co, Melbourne, 1888.

Westgarth, William, *The Colony of Victoria: Its history, commerce and gold mining and its social and political institutions down to the end of 1863*, Sampson Low, Son and Marston, London, 1864.

—— *Personal Recollection of Early Melbourne and Victoria*, George Robertson & Co, Melbourne and Sydney, 1888.

—— *Victoria: Late Australia Felix, or Port Phillip District of New South Wales; being an historical and descriptive account of the colony and its gold mines*, Oliver Boyd, Edinburgh, 1853.

PAPERS AND ARTICLES

Aborigines Protection Society, *Report of the Parliamentary Select Committee on Aboriginal Tribes (British Settlements)*, London, 1837.

Addis, CP, 'Biography of Archibald Black, 1829–1871; and of his eldest son Archibald Syme Black, 1863–1928', unpublished paper.

Australian Dictionary of Biography, <http://adb.anu.edu.au/>, articles for all named individuals who have entries.

Black, Maggie, 'Niel Black of Ardentraive: Australian pioneer', essay, 2012, at <https://sites.google.com/site/nielblackscotaustralianpioneer/home/introduction>.

—— 'The battle for the lands: Glimpses from a squatter's correspondence', *The La Trobe Journal*, no. 88, December 2011, p. 65.

Campbell, Colin, *The Squatting Question considered with a view to its settlement*, pamphlet, Melbourne, 1861.

Campbell, William, *The Crown Lands of Australia: Being an exposition of the land regulations and of the claims and grievances of the Crown Tenants; with documentary evidence appended*, Glasgow, Edinburgh and London, 1855.

Clark, Ian D, *Scars in the Landscape: A register of massacre sites in Western Victoria, 1803–1859*, Australian Institute of Aboriginal and Torres Strait Islander Studies (AIATIS), Canberra, 1995.

Colonus (Sir William à Beckett), *Does the discovery of gold in Victoria, viewed in relation to its moral and social effects, as hitherto developed, deserve to be considered a national blessing, or a national curse?*, pamphlet, Melbourne, 1852.

Eccleston, Greg, 'Niel Black's residences in Melbourne', unpublished paper, 2010.

Gray, Charles M, 'Western Victoria in the forties: Reminiscences of a pioneer', reprinted from the *Hamilton Spectator*, Melbourne, 1932.

Ireland, John, 'The Victorian Land Act of 1862 revisited', *Victorian Historical Journal*, vol. 65, no. 2, October 1994.

Lang, Gideon Scott, *Land and Labour in Australia: Their past, present, and future connection and management considered, in a letter addressed to the Hon. Francis Scott, MP for Roxburgh, and Parliamentary Agent for NSW*, printed at the Gazette office, Melbourne, 1845.

McNiven, Ian J, 'Aboriginal settlement of the saline lake and volcanic landscapes of Corangamite Basin, western Victoria', *The Artefact*, vol. 21, 1998, pp. 63–94.

Nevalainen, Alycia, 'The Massacre at Murdering Gully', chapter in draft PhD thesis, 2013.

Powell, JM, 'Gamblers by Act of Parliament: Some aspects of the first Selection Acts for Victoria', *The Victorian Historical Magazine*, vol. 39, no. 4, November 1968.

Seddon, HR, 'Eradication of sheep scab from New South Wales', *Australian Veterinary Journal*, vol. 40, December 1964, <www.onlinelibrary.wiley.com>, accessed 27 May 2013.

Vickers, Kerry, 'Claud James Farie', unpublished biographical note, 2011.

—— Niel Black and Company: Employees Index 1839–1850, Kerry Vickers, Melbourne, 1993, <https://drive.google.com/file/d/0B88nGLFinWt0N jYxMmI0YTItZGI4Yy00MGRmLThlMDgtODU5MDA3YTIxNTEz/view>.

—— *A Band of Gypsies: Employees of Niel Black & Co. in the pre-Goldrush Era*, Kerry Vickers, Kolora, 2011, <https://drive.google.com/file/d/0B88nG LFinWt0MWIwZjExNGItMTdiNy00ODg3LThhMDItMjg2OGRlM2 FiOTU4/view>.

Westgarth, William, 'Report on the Condition, Capabilities and Prospects of the Aborigines of Australia', printed by William Clarke at the Herald Office, Melbourne, 1846.

NEWSPAPERS

These have been consulted for particular episodes or events. The first year of publication is given. Except where specified, they were accessed via Trove. In some other cases, copies of particular articles, notably in the *Terang Express*, were kept by members of the Black family or collected by CP Addis.

Age (1854)

Argus (1846)

Australasian (1864)

Camperdown Chronicle (1877)

Geelong Advertiser (1840); see also entry under Baillieu, Darren

Warrnambool Examiner/Advertiser (1851), provided courtesy of Warrnambool Historical Society

ACKNOWLEDGEMENTS

Any author of a book about squatters or the squatting era in Victoria owes a huge debt to Margaret Kiddle. Her seminal work, *Men of Yesterday: A social history of the Western District of Victoria, 1834–1890*, charting the rise of pioneering graziers up the ladder of business success and gentrification, took its title from a letter written by Niel Black. More than any other character – and *Men of Yesterday* is full of them – he was her favourite. 'I think the old boy is magnificent – but he's also an old devil!' she wrote to a member of the Black family during her research.

This was Hope (née Austin), who married a grandson of old Niel Black and was prematurely widowed in 1939. During the Second World War, the government requisitioned all scrap paper for pulping and re-use. Hope Black saved the Mount Noorat estate records by hiding them in the loft of the stables. When Margaret Kiddle came calling in the 1950s, she brought down the trunks of letters, and they opened them up together. Kiddle was overjoyed by the discovery. These papers, due to their extraordinary volume and range, became the most important original source for her study. If she had lived, her next project was to produce an edited version of Niel Black's letters, but she died in 1958, three years before *Men of Yesterday* was published. I have frequently found her notes and markers among the pages of his letterbooks, and am only too aware that I am following in her footsteps, fulfilling in a different way the task she left behind.

It had always been my intention to undertake a book based on the archive of my great-grandfather. The intention crystallised in 2008, and my first major foray into scores of boxes in the Niel Black & Company archive in the State Library of Victoria took place in 2009. I can remember the first day I went into the Library escorted by my cousin-by-marriage, Greg Eccleston, who has been a tower of strength throughout the research and writing process. In fact, this book would not have been possible without the support of all of my Australian family, the descendants and partners of descendants of old Niel Black. Joanna, Greg's wife, Isabella and Richard Green, Niel and Eve Black, and Gina Black have all welcomed me and given me hospitality over many extended visits to Victoria, and their friendship, insights, assistance and goodwill have been invaluable.

Greg bore the heaviest brunt, being called on for support with technical and research issues. Niel and Gina Black gave me access to materials still in the family's possession, and helped me understand the landscape of the original Glenormiston run. Alun and Fiona Morris at Gnotuk House, originally built by old Niel's nephew Archie Black, have similarly opened their door and given me the benefit of their wisdom.

Various researchers into the history of the Western District, and into Niel Black in particular, have been extremely helpful. These include many members of historical societies, notably Susan Cole, Maree Belyea and Bob Lambell at Camperdown Heritage Centre; Margaret Macintosh at Terang; Janet MacDonald at Warrnambool; and Florence Charles at Mortlake, all of whom have patiently responded to many and various requests. Kerry Vickers, who has researched the employees of Niel Black & Company in the pre-gold rush era with extraordinary thoroughness, and Kevin Brewer, who has collected a mine of information on everything associated with Niel Black & Company in Scotland and Victoria, have been extremely generous with their time and assistance. The late Charles Addis, who researched Archie Black in the 1970s, gave me free and enthusiastic access to his collection of material; so did Robert and Margaret Gladstone of Capenoch, Dumfries, descendants of TS Gladstone's second son, Steuart. I also had useful exchanges with Alycia Nevalainen during the preparation of her thesis on Strathdownie, the Glenormiston run before Black took it over and renamed it in February 1840. I have to thank Elizabeth Newbery who photographed a full set of Black's correspondence with his nephew Archie during the 1850s for me on a visit to Melbourne at a particularly crucial moment.

For the use of illustrations, I would like particularly to thank Greg Eccleston (family photos), Gina Black (family portraits), Andrew Boyle, Kevin Brewer, Robert Gladstone, Gerard Hayes (at the State Library of Victoria), Patricia Macdonald and Anne Rowland (Ballarat Art Gallery), Ruth Pullin (on Eugene von Guérard), members of historical societies already mentioned, and Kerry Vickers. As far as the text is concerned, Alun and Fiona Morris were its first readers, and like several members of my family, offered encouragement, enthusiasm and advice.

Special thanks are due to staff in different departments of the State Library of Victoria, in particular Margot Jones in publications, Lois McEvoy in manuscripts, and John Arnold, editor of the *La Trobe Journal*. I am grateful to Professor Lynette Russell, who read the chapter on Aboriginal engagement with an expert eye. I would also like to thank Geoffrey Blainey for his generosity in providing a foreword, and Elspeth Menzies and

Paul O'Beirne at NewSouth Publishing for taking on the book and having confidence in it. Thanks also to Clara Finlay for her thoroughness in editing the text. Finally, two people no longer with us have provided special posthumous support in bringing this book to fruition, namely Jocelyn Morris and Niel Black (through Eve), and I only wish they were here to read the result.

Maggie Black
Oxford, May 2016

NOTES

1 'A run unequalled in the colony'

1. Niel Black (NB), 'Journal of a few of the first months spent in Australia, commenced 30th September 1839, the day after his first landing in Sydney', published in Maggie McKellar (ed.), *Strangers in a Foreign Land: The journal of Niel Black and other voices from the Western District*, Miegunyah Press, Melbourne, 2008 (primary source for this chapter), entries for 3 and 4 December 1839.
2. Archibald Yuille was in partnership with his cousin William Yuille: J Ann Horne, 'Yuille, William Cross', *Australian Dictionary of Biography*, vol. 6, Melbourne University Press, Melbourne, 1976, <http://adb.anu.edu.au/biography/yuille-william-cross-4909>; John Anderson to NB, 28 February 1839.
3. Journal, op. cit., 9 December 1839.
4. PL Brown (ed.), *The Narrative of George Russell of Golfhill*, Oxford University Press, London, 1935, pp. 226–7.
5. Journal, op. cit., preamble by NB on the title page, describing the object of the journal, which was to offer information and guidance to his relations at home who might think of following him to Australia.
6. John Robertson of Wando Vale, letter 9, in Thomas Francis Bride (ed.), *Letters from Victorian Pioneers*, Public Library of Victoria, Melbourne, 1898, pp. 22–35.
7. Journal, op. cit., 10 December 1839.
8. Ibid., 8, 9 and 10 January 1840.
9. *The Narrative of George Russell of Golfhill*, op. cit., p. 75.
10. This was originally called Taylor's River; the land between Camperdown and the Hopkins River was known as 'Taylor's country', according to Commissioner of Crown Lands (CCL) itinerary logs and other contemporary sources.
11. Jan Critchett, *A Distant Field of Murder: Western District frontiers 1834–48*, Melbourne University Press, Melbourne, 1990, citing itinerary of Henry Gisborne, CCL, December 1839.
12. Niel Black & Company, Station Journal and Cash Book, March 1839–March 1849.
13. Unpublished biographical note by TS Gladstone, held at Capenoch, Dumfriesshire, by his descendants.
14. 'Successful Colonists', Hon. Niel Black MLC, *The Leader*, 27 April 1872.
15. Kerry Vickers, *A Band of Gypsies: Employees of Niel Black & Co. in the pre-Goldrush Era*, Kerry Vickers, Kolora, 2011, <https://drive.google.com/file/d/0B88nGLF inWt0MWIwZjExNGItMTdiNy00ODg3L ThhMDItMjg2OGRlM2FiOTU4/view>.
16. Accounts listed on the first page in NB's first outgoing letterbook; NB to TS Gladstone, 9 April 1840.
17. Alexander Henderson, *Early Pioneer Families of Victoria and Riverina: A genealogical and biographical record*, McCarron, Bird & Co, Melbourne, 1936, p. 137.
18. Charles M Gray, *Western Victoria in the Forties: Reminiscences of a pioneer*, booklet, reprinted from *Hamilton Spectator*, 1932.
19. EM Curr, *Recollections of Squatting in Victoria*, George Robertson, Melbourne, 1883, reprinted by Melbourne University Press, Melbourne, 1965, Chapter 2.
20. Henderson, op. cit., 'The Manifolds', pp. 19–20. Manifold suggests this was when Black was on his way to take up his run; but on that occasion he took the northern route from Ballarat.
21. Journal, op. cit., 19 December 1839.
22. Ibid., 20 and 21 December 1839.
23. Lindsey Arkley, *The Hated Protector: The story of Charles Wightman Sievwright, Protector of Aborigines, 1839–42*, Orbit Press, Melbourne, 2000; Ian D Clark, *Scars in the Landscape: A register of massacre sites in Western Victoria, 1803–1859*, Australian Institute of Aboriginal and Torres Strait Islander Studies, Canberra, 1995, pp. 105–8, indicates an earlier date, but Arkley is more convincing.
24. NB to TS Gladstone, 9 April 1840.
25. Journal, op. cit., 4 January 1840.
26. Ibid., 2–4 January 1840.
27. NB to TS Gladstone, 6 January 1839.
28. Journal, op. cit., 21 January 1840.
29. Ibid., 16 and 17 February 1840.

2 'Quietly slaughtered in unknown numbers'

1. Niel Black (NB) to TS Gladstone, 6 January 1840.
2. NB, 'Journal of a few of the first months spent in Australia, commenced 30th September 1839, the day after his first landing in Sydney', published in Maggie McKellar (ed.), *Strangers in a Foreign Land: The journal of Niel Black and other voices from the Western District*, Miegunyah Press, Melbourne, 2008, entry for 9 December 1839.
3. Ibid., 25 December 1839.
4. Aborigines Protection Society, *Report of the Parliamentary Select Committee on Aboriginal Tribes (British Settlements)*, London, 1837.
5. Sir John Sinclair (ed.), *The First Statistical Account of Scotland*, vol. 5, no. XXXV, 'Parish of Inverchaolain (County of Argyle)', by the Rev. Mr Hugh Mactavish, Minister, 1793.
6. Proclamation by Lieutenant Governor Arthur of Tasmania, 26 August 1835, Historical Records of Victoria (HRV) Foundation Series, vol. i, pp. 12–14.
7. William Westgarth, *Report on the Condition, Capabilities and Prospects of the Aborigines of Australia, Melbourne*, printed by William Clarke at the Herald Office, Melbourne, 1846, p. 36.
8. Jan Critchett, *A Distant Field of Murder: Western District frontiers 1834–1848*, Melbourne University Press, Melbourne, 1990, p. 6.
9. Lindsey Arkley, *The Hated Protector: The story of Charles Wightman Sievwright, Protector of Aborigines, 1839–42*, Orbit Press, Melbourne, 2000, p. 6.
10. Journal, op. cit., 23 February 1840.
11. Ibid., 25 December 1839.
12. Ibid., 9 December 1839.
13. Ibid.
14. Ibid., 23 December 1839; information from Henry Gisborne, Commissioner of Crown Lands, camping nearby.
15. Charles M. Gray, *Western Victoria in the Forties: Reminiscences of a pioneer*, booklet, reprinted from the *Hamilton Spectator*, 1932.
16. Ian D. Clark (ed.), *Scars in the Landscape: A register of massacre sites in Western Victoria, 1803–1859*, Australian Institute of Aboriginal and Torres Strait Islander Studies, Canberra, 1995, pp. 105–12.
17. Journal, op. cit., 21 February 1840.
18. Ibid., 16 March 1840.
19. Ibid., 23 March 1840.
20. Kerry Vickers, *A Band of Gypsies: Employees of Niel Black & Co. in the pre-Goldrush Era*, Kerry Vickers, Kolora, 2011, <https://drive.google.com/file/d/0B88nGLFinWt0MWIwZjExNGItMTdiNy00ODg3LThhMDItMjg2OGRlM2FiOTU4/view>.
21. Ian D Clark, *The Port Phillip Journals of George Augustus Robinson, 8 March–7 April 1842*, Monash Publications in Geography, no. 34, Melbourne, 1988, observations of 21 March 1842.
22. 'Claud Farie: Sheriff of Melbourne', *Australian Postal History & Social Philately*, <www.auspostalhistory.com/articles/66.shtml>, accessed 16 January 2013. Farie says 90 sheep were driven off, but in Black's correspondence only nine sheep were driven off.
23. NB to TS Gladstone, 31 December 1840.
24. Journal, op. cit., 13 March 1840.
25. William Westgarth, *Personal Recollection of Early Melbourne and Victoria*, George Robertson & Co, Melbourne and Sydney, 1888, p. 44.
26. Journal, op. cit., 23 March 1840; Clark, *Scars in the Landscape*, op. cit., pp. 145–52.
27. Journal, ibid.
28. John Robertson of Wando Vale, letter 9, in Thomas Francis Bride (ed.), *Letters from Victorian Pioneers*, Public Library of Victoria, Melbourne, 1898, pp. 22–35.
29. Journal, op. cit., 23 March 1840.
30. Arkley, op. cit., pp. 46–9.
31. RA McAlpine, *The Shire of Hampden 1863–1963*, Terang Express, 1963, p. 39.
32. Biographical note on John Thomson in *These Five and Seventy Years, Thomson Memorial Church*, Terang Historical Society, Terang, 1936.
33. Arkley, op. cit., p. 66.
34. La Trobe to Gipps, 14 June 1840, letter 17 in AGL Shaw (ed.), *Gipps–La Trobe Correspondence 1839–46*, Miegunyah Press, Melbourne, 1989.
35. NB to TS Gladstone, 5 August 1840.
36. Ibid.
37. Critchett, op. cit., p. 118, citing correspondence between La Trobe and the Gentlemen signing a Representation without date, 26 March 1842.
38. NB to TS Gladstone, 5 August 1842.

39. Copy in NB's hand of a letter from AL Boursequot, dated 26 July 1842, addressed to the Port Fairy settlers.
40. Critchett, op. cit., p. 119, citing letter of NB and others to La Trobe, 1 August 1842, VPRS 19, 42/1418; copy enclosed in CSIL Port Phillip 1843, Part 1, 4/2626, in accumulated file 42/2847.
41. NB to TS Gladstone, 5 August 1842.
42. Claud Farie to NB, 9 July 1843; James Webster to NB, 9 June 1843.
43. Journal, op. cit., 25 February 1840.
44. James Dawson, *Australian Aborigines: The language and customs of several tribes of Aborigines in the Western District of Victoria*, George Robertson, Melbourne, 1881.
45. Arkley, op. cit., p. 65.
46. Four letters from Charles Sievwright to NB 1840–42.
47. NB to TS Gladstone, 5 July 1840.
48. Report of Sievwright on proceedings from 1 June to 31 October 1840, cited in Arkley, op. cit, p. 75.

49. Report of Sievwright, quoted in Journal of Reverend J Orton, entry of 12 January 1841, cited in Arkley, op. cit., p. 77.
50. Critchett, op. cit., p. 7.
51. Ibid., p. 151, citing Gary Presland (ed.), *Journals of GA Robinson March–May 1841*, Records of the Victoria Archaeological Survey, no. 6, Ministry for Conservation, Melbourne, 1977, p. 41.
52. NB to TS Gladstone, 26 December 1840.
53. Arkley, op. cit., p. 158.
54. Ibid., p. 165, citing *Journals of GA Robinson*, op. cit., entries for 21 and 22 April 1841.
55. NB to CJ La Trobe, Melbourne, 15 February 1842; also to Foster Fyans, 15 February 1842.
56. Arkley, op. cit., pp. 263 and 456–7.
57. NB to Arthur Kemmis, 11 January 1841.
58. NB, 'Notes by an Occupier of Crown Lands in Victoria, Australia', London, 21 March 1853, note in draft, NB papers.

3 'I sent for a chain to measure the distance'

1. Niel Black (NB) to TS Gladstone, 9 May 1840.
2. Margaret Kiddle, *Men of Yesterday: A social history of the Western District of Victoria, 1834–1890*, Melbourne University Press, Melbourne, 1961, p. 13; AGL Shaw, *The History of the Port Phillip District: Victoria before separation*, Melbourne University Press, Melbourne, 2003, pp. 87–110.
3. Stephen H Roberts, *History of Australian Land Settlement 1788–1920*, Macmillan, Melbourne, 1924, p. 167.
4. NB, 'Journal of a few of the first months spent in Australia, commenced 30th September 1839, the day after his first landing in Sydney', published in Maggie McKellar (ed.), *Strangers in a Foreign Land: The journal of Niel Black and other voices from the Western District*, Miegunyah Press, Melbourne, 2008, entry for 23 December 1839.
5. Stephen H Roberts, *The Squatting Age in Australia 1835–1847*, Melbourne University Press, Melbourne, 1935, p. 278, citing Gipps–Stanley letters of 1844.
6. Kiddle, op. cit., p. 133.
7. Letters to the *Camperdown Chronicle* of 1 July and 4 July 1879 on the death of Nicholas Cole, <www.trove.nla.gov.au/ndp/del/article/29098231>, accessed 28 February 2013.

8. Letter from Peter McArthur to the *Camperdown Chronicle*, 24 August 1885; Peter McArthur archive, MS 9148, SLV.
9. RA McAlpine, *The Shire of Hampden 1863–1963*, Terang Express, 1963, p. 36.
10. William Blackie, signed statement of 21 February 1840, at NB's request.
11. Journal, op. cit., 26 and 28 March 1840.
12. Ibid., 25 March 1840.
13. NB to TS Gladstone, 9 May 1840.
14. NB to TS Gladstone, 29 March 1840.
15. NB to TS Gladstone, 9 May 1840.
16. Copy of the schedules required to be filled in by the settler, including his employees, stock, holdings, etc., at every half-year, dated July 1840 in his own hand.
17. Journal, op. cit., 29 February 1840.
18. Lorne Campbell to NB, 9 January 1839.
19. Journal, op. cit., 6 and 7 March 1840.
20. Copy of a letter from Charles La Trobe to Ewen and Craig, 9 April 1840; NB to TS Gladstone, 5 July 1840.
21. NB to TS Gladstone, 9 May 1840.
22. Alycia Nevalainen, 'The Massacre at Murdering Gully', draft PhD thesis, February 2013, citing Billis & Kenyon, 1930.
23. Gipps to Russell, September 1840, *HRA*, Series I, vol. xx, p. 839, cited in AGL Shaw, op. cit., p. 87.

24. Gipps to Glenelg, 6 April 1840, *HRA*, Series I, vol. xx, pp. 90–2, and 6 April 1840, *HRV*, vol. vi, pp. 261–3, cited in AGL Shaw, op. cit., pp. 92–3.

25. Roberts, *The Squatting Age in Australia*, op. cit., pp. 348–51.

26. NB to William Steuart, 18 June 1842.

27. Shaw, op. cit., p. 95.

28. John Robertson of Wando Vale, letter 9, in Thomas Francis Bride (ed.), *Letters from Victorian Pioneers*, Public Library of Victoria, Melbourne, 1898, p. 24.

29. Gipps–La Trobe correspondence, cited in Shaw, op. cit., p. 95 and Kiddle, op. cit., p. 50.

30. Story passed down in the Black family.

31. NB to TS Gladstone, 5 July 1840.

32. Copy of letter from Fyans to Stephen Ewen, 29 July 1840.

33. NB to Fyans, 1 August 1841, 16 August 1841.

34. Fyans' evidence to the 1844 Select Committee on Crown Land Grievances, cited in Shaw, op. cit., p. 95.

35. Foster Fyans to NB, 20 August 1841.

36. Fyans to NB, 23 September 1841.

37. Itinerary of Foster Fyans, Commissioner of Crown Lands, 1–30 March 1842;

Report to the Colonial Secretary, Archives Authority of New South Wales; the entry for Keilambete is on 21 March, for Glenormiston on 20 March; given the distances he covered, there was no time for a detailed inspection, only for discussion with the run-holders.

38. Charles Sievwright to NB, 24 February 1842.

39. NB to Foster Fyans, 7 February 1842 (1).

40. NB to Foster Fyans, 7 February 1842 (2).

41. NB to Charles La Trobe, 10 February 1842.

42. NB to Charles La Trobe, 15 February 1842, and to Foster Fyans, 15 February 1842.

43. JC Riddell to NB, 17 February 1842.

44. NB to Foster Fyans, 9 March 1842.

45. Foster Fyans to FM McLachlan, a lawyer employed by NB, 24 July 1842.

46. Claud Farie to Foster Fyans, 8 March 1843.

47. Claud Farie to NB, 9 July 1843, 28 July 1843.

48. John Eddington to NB, 28 March 1843.

49. NB to Foster Fyans, written by Farie, 11 January 1843.

50. NB to TS Gladstone, 23 June 1846.

4 'Above all, I am anxious for men'

1. Niel Black (NB), 'Journal of a few of the first months spent in Australia, commenced 30th September 1839, the day after his first landing in Sydney', published in Maggie McKellar (ed.), *Strangers in a Foreign Land: The journal of Niel Black and other voices from the Western District*, Miegunyah Press, Melbourne, 2008, entry for 25 December 1839.

2. Kerry Vickers, *A Band of Gypsies: Employees of Niel Black & Co. in the pre-Goldrush Era*, Kerry Vickers, Kolora, 2011, <*https://drive.google.com/file/d/0B88nGL FinWt0MWIwZjExNGItMTdiNy00ODg3 LThhMDItMjg2OGRlM2FiOTU4/view*>. This paper has been extensively drawn on for this chapter, as has a companion paper by Kerry Vickers, *Niel Black and Company: Employees Index 1839–1850*, Kerry Vickers, Melbourne, 1993, <*https://drive. google.com/file/d/0B88nGLFinWt0NjYxM mI0YTItZGI4Yy00MGRmLThlMDgtOD U5MDA3YTIxNTEz/view*>.

3. NB to Alex Finlay, 20 September 1840.

4. Journal, op. cit., 22 February 1840.

5. Vickers, *A Band of Gypsies*, op. cit., p. 13.

6. NB to William Steuart, 18 June 1842.

7. Correspondence book for 1840–41, returns of stock 31 December 1840.

8. *These five and seventy years*, Thomson Memorial church, Terang Historical Society, Terang, 1936.

9. NB to William Steuart, 18 June 1842.

10. NB to TS Gladstone, 5 August 1840.

11. Rolf Boldrewood (Thomas Browne), *Old Melbourne Memories*, 2nd edn, Macmillan, London, 1896, pp. 87–8; Alfred Joyce, *A Homestead History, being the reminiscences and letters of Alfred Joyce of Plaistow and Norwood, Port Phillip, 1843 to 1864*, edited by GF James, 3rd edn, Oxford University Press, Melbourne, 1969, pp. 139–40 has a similar description.

12. *Geelong Advertiser*, 7 December 1847, <*http://trove.nla.gov.au/ndp/del/ article/91457620*>.

13. HR Seddon, 'Eradication of sheep scab from New South Wales', *Australian*

Veterinary Journal, vol. 40, December 1964, <*www.onlinelibrary.wiley.com*>, accessed 27 May 2013.

14. NB to TS Gladstone, 3 July 1842.
15. NB to Foster Fyans, 3 October 1842; he also wrote to Fyans complaining about Thomson's sheep on 14 June 1842 and 27 September 1842, and accounts of such incursions are mentioned in the Station Journal on 1 August 1842 and in other entries.
16. NB to William Steuart, 18 June 1842.
17. NB to TS Gladstone, 21 December 1844.
18. NB to Foster Fyans, 7 February 1842.
19. Vickers, *A Band of Gypsies*, op. cit., p. 18.
20. NB to TS Gladstone, 4 October 1842.
21. Journal, op. cit., 1 December 1839.
22. NB to TS Gladstone, 17 October 1842.
23. NB to TS Gladstone, 9 May 1840.
24. Walter Black to NB, 27 January 1941.
25. NB to TS Gladstone, 13 June 1841.
26. Vickers, *Niel Black and Company*, op. cit., pp. 14 and 19.
27. NB to Gladstone, 16 August 1841.
28. NB to TS Gladstone, 30 December 1841.
29. NB to TS Gladstone, quote compiled from letters of 4 and 17 October 1842.
30. NB to Alex Finlay, 10 December 1840.
31. John Eddington to NB, 28 March 1843.
32. Captain McKellar to NB, 28 March 1839.
33. William Campbell to NB, 5 January 1843.
34. Letters to NB from Lord Stanley, 17 June 1843, Dr David Patrick, 24 June 1843, William Houston, 21 August 1843 and 12 September 1843.
35. Margaret Kiddle, *Men of Yesterday: A social history of the Western District of Victoria, 1834–1890*, Melbourne University Press, Melbourne, 1961, pp. 152–4.
36. Letter from Mr WH Yaldwyn to Sir James Graham, enclosed with a despatch of

37. Kiddle, op. cit., p. 152, citing *Port Phillip Patriot*, 21 November 1844.
38. NB to TS Gladstone, 30 September 1846.
39. Claud Farie to NB, 9 July 1843.
40. NB to TS Gladstone, 6 January 1840.
41. Station accounts accompanying letters in the first outgoing correspondence book, 1840–41; NB to TS Gladstone, 17 October 1841.
42. NB to TS Gladstone, 9 May 1840.
43. TS Gladstone to NB, 2 November 1840.
44. TS Gladstone to NB, 5 July 1841, invoice for four bulls, shipped by *Frankfield*; copy in Margaret Kiddle archive, Baillieu Library.
45. NB to Archie Black, from Scotland, October 1851.
46. NB to TS Gladstone, 7 May 1842.
47. TS Gladstone to NB, 29 November 1842.
48. NB to TS Gladstone, 20 January 1842.
49. Adam Gladstone to NB, 22 April 1853.
50. NB to Archie Black, 6 January 1854.
51. NB to TS Gladstone, 21 January 1843.
52. NB to TS Gladstone, 21 December 1844.
53. AGL Shaw, *The History of the Port Phillip District: Victoria before separation*, Melbourne University Press, Melbourne, 2003, p. 149.
54. Vickers, *A Band of Gypsies*, op. cit., p. 14.
55. Rev Alexander Laurie, Portland, to NB, 25 January 1843.
56. RA McAlpine, *The Shire of Hampden 1863–1963*, Terang Express, 1963, p. 102.
57. NB to Thomas Storey, 7 September 1846.
58. Station Journal 1843–48.
59. NB to TS Gladstone, 16 August 1841.
60. NB to TS Gladstone, 27 October 1845.
61. Boldrewood, op. cit., p. 19.

5 'I thought it best to build a stone house'

1. Stephen H Roberts, *The Squatting Age in Australia 1835–1847*, Melbourne University Press, Melbourne, 1935, pp. 137–8.
2. Ibid., p. 287; in a letter to TS Gladstone on 5 November 1845, Niel Black (NB) said that the contemporary government estimate was 40 square miles for 8000 sheep, which amounted to 3.2 acres per sheep.
3. JM Powell, *The Public Lands of Australia Felix: Settlement and land appraisal in*

Victoria, 1834–91, Melbourne University Press, Melbourne, 1970, pp. 22–4.
4. Stephen H Roberts, *The History of Australian Land Settlement 1788–1920*, Macmillan, Melbourne, 1924, pp. 107–108.
5. James Webster to NB, 9 June 1843.
6. Gipps to Stanley, 14 April 1844, cited in Margaret Kiddle, *Men of Yesterday: A social history of the Western District of Victoria, 1834–1890*, Melbourne University Press, Melbourne, 1961, p. 164.

7. Articles in *Port Phillip Gazette* and *Port Phillip Patriot*, 3–5 June 1844.
8. Claud Farie to TS Gladstone, 17 April 1844.
9. NB to TS Gladstone, 21 December 1844.
10. NB to TS Gladstone, 7 June 1845.
11. NB to TS Gladstone, 25 June 1845.
12. NB to TS Gladstone, 25 August 1845.
13. NB to TS Gladstone, 21 December 1844.
14. NB to TS Gladstone, 25 August 1845.
15. Gideon Scott Lang, *Land and Labour in Australia: Their past, present, and future connection and management considered, in a letter addressed to the Hon. Francis Scott, MP for Roxburgh, and Parliamentary Agent for NSW*, printed at the Gazette office, Melbourne, 1845.
16. Ibid., p. 11.
17. NB to TS Gladstone, 5 November 1845.
18. Ibid.
19. NB to TS Gladstone, 2 December 1845.
20. EM Curr, *Recollections of Squatting in Victoria*, George Robertson, Melbourne, 1883, reprinted Melbourne University Press, Melbourne, 1965. In a concluding biographical note, EM Curr described his father, Edward Curr, the famous – and infamous – pioneer and speculator, as 'decidedly unpopular with the gentry, a fact which I can only account for on the supposition that an imperial manner, which was as natural to him as his skin, was not relished'.
21. NB to TS Gladstone, 16 October 1845.

22. TS Gladstone to NB, 27 April 1846.
23. William Westgarth, *Personal Recollection of Early Melbourne and Victoria*, George Robertson & Co, Melbourne and Sydney, 1888, p. 79.
24. NB to TS Gladstone, 22 November 1845.
25. AS Finlay to NB, 31 March 1846.
26. National Archives UK, Kew, Colonial Correspondence, CO 201 Book 372; this contains a special section in 'Correspondence from individuals' for Archibald Cuninghame.
27. Gideon Scott Lang to NB, 1 September 1847.
28. Daniel Curdie to NB, 29 July 1848.
29. Lauchlan Mackinnon to NB, 14 July 1848.
30. Lauchlan Mackinnon to NB, 6 November 1848.
31. NB to TS Gladstone, 3 October 1846.
32. NB to TS Gladstone, 6 August 1846.
33. NB to TS Gladstone, 18 August 1846.
34. Roberts, *The Squatting Age*, op. cit., pp. 326–30.
35. NB to TS Gladstone, 18 August 1846; the series of letters in August, October and December of 1846 in which Black expounded his ideas are long, complex, and very difficult to read and even harder to interpret.
36. NB to TS Gladstone, 12 December 1846.
37. NB to TS Gladstone, 25 February 1847.
38. TS Gladstone to NB, 7 September 1846.
39. NB to TS Gladstone, 25 February 1847.

6 'A day we hope never to see the like of again'

1. William Westgarth, *Personal Recollection of Early Melbourne and Victoria*, George Robertson & Co, Melbourne and Sydney, 1888, pp. 124–5.
2. Diary of Prince Frederick of Schleswig-Holstein, translated by Tom Durragh; personal communication from Robert Wuchatsch, 4 February 2016.
3. Niel Black (NB) to Archie Black (nephew), Birds Island, 4 August 1850.
4. James Blair to NB, 12 January 1848.
5. John C Thomson to NB, 9 December 1849.
6. NB to Walter Black, 22 July 1844.
7. NB to TS Gladstone, 25 February 1847.
8. NB to TS Gladstone, 20 January 1847.
9. NB to TS Gladstone, 26 May 1847.
10. NB to AS Finlay, 26 January 1847.
11. William Swan to NB, 22 December 1847.

12. Claud Farie to NB, 24 February 1848; Bells and Buchanan to NB, 18 May 1848.
13. Henry Bourne Foot to NB, 27 October 1847.
14. William Campbell, *The Crown Lands of Australia: Being an exposition of the land regulations and of the claims and grievances of the Crown tenants; with documentary evidence appended*, J Smith, Glasgow, 1855, p. 3, and Appendix 4, p. 29.
15. Colin Campbell, *The Squatting Question Considered with a View to its Settlement*, pamphlet, Melbourne, 1861, p. 6.
16. Margaret Kiddle, *Men of Yesterday: A social history of the Western District of Victoria, 1834–1890*, Melbourne University Press, Melbourne, 1961, p. 222.
17. NB to Jessie Black, 24 January 1849.
18. NB to Jessie Black, 23 May 1849.

19. NB to Jessie Black, 12 June 1849.
20. NB to TS Gladstone, 5 February 1849.
21. Ebenezer Oliphant, Wooriwyrite, to NB, several letters, March–September 1849.
22. NB to TS Gladstone, 2 February 1850.
23. George Rodger to NB, 14 December 1850.
24. NB to Archie Black, Glasgow, 12 July 1851.
25. Kiddle, op. cit., pp. 115–16; *Argus*, leading article, 18 August 1856; Hugh Anderson, 'Clarke, William John (1805–1874)', *Australian Dictionary of Biography*, vol. 1, Melbourne University Press, Melbourne, 1966, <*http://adb.anu. edu.au/biography/clarke-william-john-1902*>.
26. William Bell to NB, 2 September 1850.
27. Archie Black to NB, 21 November 1850.
28. Will N Gray to NB, 20 July 1851.
29. Ibid.; William Bell to NB, 14 June 1851.
30. Archie Black to NB, 16 January 1851.
31. Archie Black to NB, 5 February 1851.
32. Archie Black to NB, 10 March 1851.
33. NB to Archie Black, 12 October 1851, 12 December 1851.
34. Archie Black to TS Gladstone, 12 April 1851.
35. Archie Black to TS Gladstone, 10 June 1851.
36. Archie Black to NB, 6 August 1851.
37. Archie Black to NB, 23 September 1851.
38. Archie Black to NB, 3 October 1851.
39. NB to Archie Black, 12 October 1851.
40. Archie Black to NB, draft letter, 8 February 1852 (probably not sent).

7 'Your uncle is going to be married, as usual'

1. Niel Black (NB) to Archie Black, 6 February 1851; AS Finlay to NB, 22 February 1851.
2. NB to Claud Farie, 24 April 1851.
3. Geoffrey Serle, *The Golden Age: A history of the colony of Victoria, 1851–1861*, Melbourne University Press, Melbourne, 1963, pp. 11–12.
4. Ibid., p. 22.
5. *Geelong Advertiser*, 27 September 1851.
6. Colonus (Sir William à Beckett), *Does the discovery of gold in Victoria, viewed in relation to its moral and social effects, as hitherto developed, deserve to be considered a national blessing, or a national curse?*, pamphlet, Melbourne, 1852.
7. William Westgarth, *The Colony of Victoria: Its history, commerce and gold mining and its social and political institutions down to the end of 1863*, Sampson Low, Son and Marston, London, 1864, p. 143.
8. NB to Archie Black, 1 December 1851.
9. William Bell to NB, 14 June 1851.
10. NB to Archie Black, 12 July 1851, 3 September 1851, 21 October 1851.
11. Archie Black to NB, 3 October 1851.
12. Archie Black to NB, 24 October 1851.
13. Archie Black to NB, 12 December 1851.
14. Archie Black to NB, 23 January 1852.
15. Alfred Joyce, *A Homestead History: Reminiscences and letters of Alfred Joyce of Plaistow and Norwood, Port Phillip, 1843–1864*, edited by GF James, 3rd edn, Oxford University Press, Melbourne, 1969, p. 130, letter 5, 26 March 1852.
16. Stephen H Roberts, *History of Australian Land Settlement*, Melbourne University Press, Melbourne, 1924, p. 205; William Campbell, *The Crown Lands of Australia: Being an exposition of the land regulations and of the claims and grievances of the Crown tenants; with documentary evidence appended*, J Smith, Glasgow, 1855, p. 3.
17. Serle, op. cit., p. 132, citing *Herald*, 15 July, 12, 16 and 17 August 1852.
18. Niel Black, 'Notes by an occupier of Crown Lands in Australia', unpublished manuscript, 21 March 1853.
19. AS Finlay to NB, 1 January 1849.
20. AS Finlay to NB, 20 March 1851.
21. John Buys, 'Statistical Report of All the Land bought by Niel Black & Co in the Australian Colonies down to August 1863', ms book, NB papers.
22. NB to Archie Black, 11 July 1852.
23. Serle, op. cit., pp. 135–6.
24. Roberts, op. cit., pp. 208–11.
25. *Argus*, 15 March 1854, p. 4, report on the Duke of Newcastle's despatch on the squatting question.
26. Campbell, op. cit., p. ix.
27. *Argus*, 27 May 1854, p. 5, report on the Memorial of the Tenants of the Crown of Victoria.
28. NB to Archie Black, 25 July 1854.
29. Buys, op. cit.
30. NB to Archie Black, 6 January 1854.
31. 'A Pastoralist Pioneer. The Hon. Niel Black. Interesting historical sketch', *Terang Express*, 3 June 1927.

32. NB to Archie Black, 25 January 1854.
33. Robert Gladstone to NB, 23 May 1863.
34. NB to Archie Black, 31 May 1855, quoting a letter received by TS Gladstone from Robert Gladstone.
35. NB to Archie Black, 2 April 1855.
36. NB to Archie Black, 31 May 1855.
37. TS Gladstone to NB, 30 April 1852.
38. TS Gladstone to NB, 3 December 1852.
39. NB to Archie Black, 7 December 1852.
40. TS Gladstone to Archie Black, 28 October 1854.
41. NB to Archie Black, 6 September 1856.
42. John Eddington to Archie Black, 9 February 1856.
43. NB to Archie Black, 7 December 1852.
44. NB to Archie Black, 2 November 1855.
45. Robert Gladstone to Archie Black, 2 August 1856.
46. Robert Gladstone to Archie Black, 30 October 1856.
47. NB to Archie Black, 2 October 1856.
48. Robert Gladstone to Archie Black, 3 November 1856.
49. NB to Archie Black, 9 November 1856.
50. NB to Archie Black, 29 December 1856.
51. NB to TS Gladstone, 24 July 1866.

8 'To stem the wild torrent of Democracy'

1. James MacLehose, *Memoirs and portraits of one hundred Glasgow men who have died during the last thirty years, and in their lives did much to make the city what it now is*, No. 49, 'John Leadbetter (1788–1865)', John MacLehose and Sons, Glasgow, 1886, accessible at <*www.kosmoid.net/lives/leadbetter*>.
2. Niel Black (NB) to TS Gladstone, 28 February 1858.
3. NB to TS Gladstone, 29 March 1859.
4. NB to TS Gladstone, 9 November 1858.
5. Geoffrey Serle, *The Golden Age: A history of the colony of Victoria, 1851–1861*, Melbourne University Press, Melbourne, 1963, p. 267.
6. Ibid., p. 265.
7. NB to TS Gladstone, 25 February 1858.
8. Serle, op. cit., p. 275.
9. NB to TS Gladstone, 1 August 1858.
10. Margaret Kiddle, *Men of Yesterday: A social history of the Western District of Victoria, 1834–1890*, Melbourne University Press, Melbourne, 1961, p. 238.
11. NB to TS Gladstone, 7 July 1858.
12. NB to TS Gladstone, 9 November 1858.
13. NB to TS Gladstone, 3 March 1859.
14. NB to TS Gladstone, 15 September 1859.
15. Kiddle, op. cit., p. 227.
16. NB to TS Gladstone, 15 September 1859.
17. JM Powell, *The Public Lands of Australia Felix: Settlement and land appraisal in Victoria, 1834–91*, Melbourne University Press, Melbourne, 1970, p. 27; John Ireland, 'The Victorian Land Act of 1862 revisited', *Victorian Historical Journal*, vol. 65, no. 2, October 1994, p. 130.
18. Powell, op. cit., p. 67.
19. Ibid., pp. 54–5.
20. Serle, op. cit., pp. 271 and 301.
21. NB to TS Gladstone, 9 April 1859.
22. NB to TS Gladstone, 9 May 1859.
23. NB to TS Gladstone, 9 April 1859.
24. NB to TS Gladstone, 9 April 1859, 5 August 1859.
25. NB to TS Gladstone, 29 August 1859.
26. NB to Archibald Black (brother), 30 August 1859.
27. NB to TS Gladstone, 3 March 1859.
28. NB to Archibald Black (brother), 12 June 1859.
29. NB to TS Gladstone, 17 December 1859.
30. TS Gladstone to NB, 18 April 1860.
31. NB to TS Gladstone, 17 February 1862.

9 'We are full of corruption from head to foot'

1. Niel Black (NB) to TS Gladstone, 15 September 1859.
2. NB to TS Gladstone, 23 December 1866.
3. Geoffrey Serle, *The Golden Age: A history of the colony of Victoria, 1851–1861*, Melbourne University Press, Melbourne, 1963, p. 296.
4. NB to TS Gladstone, 9 April 1859.
5. NB to TS Gladstone, 25 October 1859.
6. NB to TS Gladstone, 11 January 1860.
7. NB to TS Gladstone, 19 February 1861.
8. NB to TS Gladstone, 11 January 1860.
9. NB to TS Gladstone, 14 April 1860.
10. NB to TS Gladstone, 23 April 1860.
11. NB to TS Gladstone, 22 June 1861.
12. NB to TS Gladstone, 16 June 1860.
13. JM Powell, *The Public Lands of Australia Felix: Settlement and land appraisal in*

Victoria, 1834–91, Melbourne University Press, Melbourne, 1970, pp. 79–80; NB to TS Gladstone, 6 July 1860.

14. NB to TS Gladstone, 20 September 1860.
15. Ibid.
16. NB to TS Gladstone, 20 December 1860.
17. NB to TS Gladstone, 6 July 1860.
18. NB to TS Gladstone and AS Finlay, 19 February 1864.
19. NB to TS Gladstone, 21 December 1860.
20. NB to JG Hamilton, 19 February 1861.
21. NB to TS Gladstone, 5 October 1870.
22. NB to TS Gladstone, 22 March 1861.
23. NB to TS Gladstone, 19 April 1861.
24. NB to TS Gladstone, 24 January 1861.
25. NB to TS Gladstone, 15 June 1861.
26. NB to TS Gladstone, 19 July 1861.
27. John Buys, 'Statistical Report of All the Land bought by Niel Black & Co in the Australian Colonies down to August 1863', ms book, NB papers; number obtained by counting the lots designated 'Occupation Licence' on Buys' hand-drawn map of lands purchased.
28. John Ireland, 'The Victorian Land Act 1862 revisited', *Victorian Historical Journal*, vol. 65, no. 2, October 1994, p. 133.
29. NB to TS Gladstone, 21 September 1861.
30. Powell, *The Public Lands*, op. cit., p. 81.
31. Ibid., p. 232.
32. Buys, op. cit.
33. Statement by Thomas Howard Fellowes on penalties under Nicholson's Act, undated, included in correspondence to NB from Klingender, Charsley and Liddle, 1862.
34. NB to TS Gladstone, 22 October 1862.
35. Victorian Parliamentary Debates (VPD), Legislative Council & Assembly, vol. viii, 1861–62, p. 993.
36. Kiddle, Margaret, *Men of Yesterday: A social history of the Western District of Victoria, 1834–1890*, Melbourne University Press, Melbourne, 1961, pp. 234–5; NB to TS Gladstone, 16 January 1862.
37. NB to TS Gladstone, 16 January 1862.

38. Kiddle, op. cit., pp. 235–7, quoting the *Age* of 18 September 1862, quoting the *Geelong Advertiser*.
39. Powell, *The Public Lands*, op. cit., p. 94, citing VPD, vol. viii, 1861–62, p. 353.
40. NB to TS Gladstone, 17 September 1862.
41. NB to AS Finlay, 18 August 1862.
42. NB to TS Gladstone, 22 February 1863.
43. NB to TS Gladstone, 22 October 1862.
44. NB to TS Gladstone, 24 November 1862.
45. NB to TS Gladstone, 18 December 1862, 10 April 1863 (final conclusion of the full bench of judges).
46. NB to TS Gladstone, 18 December 1862.
47. NB to TS Gladstone, 24 November 1862.
48. JM Powell, 'Gamblers by Act of Parliament: Some aspects of the first Selection Acts for Victoria', *The Victorian Historical Magazine*, vol. 39, no. 4, November 1968, p. 198.
49. NB to TS Gladstone, 10 April 1863.
50. NB to TS Gladstone, 20 April 1863.
51. NB to TS Gladstone, 23 April 1863.
52. Buys, op. cit., pp. 31–2.
53. Powell, 'Gamblers by Act of Parliament', op. cit., p. 209.
54. Powell, *The Public Lands*, op. cit., p. 105.
55. NB to TS Gladstone, 24 November 1862.
56. NB to TS Gladstone, 21 November 1864.
57. NB to Lauchlan McKinnon, 6 July 1865; Daniel Curdie to NB, 1 March 1865.
58. NB to TS Gladstone, 17 March 1865.
59. Buys, op. cit., map showing all the surveyed lots on Glenormiston and neighbouring runs, and their purchasers.
60. NB to TS Gladstone, 17 March 1865.
61. NB to TS Gladstone, 18 March 1865.
62. NB to TS Gladstone, 23 May 1865.
63. NB to TS Gladstone, 8 June 1865.
64. NB to TS Gladstone, 22 June 1865.
65. Buys, op. cit., supplement of 1866, p. 123 seq.
66. NB to Sam McGregor, 20 July 1865.
67. NB to TS Gladstone, 27 May 1867.
68. NB to TS Gladstone, 23 November 1861.
69. NB to TS Gladstone, 20 December 1865.

10 'All efforts to reach agreement have quite failed'

1. Niel Black (NB) to TS Gladstone, 18 May 1861.
2. NB to TS Gladstone, 17 February 1860.
3. NB to TS Gladstone, 9 February 1867.
4. NB to TS Gladstone, 20 January 1863.
5. NB to TS Gladstone, 16 August 1861.
6. RA McAlpine, *The Shire of Hampden 1863–1963*, Terang Express, 1963, pp. 6–11.
7. NB to TS Gladstone, 20 December 1864.
8. NB to TS Gladstone, 23 April 1863.
9. NB to TS Gladstone, 18 November 1860.
10. NB to TS Gladstone, 17 December 1861.

11. William Campbell to NB, 20 January 1861.
12. NB to John Hamilton, 19 June 1861.
13. William McAdam Steuart to NB, London, 22 July 1862, 25 July 1862, 26 August 1862; NB to Adam Steuart, 15 August 1863; and many others.
14. NB to TS Gladstone, 18 December 1862.
15. NB to TS Gladstone, 25 May 1863.
16. NB to TS Gladstone, 22 September 1863.
17. NB to TS Gladstone, 21 February 1866.
18. Elizabeth Steuart to NB, 26 May 1865.
19. Charles Maplestone, Heidelberg, to Mrs Marianne Miller, 24 July 1863, Camperdown Heritage Centre, Black file.
20. Claud Farie to TS Gladstone, 24 November 1861.
21. Steuart Gladstone to NB, letters 8 October 1860–9 July 1862.
22. Claud Farie to TS Gladstone, 25 August 1862; NB to TS Gladstone, 21 November 1863.
23. NB to TS Gladstone, 23 May 1864, 22 June 1864.
24. NB to TS Gladstone, 24 December 1866.
25. NB to TS Gladstone, 20 October 1865.
26. NB to TS Gladstone, 24 April 1864.
27. Claud Farie to TS Gladstone, 26 October 1867.
28. NB to TS Gladstone, 19 February 1866.
29. NB to TS Gladstone, 21 February 1866.
30. NB to TS Gladstone, 24 July 1866.
31. AS Finlay to NB, 21 May 1863.
32. NB to TS Gladstone, 19 November 1867.
33. NB to TS Gladstone, 8 November 1868.
34. NB to TS Gladstone, 24 July 1866.
35. NB to TS Gladstone, 24 November 1866.
36. NB to TS Gladstone, 17 and 24 March 1866.
37. NB to TS Gladstone, 26 June 1867.
38. Charles Sladen to NB, 1865–67.
39. NB to TS Gladstone, 25 January 1867.
40. NB to TS Gladstone, 23 December 1866.
41. NB to TS Gladstone, 22 April 1867.
42. NB to TS Gladstone, 19 September 1867.
43. NB to Claud Farie, 22 October 1867.
44. NB to TS Gladstone, 24 October 1867.
45. NB to TS Gladstone, 18 November 1867; events repeated in NB to Archibald Black (brother), 17 May 1868.
46. NB to TS Gladstone, 19 September 1867, 24 October 1867.
47. NB to Sam McGregor, 12 December 1867.

11 'I dread some fatal catastrophe'

1. Niel Black (NB) to Archie Black (brother), 21 March 1868, 17 May 1868.
2. NB to TS Gladstone, 23 April 1870. References to Finlay's attack on his honour occur in many letters from early 1868 onwards.
3. NB to TS Gladstone, 5 November 1868.
4. Greg Eccleston, 'Niel Black's residences in Melbourne', unpublished paper, 2010.
5. Claud Farie to Alexander Finlay, 5 June 1869, 20 July 1869, 3 August 1869; AS Finlay to Claud Farie, 26 May 1869, 19 June 1869.
6. NB to TS Gladstone, 11 September 1869.
7. Henry Mayers Hyndman, The Record of an Adventurous Life, Macmillan, London, 1911, p. 100.
8. Claud Farie to TS Gladstone, 20 May 1870.
9. NB to TS Gladstone, 3 October 1868.
10. NB to TS Gladstone, 11 September 1869.
11. NB to Archie Black (brother), 28 February 1869.
12. NB to Jessie Black, 8 November 1869.
13. NB to Robert Leadbetter, 18 May 1870.
14. NB to TS Gladstone, 23 March 1874.
15. Hyndman, op. cit., p. 101.
16. NB to TS Gladstone, 13 June 1870.
17. NB to TS Gladstone, 23 March 1874; also 8 June 1878.
18. Andrew Bannatyne to Robert Leadbetter, 7 October 1870.
19. NB to TS Gladstone, 18 March 1870.
20. NB to TS Gladstone, 23 April 1870, 21 May 1870.
21. Steuart Gladstone to NB, 10 October 1870.
22. Daniel Mackinnon to Rev. James Curdie, 26 February 1869.
23. NB to Sir Charles Sladen, 24 September 1878; NB to TS Gladstone, 14 April 1879.
24. NB to Robert Leadbetter, 20 March 1871.
25. NB to TS Gladstone, 1 September 1870.
26. Daniel Curdie to NB, 29 October 1870.
27. NB to Jessie Black, 29 November 1870.
28. NB to TS Gladstone, 6 December 1870.
29. Grace Black to Maggie Black (niece, Archie's sister), 27 January 1871; NB to Robert Leadbetter, in Grace Black's hand, 23 January 1871.
30. NB to Robert Leadbetter, 6 September 1871. The Tichborne case was a cause

célèbre of the time, in which an imposter posed as a lost member of the Tichborne family to claim a large inheritance.

31. Daniel Mackinnon to Mrs Walter Black, 9 September 1871.
32. Daniel Mackinnon to Rev. James Curdie, 31 December 1872.

12 'The crowning folly of my life'

1. Niel Black (NB) to Robert Leadbetter, 26 March 1872.
2. Ibid.
3. Greg Eccleston, 'Niel Black's residences in Melbourne', unpublished paper, 2010.
4. NB to TS Gladstone, 27 March 1873.
5. NB to TS Gladstone, 6 October 1873.
6. NB to Archie Black (brother), 12 June 1859.
7. NB to TS Gladstone, 23 March 1874.
8. NB to TS Gladstone, 10 June 1874.
9. NB to TS Gladstone, 23 March 1874.
10. Margaret Kiddle, *Men of Yesterday: A social history of the Western District of Victoria, 1834–1890*, Melbourne University Press, Melbourne, 1961, p. 391, citing MH Ellis, *The Beef Shorthorn in Australia*, Sydney, 1932, p. 123.
11. NB to TS Gladstone, 12 June 1873.
12. NB to John Meckle (this is how he spelled Mickle's name), 11 August 1871.
13. NB to John Meckle, 4 December 1871, 23 December 1871.
14. NB to TS Gladstone, 27 January 1874.
15. William Robertson to Daniel Mackinnon, 21 July 1870, Mackinnon family papers, MS 9470, State Library of Victoria.
16. James Sinclair (ed.), *The History of Shorthorn Cattle*, Vinton & Co, London, 1907, p. 633.
17. Harry H Peck, *Memoirs of a Stockman*, Stockland Press, Melbourne, 1942, p. 126.
18. RV Billis and AS Kenyon, *Pastures New: An account of the pastoral occupation of Port Phillip*, Macmillan, Melbourne, 1930, p. 142.
19. NB to John Meckle, 5 November 1872.
20. NB to TS Gladstone, 13 July 1872.
21. Victorian Parliamentary Debates (VPD), Legislative Council and Legislative Assembly, vol. xv, 15 October 1872, pp. 1767–9.
22. James T Critchell and Joseph Raymond, *History of the Frozen Meat Trade*, Constable, London, 1912, pp. 7–8.
23. NB to Archie Black (brother), 4 October 1868.
24. NB to TS Gladstone, 2 December 1868.
25. Robert Leadbetter to NB, 24 March 1870.
26. NB to TS Gladstone, 2 December 1868.
27. NB correspondence with his agents Eaglestone & Ettishank, and the Ballarat Meat Preserving Company, 21 December 1871.
28. NB to TS Gladstone, 6 December 1869.
29. Correspondence from Eaglestone & Ettishank to NB, May and June 1875.
30. 'The Mount Noorat Herd of Shorthorns', *Australasian*, 23 October 1875, p. 22.
31. Correspondence between Robert McDougall and NB, October 1872.
32. Robert McDougall to NB, 13 November 1875.
33. NB to TS Gladstone, 27 November 1875.
34. NB to TS Gladstone, 30 November 1875, and to John Meckle, same date.
35. *Australasian*, 8 January 1876; the report on the Robertsons' sale follows that on Black's.
36. *Australasian*, 23 October 1875.
37. NB to John Meckle, 23 January 1876.
38. NB to TS Gladstone, 24 January 1876.
39. *Australasian*, 13 January 1877.
40. NB to TS Gladstone, 22 January 1877.
41. NB to John Meckle, 17 January 1878.
42. *Camperdown Chronicle*, 14 January 1879, p. 3; NB to TS Gladstone, 20 January 1879.
43. NB to TS Gladstone, 27 November 1875, 13 March 1877; many other letters in this period cover the same topics.
44. NB to TS Gladstone, 13 March 1877.
45. Charles Webb to NB, 11 November 1876, 28 December 1876.
46. NB to Robert Leadbetter, 14 April 1877.
47. NB to TS Gladstone, 31 July 1877.
48. NB to TS Gladstone, 23 December 1877.
49. NB to Robert Leadbetter, 4 November 1877.
50. NB to TS Gladstone, 30 August 1878.
51. NB to (Archibald John) Ian Black (son), 5 July 1879.
52. NB to AS Finlay, 21 February 1864.
53. NB to (AJ) Ian Black (son), 22 February 1880.
54. NB to TS Gladstone, 18 February 1880.
55. Obituary of the Hon. Niel Black, *Warrnambool Standard*, 20 May 1880.
56. Grace Black to (AJ) Ian Black, 17 May 1880.

INDEX